Edgar J. Goodspeed,
America's First Papyrologist

CALIFORNIA CLASSICAL STUDIES

NUMBER 8

Editorial Board Chair: Donald Mastronarde

Editorial Board: Alessandro Barchiesi, Todd Hickey, Emily Mackil, Richard Martin, Robert Morstein-Marx, J. Theodore Peña, Kim Shelton

California Classical Studies publishes peer-reviewed long-form scholarship with online open access and print-on-demand availability. The primary aim of the series is to disseminate basic research (editing and analysis of primary materials both textual and physical), data-heavy research, and highly specialized research of the kind that is either hard to place with the leading publishers in Classics or extremely expensive for libraries and individuals when produced by a leading academic publisher. In addition to promoting archaeological publications, papyrological and epigraphic studies, technical textual studies, and the like, the series will also produce selected titles of a more general profile.

The startup phase of this project (2013–2017) was supported by a grant from the Andrew W. Mellon Foundation.

Also in the series:

Number 1: Leslie Kurke, *The Traffic in Praise: Pindar and the Poetics of Social Economy*, 2013

Number 2: Edward Courtney, *A Commentary on the Satires of Juvenal*, 2013

Number 3: Mark Griffith, *Greek Satyr Play: Five Studies*, 2015

Number 4: Mirjam Kotwick, *Alexander of Aphrodisias and the Text of Aristotle's* Metaphysics, 2016

Number 5: Joey Williams, *The Archaeology of Roman Surveillance in the Central Alentejo, Portugal*, 2017

Number 6: Donald J. Mastronarde, *Preliminary Studies on the Scholia to Euripides*, 2017

Number 7: Olivier Dufault, *Early Greek Alchemy, Patronage and Innovation in Late Antiquity*, 2019

The present volume is simultaneously the inaugural number (Number 1) in the series Publications of the Center for the Tebtunis Papyri.

EDGAR J. GOODSPEED, AMERICA'S FIRST PAPYROLOGIST

Todd M. Hickey — James G. Keenan

CALIFORNIA
CLASSICAL
STUDIES

Berkeley, California

© 2021 by Todd M. Hickey and James G. Keenan

California Classical Studies
c/o Department of Ancient Greek and Roman Studies
University of California
Berkeley, California 94720–2520
USA
https://calclassicalstudies.org
email: ccseditorial@berkeley.edu

ISBN 9781939926142 (paperback), 9781939926159 (eBook: Adobe PDF)

Library of Congress Control Number: 2021944994

CONTENTS

Preface	vii
List of Illustrations	xi
Prologue	1
1. Chicago Beginnings and an American Abroad	7
2. Egypt, a "Lost" Epic, and "the Treasure of Leviathan"	35
3. An Oxford Summer	69
Epilogue	108
Appendix A: The Ayer Papyrus and Goodspeed's "Last Graduate Year"	120
Appendix B: Edgar's Letter to His Mother about His Visit to Tebtunis	125
Appendix C: Grenfell and Hunt's Account of the Tebtunis Excavations (*New York Journal*)	133
Appendix D: Grenfell's Letter to Goodspeed about His Contribution to *P.Tebt.* II	141
Appendix E: Concordance: T-numbers Assigned to Goodspeed and Their *P.Tebt.* II Publication Numbers	145

Appendix F: Hunt's Letters to Gertrude Caton-Thompson concerning the Pharaonic Remains at Tebtunis and the Level of Lake Moeris   146

Appendix G: Goodspeed's Proposal to Transfer Some Tebtunis Papyri from Berkeley to U.C.L.A.   149

Works Cited   154

Index   166

PREFACE

This project had two essentials, *sine quibus non*. Obviously indispensable was the concern of our titular persona, Edgar J. Goodspeed, to create and preserve the extensive written and photographic records touching upon his long and eventful life. But equally crucial was the careful curation of the lion's share of the resulting archive, now known as the Edgar J. Goodspeed Papers, in the Hanna Holborn Gray Special Collections Research Center (hereafter SCRC) of the University of Chicago Library. We thank Daniel Meyer, Director Emeritus of the SCRC, for his permission to reproduce, quote, and cite the archival materials that are the heart of this book.[1] We are also grateful to Julia Gardner, former Head of Reader Services, Christine Colburn, Reader Services Supervisor, Barbara Gilbert, Reading Room Coordinator, and their colleagues for their assistance during our ten-plus years of research on this project. They have bestowed upon us every possible courtesy, thereby making the SCRC more than just an ideal physical space for our work.

For guidance and for permission to use materials from a valuable secondary source, the Edgar J. Goodspeed Collection, Denison University Archives and Special Collections, Granville, Ohio, we thank Sasha Griffin, University Archivist and Special Collections Librarian, and Colleen Goodhart, Reference Archivist. We are also indebted to the Bentley Historical Library, University of Michigan, for permission to cite or quote from the papers of Wooster Woodruff Beman, Francis Willey Kelsey, and the Kelsey Museum of Archaeology, and to reproduce a photograph preserved in the Easton Kelsey Papers. For permission to cite or quote from the correspondence of J. Gilbart Smyly, we thank The Board of Trinity College Dublin, The University of Dublin. Quotations from Emma Andrews's unpublished "Journal on the Bedawin" appear courtesy of the American Philosophical Society.

For the opportunity, 9 January 2020, to consult records of the Field Museum of Natural History, Chicago, regarding Edward Ayer's Egyptian travels and acquisition of the papyrus named in his honor (cf. Appendix A), we are grateful to

---

[1] For precise credits for the visual materials reproduced from the Goodspeed Papers and other sources, see the List of Illustrations.

Gretchen Rings, Museum Librarian and Head of Library Collections, the Field Museum Archives in the Marie Louise Rosenthal Library; Jamie Kelly, Anthropology Collections Manager; and Armand Esai, Museum Archivist. Permission to use these documents was furnished by Gretchen, while Emma Turner-Trujillo, the Museum's Assistant Registrar, aided us with the permission for the image of the Ayer Papyrus.

For his permission to cite Crum Notebook 67 and, especially, to publish Hunt's letters to Gertrude Caton-Thompson in full (Appendix F), we thank Jaromír Málek, Keeper Emeritus of the Griffith Institute Archive, University of Oxford. We are also indebted to Stephanie Jenkins, former secretary at the Oxford Centre for Late Antiquity, for helpfully scanning and sending an image of a vintage postcard depicting the "Isis" Boarding Establishment.

This book took life as a long two-part article, kindly read and improved by Michael Zellmann-Rohrer. The suggestion to transform it into a book came from Ellen Bauerle of the University of Michigan Press. We are grateful to Donald Mastronarde for his receptive response to our inquiry about publishing the expanded work in the series California Classical Studies (CCS) and for the significant time and energy he has devoted to shepherding the manuscript through to publication. Dorothy J. Thompson read the penultimate version of our text and offered important advice and corrections. To her, and to the two anonymous readers for CCS, who opened our eyes to aspects of the manuscript that had escaped our notice and provided an occasion to rethink and emend a number of particulars,[2] we offer thanks for their contributions to the project as a whole. For specific assistance, we acknowledge in our footnotes the helpful expertise of Magdy Aly, Emily Cole, Holger Essler, Marius Gerhardt, Brendan Haug, Alice Mulberry, Dominic Rathbone, Gil Renberg, Christina Riggs, Paul Schubert, John-Mark Smith, Alice Stevenson, and (again) Michael Zellmann-Rohrer. They are not of course responsible for any lingering mistakes on our part.

It was a delight to work with Alison DeGraff Ollivierre, Senior Cartographer and GIS Specialist, Tombolo Maps and Design. Since the maps that Aly created for our volume are meant to illustrate Goodspeed's personal experience, to enable the reader to follow his footsteps in Oxford, Cairo, and the Fayyūm (cf. Holmes 1985), and since we consider the names in those places to be part of that experience, we have used his preferred spellings when others would have been more technically correct (cf. Lawrence 1935, 24). Similarly, if another of our documentary sources refers to a place, we privilege its spelling, giving priority, after Goodspeed, to the choices of Bernard P. Grenfell.[3] In our text, the transliterations of Arabic present in sources typically appear within quotation marks when used outside of

---

[2] One reader was later revealed, at our request and with his consent, to be Nick Gonis. It had seemed inappropriate to leave certain important observations anonymous.

[3] When Goodspeed is inconsistent, we have endeavored to use the form most frequently employed.

their original contexts. The source of first resort for our own spellings of Arabic geographic names has been Office of Geography 1959, though we have also consulted various maps (e.g., Egyptian Ministry of Finance 1914, Army Map Service 1947). Certain common placenames offer an exception, appearing in the forms by which they are well known. For Arabic transliteration we have endeavored to follow Library of Congress recommendations, though some inconsistencies no doubt remain, and we have not attempted to normalize the spellings of personal names, preferring instead to use the forms that seem prevalent in scholarship and to discuss discrepancies or problems as necessary.

The transcriptions of the letters and documents appearing herein draw their practical inspiration from Mark Twain Project 2007, though we have felt free to modify that to suit our needs. They preserve the quotation marks (single or double) of our sources as well as their punctuation and (less rigorously) spacing.[4] In earlier versions of the text, *sic* was employed much more liberally, but on Dorothy Thompson's recommendation, we decided not to flag some features of the documents as written, leaving unmarked words unnecessarily or inconsistently capitalized by current standards, nor entering apostrophes in possessives and contractions where they are missing in the originals. We have attempted to be true to the originals in their specifics and, obviously, as accurate as possible overall, indicating mistakes by *sic* only in cases that seemed ambiguous or puzzling or were genuine authorial mistakes.

Our footnotes, readers will quickly notice, are often lengthy; they provide a running commentary on the main text, especially when it comes to explicating details of Goodspeed's correspondence. This is a papyrologists' practice that is hard to shed. The combination of text and notes, though not strictly amounting to a history of papyrology, is meant, as a byproduct of the book's biographical framework, to recreate a sense of what the emergent field of papyrology was like insofar as it was experienced by Goodspeed in the late 1890s and early 1900s.[5] But as our research progressed, we found it impossible, indeed unfair to him, to separate his endeavors in papyrology from his other professional work or even from the ambient course of his personal life. Thus, as Nick Gonis astutely noted, there are several ways to read the book, including—to give but one example—as a travelogue narrating a young American academic's experiences abroad, in effect

---

[4]Thus the reader will frequently see double quotes (Goodspeed's) within double quotes (ours). Ellipses in published sources are ours unless otherwise noted; in manuscript sources, we enclose our ellipses within square brackets. Hyphens at the end of manuscript lines are usually omitted (cf. also App. B, n. 1).

[5]Appendixes C and F are fossils from the earliest days of the project, when its focus was the excavations at Tebtunis (cf. Prologue). After our emphasis shifted, we decided to retain them since they include information that we feared could be lost if they were excised. (Neither appendix can stand on its own.) Their presence continues to seem justified by their contribution to our understanding of Goodspeed's experience of the nascent discipline, an experience in which Tebtunis was central.

a *Bildungsroman* with a narrative arc and its own human interest, set against the scholarly, cultural, and political background of his time.

Goodspeed's was an era, as many readers will know, when Egyptian antiquities, their discovery and dissemination, were subject to colonialist occupation and control (see the Prologue). Though fully aware of the increasing sensitivity about the sometimes ethically questionable origins of papyrology under those conditions, we here concentrate on presenting the narrative that our research has surfaced, without explicit judgement or condemnation, expecting that the Goodspeed story will provide ample scope for further ethical evaluation of the practices then prevailing.

References to publications of papyri employ a series of abbreviations (sigla) that are standard for the field of papyrology. These may be decoded using Oates et al. 2021, freely accessible online. References in the format "box x, folder y" without further specification refer to the Goodspeed Papers archived in the SCRC at the University of Chicago.

Todd M. Hickey and James G. Keenan
Benicia and Chicago, July 2021

LIST OF ILLUSTRATIONS

For Figs. 6–13, the quoted titles are those of the photographers. The quotes in the captions for Figs. 3, 16, and 17 are drawn from Goodspeed's correspondence.

Figure 1: Edgar J. Goodspeed's portrait from the "Student Travel Letters," p. 6
  Unknown photographer; courtesy of the SCRC, University of Chicago.
Figure 2: Bernard P. Grenfell, ca. 1897, p. 15
  Public domain; sourced from *McClure's* 9 (1897) 1023 (personal copy of T. M. Hickey).
Figure 3: 10 Bedford Place, "where I hang out when in London," p. 23
  Edgar J. Goodspeed photo; courtesy of the SCRC, University of Chicago.
Figure 4: Grenfell and Hunt's dedication to Jules Nicole, p. 34
  Public domain; sourced from Grenfell and Hunt 1898 (copy from the Library of the University of California, Berkeley).
Figure 5: The Hotel Karoon with waterwheels in the foreground, ca. 1900, p. 58
  Photographer unknown; photographic print owned by T. M. Hickey.
Figure 6: "An Egyptian rialto," p. 59
  Edgar J. Goodspeed photo; courtesy of the SCRC, University of Chicago.
Figure 7: "Sebbakhin at mound of Arsinoe," p. 60
  Easton T. Kelsey photo, 1920; courtesy of the Bentley Historical Library, University of Michigan.
Figure 8: "An Egyptian train (and Mohammed Mansour?)," p. 61
  Edgar J. Goodspeed photo; courtesy of the SCRC, University of Chicago.
Figure 9: "Mr. Grenfell in the Field," p. 64
  Edgar J. Goodspeed photo; courtesy of the SCRC, University of Chicago.
Figure 10: "Grenfell and Hunt's camp," p. 67
  Edgar J. Goodspeed photo; courtesy of the SCRC, University of Chicago.
Figure 11: "Encampment photo (with Hunt)," p. 68
  Edgar J. Goodspeed photo; courtesy of the SCRC, University of Chicago.
Figure 12: "Medinet el-Fayum," p. 70
  Edgar J. Goodspeed photo; courtesy of the SCRC, University of Chicago.

Figure 13: "Medinet," p. 71
Edgar J. Goodspeed photo; courtesy of the SCRC, University of Chicago.
Figure 14: An advertisement for the "Isis" Boarding Establishment, 1900, p. 81
Public domain; sourced from *Alden's Oxford Guide* (personal copy of T. M. Hickey).
Figure 15: Postcard for the "Isis" Boarding Establishment, ca. 1900, p. 82
Public domain; courtesy of its owner, Stephanie Jenkins.
Figure 16: Goodspeed's "extraordinary magical" papyrus, the future *P. Tebt.* II 275, p. 98
Courtesy of the Center for the Tebtunis Papyri, University of California, Berkeley.
Figure 17: The "letter of the Emperor Gordian," the future *P. Tebt.* II 285, p. 99
Courtesy of the Center for the Tebtunis Papyri, University of California, Berkeley.
Figure 18: The Ayer papyrus, p. 123
© The Field Museum, image no. 31327, cat. no. 31327, photographer Lauren Fitts.
Figure 19: Goodspeed in the year in which *As I Remember* appeared, p. 153
Unknown photographer, 14 March 1953. *Los Angeles Herald Examiner* Photo Collection/Los Angeles Public Library.

Maps

1. Goodspeed's Cairo, p. 37
2. Goodspeed's Fayoum, p. 57
3. Goodspeed's Oxford, p. 80

For Mary and Laurie

"The thing seems nearly ready: but it always seems so."
– Edgar J. Goodspeed to his brother Charles, 24 May 1900

Edgar J. Goodspeed,
America's First Papyrologist

Prologue

The fascination with the quotidian is one of the habits for which biographers are regularly chided by critics, who, craving plot and dramatic tension, dismiss the daily as mere besotted inclusiveness. Yet a biographer's first duty is to recover the actual; and what is more powerful in a man's life than the details of his days?[1]

The project that was an indirect and unintended inspiration for the present work was Hickey's endeavor to collect as much testimony as possible on the excavation of Bernard P. Grenfell and Arthur S. Hunt at the ancient village of Tebtunis on the southern edge of the Fayyūm province of Egypt in the winter of 1899–1900. This was the source of the papyrus collection now housed in the Center for the Tebtunis Papyri in The Bancroft Library of the University of California, Berkeley. A visitor to the excavation in progress had been a newly appointed faculty member of the University of Chicago, Edgar J. Goodspeed, who had written about the experience in a popularizing article published in 1904 with photographic accompaniment.[2] It seemed from this a likely wager that correspondence between the parties would be found in the Edgar J. Goodspeed Papers at the University of Chicago, where Goodspeed had been a longtime faculty member (1898–1937) specializing in the New Testament and its Apocrypha. Keenan's visit to the Special Collections Research Center in the Regenstein Library, 13 July 2004, discovered only a few items from Hunt, but a substantial number of letters and postcards to Goodspeed from Grenfell, including a few in advance of and in preparation for his visit to Tebtunis, and others principally concerned with the terms of his assistance in editing and publishing the excavation's papyrus finds.[3]

Although the original project on the Tebtunis testimonia remains alive, and in

---

[1] B. L. Reid 1990, 5. Cf. Kimber 2021, 3: "The best biographers appreciate trivia, too. They write books that don't just provide us with dull, chronological exposés of dates, places and names, but which also include those seemingly irrelevant details that reveal the absolute essence of their subject, and which most of us, if we're honest, find compulsively fascinating."

[2] Goodspeed 1904b. Goodspeed 1902a was not yet known to us.

[3] Reported to Hickey in an email on the same date.

some measure is fulfilled below, it took a radical detour six years later following discovery of Goodspeed's "Student Travel Letters vol. 2" (vol. 1 is lost), which make it possible to track his daily and sometimes by-the-hour progress during the second half of two years (1898–1900) of study and travel abroad, in Europe, Egypt, and the Holy Land. For the excavation, the gem of vol. 2 is the letter to his mother with its immediate narrative of his visit to Tebtunis, 17–19 February 1900, providing intimate details not included in his article of 1904.[4] But the letters also allow for tracking Goodspeed's early career in far greater depth and detail than that allotted in his 1953 memoir, *As I Remember,* or anywhere else, particularly regarding his progress in the newly prominent discipline of papyrology, putting much additional substance to the claim that Goodspeed was indeed "America's First Papyrologist." The result is a "thick description" of his youthful engagement with the fledgling field from the late 1890s into the first decade of the twentieth century. It is not a direct history of papyrology during those years but an account of one budding scholar's experiences in pursuit of recognition in that subject, a story that, as persevering readers will discover, has its own particular complications, narrative arc, and human interest.

Those readers for whom the terms papyrology and papyrologist are unfamiliar will still sense that they are half based on the word papyrus, which refers, in first instance, to the tall, flowered, aquatic sedge that grew in Egypt's swampier regions, especially the Nile Delta. In second place it refers to the ancient form of paper that was manufactured from strips of pith cut from the plant's long stem after peeling. In third, but most important place for present purposes, it refers to any such piece of "paper" that has been inscribed with writing; its plural is papyri. Papyrology is therefore the study of such writings, while the papyrologist is one who engages in such study. Until recently—at least in the English-speaking world—the terms implied (mostly) study of writings in Greek, the administrative language of Egypt for the long millennium stretching from the late fourth century BC into the early eighth century AD, papyrology itself being initially (and for the most part still) an extension of the field known as classical philology.[5] Papyri inscribed in Egyptian scripts were the preserve of the field known as Egyptology, classical philology and Egyptology historically having pursued separate disciplinary paths.

The borders between the disciplines have recently softened, but this was not the case when Goodspeed entered upon the scene in the late 1890s. His arrival coincided with the time when papyrology in the traditional sense, the study of mainly Greek documents written mainly on papyrus, was experiencing its first steps toward becoming an acknowledged scholarly science, thanks in part to a rash of manuscript discoveries. Some would even date the field's takeoff to a specific year,

---

[4]Excerpted toward the end of Ch. 2 below, edited in full as App. B.
[5]J. Turner 2014, esp. at 299.

1891, marked by the landmark publication of the British Museum's recently acquired Aristotelian *Constitution of Athens*.[6]

Many readers will know that the source country of these discoveries was Egypt, this as a consequence of the country's unique combination of geography and climate. For historical perspective it is helpful to recall that when Goodspeed was in Egypt, in 1899 and 1900, William McKinley was president of the United States, his assassination an event yet to come (1901). Victoria was queen of England and empress of India, *regina et imperatrix*, memory of her 1897 Diamond Jubilee recent and fresh, a defining moment for the British Empire.[7] Egypt's ostensible head of state was the khedive, based in Cairo, who functioned nominally as viceroy under the sultan of the Ottoman Empire based in Istanbul. But the real administrative and policing power had, since 1882, vested in Britain and its consul-general, while the directorship of the Antiquities Service and the Egyptian Museum was the preserve of the French, the director's nomination being subject to the consul-general's approval—by "gentlemen's agreement" until formalized in 1904.[8] In 1899–1900 the relevant personnel in Egypt were, respectively, ʿAbbās Ḥilmī II (1874–1944), reigned 1892–1914; Sir Evelyn Baring, Lord Cromer (1841–1917), "reigned" 1883–1907; and Gaston Maspero (1846–1916), just beginning a second term as director, 1899–1914.[9] Between 1890 and 1902 the Egyptian Museum was housed in Gizeh, across the Nile from Cairo, in a former palace of the Khedive Ismāʿīl (reigned 1863–1879), an ornate, dilapidated "old tinder-box."[10] There, in November 1899, Goodspeed met Maspero and other important Egyptologists and was allowed to practice his craft by copying any Greek-language papyri he liked

---

[6] Keenan 2009.

[7] Morris 1979. For the pageantry in London on 22 June 1897 and the empire-wide participation: ibid., esp. ch. 1. Victoria's "supreme moment of earthly apotheosis" amid "widespread imperial rapture": Cannadine 2001, 109, 147.

[8] D. M. Reid 2002, *passim* but esp. 196; D. M. Reid 2015, *passim*.

[9] Goldschmidt 2000, 2–3 (ʿAbbās Ḥilmī II); Bierbrier 2012, 40, and Morris 1979, 244–246 (Baring); Bierbrier 2012, 359–361 (Maspero). Synopsis of the political arrangements and social conditions in Egypt in and around 1897: Morris 1979, 206–209. A contemporary British journalist tells his readers (Steevens 1899, 63–64), Lord Cromer "is, as you know, the mouthpiece of our policy and, in practice, the ultimate ruler of Egypt … In theory, he has no more right to tell the Khedive what is, or is not, to be done than you have. He just happens to give advice, and the Khedive happens to take it." He praises the imperial project in Egypt in a chapter entitled "Lord Cromer and His Work" (Steevens 1899, ch. XVI, 185–196) and throughout his book, loaded as it is with paternalistic, cultural, and racial bias.

[10] D. M. Reid 2002, esp. 192–195 with fig. 36 on 194 (cf. map 2 on 105); Abt 2011, 43–44 ("old tinder-box": James Henry Breasted based on a visit in fall 1894, though the palace was then only twenty-five years old, having been built in 1869 in connection with the celebratory opening of the Suez Canal); cf. Drower 1995, 169–170. Goodspeed, on the contrary, from 17 November 1899 onward, expressed admiration for its stately features (Ch. 2).

(though without blanket rights of publication), while he also continued to work on his personal collection, whose acquisitions are described in Chapters 1 and 2.[11]

Papyri that Goodspeed was copying in Gizeh came into its inventory in various ways, one of which was through *partage*, that is, the sharing of finds between the Egyptian Museum and the foreign sponsors of licensed excavations, roughly on a 50/50 basis.[12] In theory, the Antiquities Service and its director controlled this apportioning and could lay claim to any particularly significant cultural objects, but one can see (for example) from a letter from Bernard P. Grenfell to Flinders Petrie, written during the first season's dig at Oxyrhynchus (1896–1897), how excavators might try to "game the system," albeit for, in their view, worthy scholarly aims.[13] Other papyri were being channeled both into the Museum and onto a worldwide, or more precisely, a European market through a chain of less formal excavation (especially by Egyptian farmers digging for the kind of fertilizer known as *sebākh*) and the buying of antiquities, whether by private individuals or institutional agents. There was a bit of a competitive "Wild West" atmosphere in this, with national interests at stake.[14] Some of the activity was legal, controlled by licensing and export permits. In this way, for example, antiquities could be sold openly, and legally, in shops near the famous Shepheard's Hotel in Cairo, subject to customs duties upon exportation.[15] But there were also "clandestine" excavations that were not always so clandestine, and attempts to evade the law and its requirements through circumvention of the Antiquities Service's rights of first claim. Undoubtedly the most successful of the institutional agents, operating both within and beyond the law, was the controversial E. A. Wallis Budge, whose two-volume account of his activities on behalf of the British Museum, *By Nile and Tigris*, published in 1920, the year of his knighthood, often reads like an adventure novel from high imperial times.[16]

---

[11] Results of these labors include *P.Cair.Goodsp.*, *P.Chic.*, and *P.Kar.Goodsp.* For the Goodspeed papyri in general: Allison 1975; a re-edition of *P.Cair.Goodsp.* 3: Renberg and Naether 2010.

[12] An apparent ideal in the 1890s, made official by law in 1912: Kersel 2010, 87. Cf. Grenfell's reference (letter of 30 January 1897 to E. M. Thompson of the Egypt Exploration Fund, Hickey and Keenan 2016, 361) to "the full half to which they [sc. the Museum authorities] are entitled," in reference to the first season's finds at Oxyrhynchus. See also next note.

[13] Hickey and Keenan 2016, 365–375, at 369: "At the worst they [sc. the Museum authorities] cant I suppose collar more than half, we shall take care it is the worse half[.]" Nevertheless, Grenfell would later report to the EEF (1896–1897, 10) that "[o]ne hundred and fifty of the largest and best preserved rolls … were retained for the Gizeh Museum." For the division of the Tebtunis finds, see App. C.

[14] For the perspective of an agent for one of the smaller players in the competition, see Raven 2018.

[15] See Sattin 1988, 179–182 and *passim*, for the hotel; Hombert 1933 for a parodic description of the chaotic scene outside the hotel in the next generation (recapitulation in Keenan 2009, 69). Apparently things in Cairo had not changed from the turn of the century: Sattin 1988, 199–200.

[16] As in a way it is: Budge 1920. Synopsis of Budge's smuggling methods: Hagen and Ryholt 2016, 142; for a specific example (the famous roll of Bacchylides), see Budge 1920, 345–355. Heroizing résumé in Deuel 1965, ch. VII ("The Traffic in Papyri: Wallis Budge").

Budge, incidentally, met Goodspeed in July 1899 during one of the latter's stops at the British Museum, months before he (Goodspeed) set out for Egypt. Nevertheless, the Goodspeed story does not start in London with his introduction to Budge, or in Gizeh with his introduction to Maspero, but with a chance encounter with a papyrus during his "last graduate year" in the 1890s boom town of Chicago.[17]

---

[17] "[L]ast graduate year": Goodspeed 1953, 98, initiating a chronological problem whose parameters we try to define in App. A. "[B]oom town": It only became "that toddlin' town" in 1922 with Fred Fisher's famous popular song.

Figure 1: Edgar J. Goodspeed's portrait from the "Student Travel Letters."
Unknown photographer; courtesy of the SCRC, University of Chicago.

Chapter 1

Chicago Beginnings and an American Abroad

> We shall decline having any inexperienced person mixed up with our papyri, and so far as I know you are the only American who has worked at the subject.

So writes Bernard Pyne Grenfell near the close of a letter written from "Gharak, Fayoum, Feb. 10 [1900]" and transcribed below (Chapter 2) in full. The letter's recipient, Edgar Johnson Goodspeed (1871–1962; Fig. 1), was at the time a traveling scholar, temporarily based in Cairo, not quite thirty years old. He had been born in the Mississippi River town of Quincy, Illinois, 23 October 1871, the month and year of Chicago's Great Fire, son of Baptist minister Thomas Wakefield Goodspeed and his wife, Mary Ellen Goodspeed (née Ten Broeke).[1] Soon after the birth of Edgar, named for his father's oldest and much revered brother, the family moved from Quincy to Chicago. Another move, in 1876, placed the family in Morgan Park, now a neighborhood on Chicago's far south side but then a newly founded Baptist community in Calumet Township.[2] Seventeen years later, in 1893, still years before stables gave way to garages, the Goodspeeds settled in Hyde Park, a former township recently (1889) annexed by referendum to the city of Chicago and home to the newly resurrected University of Chicago, then in full excitement of building and growth.[3] That summer the World's Columbian Exposition was in full swing in nearby Jackson Park with exciting and exotic attractions—including the first Ferris Wheel and "Street in Cairo," "a tawdry commercial exhibit" with camel rides, snake charming, and belly dancing—spreading westward along the

---

[1] For the opening biographical details, we rely principally on Cook 1981, 1–2, and Cobb and Jennings 1948, 1–2, which quotes an unpublished account written by Goodspeed's father. For Thomas's life and career, first in ministry, then in education, the latter much concerned with fundraising, see C. T. B. Goodspeed 1932. Chicago fire: as Goodspeed himself noted (Goodspeed 1953, 11).

[2] Skerrett 2008.

[3] Hart and Pacyga 1979, 73–86. The first of the University's original buildings, the Gothic-style Cobb Lecture Hall, had opened for classes on 1 October 1892 (architecture.uchicago.edu, consulted 13 June 2018). For this and the other early constructions, see the firsthand account in T. W. Goodspeed 1916, ch. VIII; cf. Pridmore 2013, chs. I–III with their lavish illustrations.

Midway Plaisance just south of the burgeoning campus.[4] The Exposition was in one respect a coming out party for the city of Chicago, but contemporaries also came to see it as an inflection point in American history. "Here was a breach of continuity—a rupture in historical sequence!" wrote historian Henry Adams (1838–1918), a two-time visitor from the East Coast. "Chicago asked in 1893 for the first time the question whether the American people knew where they were driving ... Chicago was the first expression of American thought as a unity; one must start there."[5]

In the years leading up to this pivotal event, Edgar studied Latin, then Greek in preparation for attending college. In due time he matriculated at Denison University, a Baptist foundation in Granville, Ohio, earning his A.B. in 1890 with distinction in Classics.[6] He next pursued a year's graduate study (1890–1891) at Yale (Hebrew, Arabic, legal literature of the Old Testament) under William Rainey Harper, soon to become the new University of Chicago's first president.[7] Edgar returned from New Haven to Illinois, first teaching Latin and Greek at the Owen Academy in Morgan Park and then, in the following year (1892), enrolling

[4] For the Exposition, 1 May–30 October 1893 (it was a year late in getting started), and its significance, see, e.g., Cronon 1991, 341–369; Larson 2003; and Olson 2017, 43–47 ("Interlude: Chicago, October 21, 1892"). Locations of the many exhibits may be found on Heinze et al. 1892 and Rand, McNally and Co. 1893. (We thank John-Mark Smith for resources on the Exposition.) "[T]awdry commercial exhibit": Abt 2011, 58; cf. Teeter 2010, 304. "Street in Cairo" (variously named in the literature) is the name as given on the Rand McNally map under no. 18. It was immediately northeast of the Ferris Wheel, no. 15. See Grossman 2016 and 2018 for pertinent archival photographs.

[5] H. Adams 1918, 340, 343. The most celebrated contribution to that "conversation": Frederick Jackson Turner's lecture at the Art Institute of Chicago, 12 July 1893, on "The Significance of the Frontier in American History" (reprinted in F. J. Turner 1986, 1–38). "It is no real exaggeration to state that after the presentation of Turner's theoretical argument, the telling of American history was never quite the same": W. R. Jacobs in F. J. Turner 1986, ix–x. Later that summer, at the Exposition's Festival Hall, Frederick Douglass would evaluate the course of American history from a much different perspective (Blight 2018, 734–739).

[6] Denison was chosen because the first ("Old") University of Chicago had failed in 1886, despite the efforts of the elder Goodspeed, an alumnus and indefatigable fundraiser (above, n. 1), to save it (cf. C. T. B. Goodspeed 1932, esp. chs. II–III; Boyer 2015, ch. I). His brother Charles (see below) also attended Denison, rooming with Edgar. Edgar would later give the keynote address at Denison's centennial celebration (1931) and be awarded honorary doctorates of Divinity and Letters. The Edgar J. Goodspeed Collection at Denison contains manuscripts and letters touching upon the Goodspeeds' connections with Denison, Edgar's graduation photograph, a biographical sketch by Walter Eisenreis (dependent on Goodspeed 1953), and a February 1973 typescript for Allison 1975. Later correspondence concerns books donated to Denison by Goodspeed and the transfer of Goodspeed papyri from Denison to Chicago—but there is rather more than this, much of it, however, as far as Goodspeed himself is concerned, late (from his California years) and even posthumous.

[7] A memoir of the untimely deceased Harper (1856–1906) was begun by Thomas Goodspeed—it was to be his life's final work (C. T. B. Goodspeed 1932, 70). Upon Thomas's death (1927), Edgar helped bring it to completion (T. W. Goodspeed 1928). For an account of Harper and the founding of the University with more emotional distance, see Storr 1966. The years of Harper's presidency (1892–1906) were academically inventive but financially anxious: Boyer 2015, ch. II.

at Chicago and continuing his studies in Semitics, earning a Bachelor of Divinity degree that was capped by an 1897 thesis on an unedited Syriac manuscript of the New Testament.[8] Two years previously, however, with some friendly pressure applied by Ernest De Witt Burton,[9] and having been inspired in the summer quarter of 1895 by Caspar René Gregory's visiting lectures on New Testament manuscripts,[10] he had changed his doctoral concentration to New Testament Studies in the Department of Biblical and Patristic Greek. This would lead to his Ph.D. *summa cum laude* in that field on 1 April 1898.[11] It was Gregory who had pointed him toward his dissertation topic on "The Newberry Gospels."[12]

With his Ph.D. fresh in hand, Goodspeed was added to Chicago's faculty as an "Assistant in Biblical and Patristic Greek,"[13] but with President Harper's insistence that he spend time abroad, studying, visiting universities, traveling and "networking" with European scholars in preparation for a fully engaged life of teaching and research (the extension to Egypt and the Holy Land was not part of any original

---

[8] Goodspeed 1897. This is catalogued in the Regenstein Library as an M.A. thesis, but it was the capstone for his B.D. (and is thus recorded in Cobb and Jennings 1948, 7, and Cook 1981, 81). The language (Syriac) perhaps looks back to Goodspeed's past studies in Semitics, the substance (New Testament) to his new concentration.

[9] Burton was professor of New Testament interpretation and department head at this time. He would later become the University's third president, 1923–1925, years of "renewal" according to Boyer 2015, 163–185. He was the subject of one of the elder Goodspeed's biographies of Chicago colleagues and benefactors (T. W. Goodspeed 1926). In 1933 Edgar became the Ernest De Witt Burton Distinguished Service Professor of the University of Chicago (Cook 1981, 4).

[10] Goodspeed 1953, 94: "It was Dr. Burton's bringing of Professor Gregory [to the University of Chicago] ... that gave a new direction to my studies." Cf. Metzger 1997, 39. Caspar René Gregory (1846–1917) was a Germanized American of French descent (Grégoire), a distinguished New Testament textual critic, professor at Leipzig, teenage veteran of the American Civil War, and aged casualty (on the German side) in World War I. There is an odd little obituary for him in *Biblical World* 50 (1917) 300–301. After Chicago, Goodspeed and Gregory renewed their acquaintance when the former stopped to visit the latter at Leipzig while touring German universities: Goodspeed 1953, 108. Details of the visit would have been recorded in the lost "Student Travel Letters vol. 1." Gregory reappears in a cameo role, though offstage, in Ch. 3. Goodspeed 1953, 96–97, offers a glowing assessment of his former teacher as a scholar and person.

[11] "[S]*umma*": Goodspeed 1953, 94, for the circumstances behind the distinction. "1 April 1898": University of Chicago 1897–1898, 151 (Chicago was on the quarter system). We are inclined to accept this date over Goodspeed's own more general recollection in Goodspeed 1953, 94 ("I took my Doctor of Philosophy, in the spring of 1898 ...") and 95 ("At an evening convocation at which I took my degree in March of 1898 ..."). If his recollection is correct, there must have been a separate, slightly earlier convocation for his award, a hypothesis for which we have no support. In any case, a letter of James Henry Breasted to Goodspeed, 4 April 1898 (see below), addressed to "My dear Doctor!" suggests fresh receipt of the degree, which was awarded through Chicago's Divinity School. See further App. A.

[12] Goodspeed 1899a (the first publication of the thesis), at 116. The gospels in question were on a twelfth-century parchment codex in Chicago's Newberry Library; the dissertation was subsequently republished as Goodspeed 1902c.

[13] University of Chicago 1904–1905, 22–23. He held this title during his time abroad; on his return he was promoted to "Associate."

plan, nor was the return to Oxford in summer 1900). He began his sojourn abroad at Berlin, where he spent six months studying early Christian literature and the history of dogma.[14] During this period and the nearly year and a half that followed, in a project that was planned before his departure (he was "to post twice a week, news or no news"),[15] Edgar maintained a richly detailed correspondence with his father and mother (separately), and with his older brother, his only sibling, Charles Ten Broeke Goodspeed (1869–1949), a Chicago attorney whose clients included the Y.M.C.A. and the Hyde Park Baptist Church.[16] He wrote his letters in sequential rotation—with each covering a series of days rather than a single day—to brother, father, and mother, the latter sometimes addressed or referred to as "Pater" and "Mater"; but it is thanks specifically to brother Charles that this correspondence was gathered, arranged chronologically, and "thoughtfully" bound in two volumes.[17] The first volume of the collected letters has vanished. Its expected place of deposition would have been box 47 of the Edgar J. Goodspeed Papers in Chicago. What will be found there today, in two folders (20 and 21), is in fact labeled "Book of Travel Letters 1889[sic]–1900." The letters there, however, do not amount to a book; moreover, they all concern Edgar's working excursion in Europe in the company of his wife Elfleda dating to 1903.[18] On the contrary, the second volume with its 308 sheets, approximately 600 sides, of handwritten

---

[14] For the German research institution as a model for newly developing American graduate programs, see Clark 2006, 463–465, with specific mention of Johns Hopkins, Chicago, Harvard, and Columbia. For the model's influence on Harper: Boyer 2015, 131–144 ("Chicago and the World: A German Research University?"). At the time Berlin was the pinnacle of the German system, and Goodspeed was not the only one Harper encouraged to study there; James Henry Breasted had preceded him (Abt 2011, esp. 23–24).

[15] Letter to Father, begun on 24 June 1900 (Goodspeed box 48, folder 1).

[16] The family joined this church, "meeting in a little frame building at Fifty-fourth Street and Madison (now Dorchester) Avenue," in 1893 (C. T. B. Goodspeed 1932, 56). In 1961, Edgar donated a stained-glass window in memory of his parents and brother to the successor of the Hyde Park Baptist Church, the Hyde Park Union Church, 5600 South Woodlawn Avenue, where it can still be seen. It is described along with the other windows in a booklet available at the church (*Hyde Park Union Church* [1989], 16–17 for the Goodspeed window; our thanks to Alice Mulberry for this lead).

[17] Goodspeed n.d., ch. II, p. 2 ("thoughtfully," though disposing of the envelopes with their stamps and postmarks; for an exception see the 1 July 1899 letter to Father). Cf. Goodspeed's own later binding of Burton's "journal letters" sent from China in 1909: Goodspeed 1953, 126–127. While abroad, Goodspeed tended to receive letters from home in batches—he does not seem to have saved these—and this correspondence conditioned responses in his own letters, giving occasional glimpses of what had been written to him by his family, friends, and associates. He did preserve letters and postcards from B. P. Grenfell (see Chs. 2 and 3), two letters from Caspar René Gregory (Ch. 3), one from B. L. Gildersleeve (Ch. 3), and a postcard from Theodor Nöldeke (below in this chapter, n. 65), no doubt because of their professional significance.

[18] Summarized in Goodspeed 1953, 136–139. The centerpiece concerns eventually successful efforts to gain access to the Chapter Library in Toledo in search of medieval manuscripts. He would receive general advice about this excursion from A. S. Hunt; relevant correspondence survives in Goodspeed box 5, folder 4.

letters does survive as "Student Travel Letters vol. 2" in box 48, folder 1.[19] Its first letter dates to 5 June 1899; the last concludes with the underlined notation "5 p.m. Aug. 27, 1900." The volume's cover, a light brown, measures 11" high x 8" wide x 2¾" thick. A challenge for Edgar was to provide his recipients and the prospective collection with sheets of paper of uniform size for ease of binding. At this he was almost always successful,[20] but even though of uniform size, the sheets of paper varied in thickness, quality, and tint;[21] they were sometimes so thin as to cause see-through or bleed-through effects. In filling these pages, Edgar left little or no room for margins, habitually packing them to all edges with writing and, sometimes, drawings and sketches. On his end Charles used sheets from a book on *Commercial and Banking Law* as backing for photographs and other special inserts. He used pages 525–676 of the lawbook after the last of Edgar's letters to extend the compilation's thickness to fit the cover he had provided. Underlines on the letters in red seem to be by Edgar himself, perhaps made as he later consulted them while composing his memoir *As I Remember* (Goodspeed 1953).[22] Filed at the end of Edgar's letters is a sheaf of seven letters on small stationery addressed to cousins named Sarah (five letters) and Sue (two).[23]

---

[19]Unless otherwise noted, all letters cited herein come from this source. Goodspeed himself (Goodspeed n.d., ch. II, p. 1) later estimated this epistolary output at 300,000 words, enough to fill "three or four fair sized volumes" ("three or" is a later insertion in ink). That the letters were bound in only two volumes, with the second not filled to the space available (see below), is suggestive of how large vol. 1 must have been. Strangely, writing about his letters on 27 April 1900 (in continuation of 25 April), he says to his mother, "I hope that 2d vol. is full"—this when he had three and a half months left before coming home. Numerous photographs from the period covered by vol. 1 are in box 52, folder 2; see also Goodspeed 1953, 107–109.

[20]He sometimes resorted to hotel stationery and once used the undersized stationery of the "Friends' Summer School, Birmingham, Sept. 4th to 15th 1899" in a 15 September 1899 letter to Father.

[21]"[T]int": usually in a white to yellowish range, but once early on making do with slightly undersized blue paper, while the final 31 sheets, in proper size, beginning with a 4 July 1900 letter to Father, are light blue.

[22]The Goodspeed Papers contain two typescripts of *As I Remember*, one in box 19, folders 6–9 (version 1), the other—with some markup for typesetting—in box 20, folders 1–4 (version 2). As for the red underlinings, it is perhaps even more likely that they helped him prepare Goodspeed n.d. (see next paragraph). It is also conceivable that they are the product of an effort by Charles to index the correspondence, though Edgar discouraged him from this task ("[D]ont kill yourself on that index.") in a letter of 27 June 1899.

[23]"Sarah" is surely Goodspeed's maternal cousin, Sarah Ellen Mills, b. 24 October 1869 in Quincy and mentioned in Goodspeed 1953, 33. She would work in various librarian positions in Morgan Park and, eventually, on the Hyde Park campus (cf., e.g., University of Chicago 1904–1905, 32, and *American Library Annual* 1916–1917, 333). The 1920 U.S. census documents her as a resident in the home of Goodspeed's parents on South Blackstone Avenue. It spells her name, incorrectly, as "Sara" and places the family at 5761 S. Blackstone; this should be 5765. The identity of "Sue" is less certain, but it seems probable that she is also the addressee of a 30 November 1890 letter (box 13, folder 5) sent from New Haven, which Goodspeed closes with "Your affectionate Cousin." The letter's reference to "Aunt Sarah" (Sarah Mills née Ten Broeke, the mother of Sarah Ellen Mills) suggests another maternal cousin.

Goodspeed also reviewed his "Student Travel Letters" as he was composing "Abroad in the Nineties," an unpublished and undated typewritten memoir that is likewise preserved among his papers (box 19, folder 1). This covers the same two years abroad in briefer compass than in the "Student Travel Letters," but in richer detail and with greater candor than in *As I Remember*. It may have been composed simultaneously with that book, its ninety-plus pages eventually reduced for publication to the ten pages (106–115) of *As I Remember*, chapter VIII, "Foreign Shores."[24] Nevertheless, the typescript also bears signs that Goodspeed returned to it *after* his memoir's publication, clues that events that had once been fifty years old had turned sixty.[25] Whatever the circumstances and timing of composition and revision, one of the values of "Abroad in the Nineties" lies in its partial compensation for the missing "Student Travel Letters vol. 1." Of course, it further complicates the problem of collating Goodspeed's immediate reactions to events as conveyed in the letters with his reflections in his published and unpublished reminiscences more than half a century later, susceptible as they seem to have been, at times, to "the forgetfulness or the sensibility of advancing years."[26]

❄ ❄ ❄ ❄

As he describes the experience in *As I Remember*, it was in his "last graduate year at Chicago" that Goodspeed saw his first papyrus:[27]

> I heard of it one night at the New Testament Club when Dr. Clyde W. Votaw said there was a Greek papyrus in Dr. Breasted's office.[28] Next morning I called on my

---

[24] It is divided into named chapters, starting—significantly—with VIII ("I Go to Sea," in type), corrected to I ("A German University of Yore," handwritten), ending with VII (with a two-line heading in typed capitals: "THE TREASURE OF LEVIATHAN | AMONG THE CROCODILES"). The manuscript obviously had been reconceived and was being revised as a standalone work.

[25] The cover sheet changes the typewritten title from "TRAINING FOR TRANSLATION -- PALESTINE, PAPYRI, AND PEOPLE" to "Abroad in the Nineties or 'Tis Sixty Years Since' with Apologies to Sir Walter," a reference to the alternative title of Sir Walter Scott's *Waverly* (1814); cf. Goodspeed 1953, 61, using this tag again but in a different context, the 1951 Yale commencement—i.e., sixty years since Goodspeed's 1890–1891 year at Yale. Elsewhere, there is a reference to fifty years, not sixty, ch. V, p. 14; "more than fifty years," ch. III, p. 7. In ch. V, p. 9, "fifty years ago" has been corrected by hand to "sixty years ago" by the neat overwriting of the two f's. To make this absolutely clear: Fifty, in referring back to events of 1898–1900, suggests a time of writing of 1948–1950, before *As I Remember*'s 1953 publication; sixty indicates a time of writing of 1958–1960.

[26] Gosse 1984, 33.

[27] "[L]ast graduate year": Goodspeed 1953, 98, but his recollection about the timing is wrong; see App. A.

[28] Votaw was then Instructor of New Testament Literature; he received his Ph.D. from the University two years before Goodspeed. The New Testament Club was founded in 1892–1893. In the club's records in the SCRC (one box), folder 11 contains a letter, dated 22 November 1943, from Goodspeed to Harold H. Platz, in which he recalls the incident with Votaw. This letter also indicates that Goodspeed remembered beginning his involvement with the Club in 1894–1895.

old friend James Henry Breasted and asked about it.²⁹ He got it right out and in five minutes there I was, well started on the downward path to papyrology.

The papyrus in question was the Ayer papyrus, named for its purchaser, Edward E. Ayer, Civil War veteran (in the Far West), broker of railroad ties and telephone poles, collector of antiquities and rare ornithological books, co-founder and first president of Chicago's Field Columbian Museum.³⁰ He had obtained it in Cairo in 1894.³¹ As Breasted made no claims on the papyrus, it was turned over to Goodspeed for publication.³²

As soon revealed to the scholarly world,³³ the Ayer papyrus presents a mathematical text with a host of problems, geometrical and palaeographical. Toward resolving these, Goodspeed had conferred with experts at home (mathematicians in America) and abroad (England, Germany). Among those consulted by mail was Bernard Pyne Grenfell, who had recently made his first big splashes in the yet-to-be-named field of papyrology.³⁴ Goodspeed later described his impressions

---

²⁹On Breasted (1865–1935), see Abt 2011, Bierbrier 2012, 78–79. "[M]y old friend": Goodspeed first met Breasted when the two Illinoisans (Breasted was from Rockford; he is buried there in Greenwood Cemetery: Abt 2011, xi–xv, 397–402) were studying at Yale under Harper's guidance, 1890–1891 (Goodspeed 1953, 59). Reference to "my old friend" was therefore perhaps written from the octogenarian memoirist's perspective rather than the young graduate student's. Nevertheless, Goodspeed was innately quick to identify friends, and there is no doubt that in time the friendship with Breasted was mutually and deeply felt. See Breasted's affectionate letter to Goodspeed, 28 April 1930 (box 1, folder 21), addressed to him as an "old friend" whose memory like Breasted's "reaches back to the old Yale days when the University of Chicago was still a dream." See also the incident (unrolling the papyri) described below. Still the friendship was not without its bumps, as incidents mentioned in Chs. 2 and 3 will show.

³⁰Today's Field Museum of Natural History. For Ayer (1841–1927), see Lockwood 1929; Hickey and Worp 1997, 80–81.

³¹For the year, the source of the funds, and other details, see App. A. Price: £3 (whether British or Egyptian is not specified) according to a letter from Ayer to Goodspeed, 29 October 1897 (box 1, folder 13); "five pounds": Goodspeed 1953, 98. For the provenance, see below in this chapter, n. 36; for the dealer, see Ch. 2, n. 60. Ayer was also the source for ostraka now housed in the Field Museum and the Oriental Institute of the University of Chicago (cf. Goodspeed 1904a, 45–46).

³²Ayer in his letter of 29 October 1897 (preceding note) indicates he had given the rights to Breasted: "I talked to Dr. Breasted about it, and told him he could publish it if he desired, of course giving the Field Columbian Museum the credit of being the possessor."

³³Thanks to Goodspeed's prompt publication: Goodspeed 1898a (republication: P.Chic. 3). Five years later, a brief account geared to non-specialists followed: Goodspeed 1903b. A second letter from Ayer (also from box 1, folder 13), written from his vacation home in Lake Geneva on 27 June 1898, thanks "Dear Mr. Goodspeed" for sending a copy of the 1898 publication; he seems pleased at having the papyrus named for him.

³⁴For Grenfell (1869–1926), see the brief treatments of Bierbrier 2012, 225–226, and Lehnus 2007, 115–120. "[F]irst big splashes": P.Rev. and P.Grenf. I of 1896. Grenfell's advance separate publication, with A. S. Hunt (Grenfell's slightly younger colleague), of P.Oxy. I 1 as ΛΟΓΙΑ ΙΗΣΟΥ, Sayings of the Lord (Grenfell and Hunt 1897), would appear in July 1897, selling more than 30,000 copies at 2 shillings apiece: E. G. Turner 2007, 19; cf. Nongbri 2018, 338 n. 11, citing the Egypt Exploration Fund's

of Grenfell in a letter to Sarah, 18–19 December 1899:

> Do you know about him? He's an Oxonian, Queen's college, 30 years old, of a most taking presence: has the most brilliant smile I ever beheld, and is clever clear through. He publishes 1 large book and 1 small book every year; has dug five or 6 years in Egypt, + found more Greek papyri than any living man. These he edits in a manner that puts other Englishmen in the shade and the Germans + French to positive shame and confusion.[35] [Fig. 2]

Grenfell wrote back cordially lending some ideas and offering apologies for not (he said) being able to offer more assistance: "I am afraid that, not being a mathematician, I am unable to help you much."[36] His letter's 15 November 1897 date provides the *terminus ante quem* for the beginning of what would become Goodspeed's relationship with Grenfell, a major influence during the early years of his professional career.

Goodspeed, by the way, also found it ironic that he, like Grenfell, should be contending with a papyrus on a topic for which he felt little aptitude. Nevertheless, the Ayer papyrus was his

> introduction to a new field, in which no American had up to that time taken a hand,[37] and it also served to introduce me to a whole string of European workers in Greek papyri, most notably Bernard Grenfell and Arthur Hunt at Oxford, who later became my generous friends.[38]

At the same time, Goodspeed recalls, he had himself caught the collecting bug:

---

secretary's report (25,800 copies within the first year of publication). For the impression made upon Goodspeed by the *Logia*, see Goodspeed 1953, 99, 110. "[Y]et-to-be-named field": Cf. Keenan 2009, 61.

[35] Goodspeed box 48, folder 1. A bit later this letter states, "His friend Hunt is less brilliant perhaps, but even nicer, if possible than B.P.G." Andrews n.d., 2:2, may be compared regarding the appeal of Hunt: "Dr. Hunt and Dr. Grenfell were on the boat and we found them as always – delightful and interesting. The former especially I like." Note also Goodspeed's later remarks to his mother about Grenfell and Hunt (letter of 17 May 1900, in continuation on 18 May): "They are certainly the most incorrigible and incomparable bookmakers anywhere"—a likely nod to Eccles. 12:12, "Of making many books there is no end" (*KJV*; cf. below in this chapter, n. 89).

[36] Goodspeed box 4, folder 9. Grenfell's letter included information that Goodspeed would use in Goodspeed 1898a, 26: "The only precise information obtainable as to the place where the papyrus was found comes from Mr. Grenfell, of Oxford. Mr. Grenfell kindly writes me that he saw the fragment in Egypt some four years ago, in the hands of a dealer who said that he found it at Hawara, in the Fayum, near the pyramid; and as he was known to have been digging there, his story may have been true. This accords with what was said to Mr. Ayer, at the time the fragment was purchased." For the identity of the dealer, see Ch. 2, n. 60.

[37] Cf. Cobb and Jennings 1948, 2: "the first American to collect, decipher, and publish Greek papyri."

[38] Goodspeed 1953, 99–100.

Figure 2: Bernard P. Grenfell, ca. 1897
Public domain; sourced from *McClure's* 9 (1897) 1023 (personal copy of T. M. Hickey).

Having tasted research, I soon became the victim of it. I felt I must have more papyri to decipher and if possible publish. I wanted pieces that had not been deciphered to see what I could make of them.[39]

In satisfaction of this aim, he managed to purchase papyri, "a small collection that had not been studied,"[40] from a dealer through one of Breasted's connections, the Rev. J. R. Alexander, D.D., a missionary of the United Presbyterian Church of North America, stationed in Asyūṭ since 1875, now at the beginning of his service (1896–1909) as president of the mission school, Assiut College for Boys.[41] Archival letters confirm the information Goodspeed himself gave readers about provenance in Goodspeed 1902b, but they add significant details about the papyri and their acquisition.[42]

5 February 1897, Breasted writes to "My dear Goodspeed" confirming that he (Breasted) had in Goodspeed's name sent £25-11-9, English exchange, to "Mr. J. R. Alexander, Assiût, Egypt, with explicit instructions as to packing." Breasted's 4 February cover letter to Alexander has not survived, but reference to it establishes a date before which negotiations about purchasing the papyri must have occurred, presumably reaching back into 1896.

22 April 1897, Alexander writes acknowledging receipt of Breasted's letter and its enclosure, which he calls "exchange for $125."[43] He proceeds to describe the purchase as featuring an *Iliad* fragment of Book VIII ("with accents in place, time of Vespasian, middle of third [sic] Cy."), letters and fragments thereof, "two or three dilapidated rolls," unopened, and 50 or 60 tax or business receipts ("all dated and all in very perfect condition"). The cost was $135, and so over budget, but still presented as a good deal—as confirmed by A. H. Sayce, who happened to be present to advise the reverend concerning the contents.[44] Alexander frets over

---

[39] Goodspeed 1953, 100.

[40] Goodspeed 1953, 100.

[41] See for these details *Annual Report* 1907, 6, 79–82 (separate photographs of faculty, above, and students, below, between 80 and 81; in the former Alexander must be the bearded gentleman, front row center), 129, 211; *Annual Report* 1916, 6, 80, 134, 138, 140, 263. In full on the North American missionary movement and its aim to "occupy" (D. M. Reid 2015, 201) Egypt: Sharkey 2008, in which Alexander is a prominent figure. For more on his purchasing activities, see Packman 1992, 42. Another American Presbyterian missionary was at this time engaged in antiquities collection and transactions on a much grander scale than Alexander: Chauncey Murch (1856–1907; Bierbrier 2012, 392), based in Luxor and agent in some of E. A. W. Budge's acquisitions for the British Museum. "Murch helped Budge to make useful connections with local dealers and later received and cashed the treasury warrants sent out by the Trustees of the British Museum to pay the locals for what Budge had purchased": Wilson 1964, 78–79.

[42] The pertinent letters are in Goodspeed box 1, folder 3.

[43] According to Officer 2018, the exchange rate was $4.86/£1, i.e., the conversion quoted by Alexander is almost exact (too high by only 64¢).

[44] Sayce (1845–1933) was a clergyman and famed Assyriologist, but one who spent much time in Egypt, especially in winter, traveling the Nile in his own boat (*dhahabīyah*), the *Ishtar*. Emma Andrews

the difficulty of getting the papyri out of Egypt ("You know that such things are contraband"), but envisions bringing them to Alexandria in June and clearing customs for dispatch to Chicago.[45] (The $125 later prompted Goodspeed's recollection of his financial condition in 1897: "Into this enterprise," he recalls, "I poured my modest student savings."[46])

14 March 1898, Alexander writes to Goodspeed ("Dear Mr. Goodspeed"), responding to a (lost) letter from Goodspeed seeking information about his purchases. The letter is courteous, apologetic for the long delay (he had great trouble getting the information desired—his sources remain anonymous), but at last reveals the following: "(1) The papyri were found in the Faiyum at a town called Washim. (2) They were found by people digging in the heaps or "tells" of dirt and rubbish at the edge of the town. As they dug down they found walls of houses standing in position. In the rooms of these houses or some of them they found the papyri -- some were in sacks, others in piles in corners, etc. (3) The pieces are all from that one town but probably not all from the same old ruin -- but from different houses." Alexander concludes with repeated "regrets at the great delay" and "kind regards."[47]

4 April 1898, Breasted, regretful and surprised at having just received another letter from Alexander (lost) enclosing a bill for duty on the papyri, thinks Alexander is mistaken about his cost—rather a "charge [...] by customs brokers"—and so informs "My dear Doctor!" The exclamation point in the address must stress its congratulatory allusion to Goodspeed's just earned Ph.D.

Whether the extra invoice was ever paid is unknown, but Alexander was good to his word of 22 April 1897 about shipping the papyri. Having been safely packed in two tin cigarette boxes stuffed with cotton, they arrived in Chicago in October.[48] When opened they proved to contain the papyri as Alexander had described

---

(n.d., 1:101) noted the vessel's "very large" stern cabin, "fitted as a library – with bookcases to the ceiling – a charming, scholarly room – and here Prof. S. says he really does his work for the whole year." For Sayce, see further Bierbrier 2012, 489–490, D. M. Reid 2015, 180–181, 213.

[45] This letter's original has not been located. We cite from a copy in Goodspeed's hand.

[46] Goodspeed 1953, 100; equivalent in 2019 to $3,970 according to the Consumer Price Index (Williamson 2021).

[47] For this letter, we rely on the typewritten transcript by R. W. Allison, dated February 1973, in the Goodspeed Collection at Denison. The letter, not incorporated in Allison 1975, is missing from its proper location (box 1, folder 3) in the Goodspeed Papers in Chicago. "Washim" (Kawn Aushīm) is the modern equivalent of the ancient village of Karanis.

[48] October receipt: *P.Kar.Goodsp.*, p. 1. An article about Goodspeed's papyri, described as reaching Chicago "within the last few weeks," appeared in the local press: "Old Papyri in Town," *Chicago Daily Tribune*, 6 December 1897, p. 46. One of its subheads reads "Best Ever in America," and it identifies the source of the manuscripts as an "old Arab Sheik," who was "digging about in the sands somewhere along the Nile. He took pains to conceal the place of discovery, but he offered the bundle of old papyri for sale, and at length it found its way to Dr. [William Matthew Flinders] Petrie." Of course, the Fayyūm is not strictly "along the Nile," and sheikhs are old by definition. The links between the sheikh, Petrie (for whom see below in this chapter, n. 81), and Alexander are unclear. The appearance

them.⁴⁹ Goodspeed and Breasted ("James"), in Goodspeed's later words, "repaired to my mother's kitchen, and with a steaming kettle carefully softened and unrolled the two sizable rolls which were the most impressive pieces [the boxes] contained."⁵⁰ Upon opening they proved to preserve, not any hoped-for pieces of Greek literature, but, combined, a nearly twelve-foot length of estate accounts from the second century AD.⁵¹ And thus if it was the Ayer papyrus that had started Goodspeed "on the downward path to papyrology," it was his own collection, with its Homer, its grain receipts, and its freshly unrolled accounts, that sped him on his way.⁵²

✣ ✣ ✣ ✣

Not quite a year after receiving his papyri, Edgar began his foreign adventure, headed for Berlin, departing by train, "the night train over the Erie road," for New York from Chicago's Rock Island Depot on 15 September 1898.⁵³ His luggage included a thoughtful parting gift from Charles, a camera that "became the constant companion" of his journeys, affording him, as he later wrote, "much pleasure as an amateur photographer" and the means to illustrate the articles he planned to write.⁵⁴ He also brought papyri from his personal collection.⁵⁵ In Berlin, he strove to improve his German language skills, verbal and reading,⁵⁶ pursued theological

---

of Fayyūm papyri on the market so far south in Asyūṭ should not give pause; cf. Hickey 2014, 46 n. 8.

⁴⁹Cf., e.g., Goodspeed 1898b, 1902b (= *P.Kar.Goodsp.*), 1908, 1953, 100–103. Alexander also acquired some papyri of his own from this lot but soon deposited them in the Museum of Westminster College, New Wilmington, Pennsylvania (*P.Cair.Goodsp.*, p. 23). These became *P.Cair.Goodsp.* 16–27, "The Alexander Papyri." Other Alexander pieces at Westminster, small fragments, are published in Packman 1992.

⁵⁰"[M]other's kitchen": evidently a large one, "eat-in" in today's terms, in the family home, an Italianate frame structure dating to 1865 at 5630 South Kimbark Avenue (C. T. B. Goodspeed 1932, 55–56, 67; www.zillow.com, consulted 7 June 2018).

⁵¹Goodspeed 1953, 100–101. The longer roll (47 columns, roughly 8¼ feet in length) was destined to become *P.Cair.Goodsp.* 30; for the shorter, see Goodspeed 1908.

⁵²For the unrolling, see also Danker 1988, 126–127.

⁵³Goodspeed n.d., ch. I, p. 1. "Erie road": in reference to the then-named Erie Railroad Company, which operated between New York and Chicago via Buffalo (britannica.com, consulted 21 July 2020). "Rock Island Depot": letter to Father, [15 June] 1900. Chicago's famed Union Station would not open for another twenty-five years.

⁵⁴The camera's case would also serve as a desk; see, e.g., 26 July continuation of 24 July 1899 letter to Mother: "I am writing on my camera case as usual."

⁵⁵Goodspeed n.d., ch. I, pp. 7–8. Their number excluded ten receipts already sent ahead to Berlin (below in this chapter, n. 61).

⁵⁶For his knowledge of German: Goodspeed 1953, 33, childhood study guided by his "charming cousin," Florence Mills, for whom see Ch. 2, n. 36. This and other details, including two years of college study and a graduate school reading group, are mentioned in Goodspeed n.d., ch. I, pp. 9–10, but cf. p. 5: Formal dinners were a strain on his German. Nevertheless, regarding a later occasion, he writes (17 November continuation of a 15 November 1899 letter to Father) about being "jolly in English and Ger-

studies, principally under the direction of Adolf von Harnack,[57] and, while sharing the workroom with Wilhelm Schubart, worked on his own papyri and on some Berlin material under the kindly guidance of Fritz Krebs.[58] Although in a letter to Sarah, 11 February 1899, he confessed to some discouragement with his progress on the Berlin "Urkunden," he kept at it, convinced that he would acquire a certain cachet by association if some of his work, "at least 2 pieces," were included in one of the *BGU* volumes then in production.[59] In the event, the third volume of the *Urkunden* did include editions of two papyri by Goodspeed (nos. 810 and 811),[60] and led to publication of the edition now abbreviated as *P.Kar.Goodsp.*, which presented most of Goodspeed's Chicago pieces for the first time and reprinted forty-three related pieces previously published in *BGU*.[61]

---

man" at lunch with his companions at the Gizeh Museum. It is amusing to note that in Goodspeed's literary thriller (Goodspeed 1935), the hero, from Chicago (p. 204), a barely concealed representation of the author, is obviously at ease speaking "in that melodious tongue" (p. 141).

[57] For the influence and career of Lutheran theologian and Church historian Carl Gustav Adolf von Harnack (1851–1930), see, in brief, Clark 2006, 466–471. Goodspeed found Harnack distant and uncooperative (Goodspeed n.d., ch. I, pp. 5–6).

[58] Goodspeed 1953, 107. For Friedrich ("Fritz") Maximilian Krebs (1867–1900), see Schubart 1901; note also Wilcken 1901. About this papyrological mentor Goodspeed writes, "This man Krebs, the acting director here, is a very good friend of mine, indeed. I shall bid him farewell with regret. His kindness to me has been absolutely unvarying and unqualified" (letter to Sarah, 11 February 1899; Goodspeed box 48, folder 1). Similar sentiments, written much later and tinged with regret over Krebs's early death: Goodspeed n.d., ch. I, pp. 7–9, though confused about Krebs's first name: Karl canceled, replaced with Franz. For Schubart (1873–1960), see Poethke 2007b.

[59] Goodspeed box 48, folder 1.

[60] The volume as a whole was not assembled until 1903, but fascicle 4 with Goodspeed's two pieces was shown to him on 31 July 1899, freshly published, when he visited Grenfell (and Hunt) in Oxford (31 July continuation of a letter to Charles begun on 27 July; Goodspeed n.d., ch. III, p. 5). "It hardly seems credible," he wrote at the time, "that Krebs should have run my thing : I find it difficult to realize it. It seems a great thing to me, you know, and I greatly hope will to you and Pater, and worth 3 weeks in Berlin." (His "3 weeks" must refer solely to the time spent editing these Berlin texts.) Copies of the fascicle, apparently sent by Krebs, eventually reached home; in a 31 August continuation of a 30 August 1899 letter to Mother, Edgar remarked, "Yes, it looks fine : the man who copies Wilcken's things copied it, & his hand is very good. I think you'll recognize the hand of the signature! I see you refer to it as my "article" : I fear you were disappointed when you really saw its meager proportions." (We thank Marius Gerhardt for the dates of the *BGU* fascicles, drawn from notes by Fritz Uebel preserved by Günter Poethke. Libraries, we have found, in binding the fascicles into volumes have typically disposed of their covers with their information about dates.)

[61] For *P.Kar.Goodsp.*, see above with nn. 48–49. The Berlin and Goodspeed shares of these granary receipts (and the Rev. Alexander's granary receipts, *P.Cair.Goodsp.* 16–24; see above, n. 49) must therefore have come from the same lot, divided after discovery and before sale. Reprints: *BGU* I 31, 104–105, 107, 152, 160, 167, 169–172, 201–211, 262–263, 278–280, 284–285, 294, 331; II 438–443, 516–517, 626; III 701, 720–721. Letters from Krebs to Goodspeed, 10 November 1897, 5 May 1898, and 7 July 1898 (box 5, folder 18) indicate, among other things, that before Goodspeed left for Berlin he knew that there was a connection between his purchase and papyri in the Berlin collection. Goodspeed 1953, 102, credits his knowledge of this to Frank Bigelow Tarbell, then professor of classical archaeology at Chicago. The letter of 7 July 1898 reveals that Edgar had sent Krebs ten of his own papyri in advance of his arrival.

Despite this scholarly progress and Krebs's personal kindness and professional assistance, Goodspeed, while conceding the beauties of the Thiergarten (his preferred spelling) and Unter den Linden and the stateliness of the Brandenburg Gate, in later reflection based on a review of letters now lost, concluded that he had found Berlin so "drab" and "dull" that he was happy to leave it, on 15 February 1899, for "a tour of the Luther country" and "a dozen German universities."[62] For our purposes the tour presents three highlights, all from its latter half:

(1) Goodspeed arrived at Vienna, the southernmost "German" city on his list, early in April (exact date uncertain). There he visited the Archduke Rainer Collection, already then with more than 100,000 papyri, making the acquaintance of Carl Wessely, "a poor gymnasium teacher," who nonetheless was "the veteran papyrographer of Europe."[63] After having Goodspeed home for supper, Wessely blessed him on departure with a stack of offprints.[64]

Krebs proposes, following Berlin practice, to mount Goodspeed's papyri between "airtight" ("<u>luftdicht</u>") glass panes at no cost.

[62] Goodspeed n.d., ch. I, p. 13: "dull, drab and distressing to a degree [...] almost intolerably drab and dull." His assessment may have been influenced by hindsight after two world wars, but the "Student Travel Letters" make clear that already in 1899 there were negative feelings; one very brief example from a 7 August continuation of a 4 August letter to Mother: "I dread the continent <u>indescribably</u>." For Berlin specifically, Henry Adams's harsh conclusions from his experience of the city forty years earlier may be compared. Berlin, according to the "deplorably Bostonian" Adams, was in 1858 "a poor, keen-witted, provincial town, simple, dirty, uncivilized, and in most respects disgusting. Life was primitive beyond what an American boy could have imagined" (H. Adams 1918, 371, 77, respectively). "[T]our of the Luther country," consisting of four sites: Goodspeed 1953, 107; "German universities": Goodspeed n.d., ch. II, p. 2, where the handwritten insertion of "Giessen" raises the dozen to thirteen. And the number climbs still higher, for version 1 of *As I Remember* (ch. VIII, p. 110) counts Bonn as "my fifteenth German university" in an above-the-line insertion; version 2 (ch. VIII, p. 102) incorporates this into the text on the line, and it makes its way into Goodspeed 1953, 109. He had chosen university cities where "serious Greek and biblical research was carried on" (Goodspeed 1953, 107).

[63] "[P]apyrographer": The earliest reference to "papyrographer" in *OED* (s.v. "papyro-, combining form") dates to 1906, but note Haeberlin 1897, 5: "Denn wer ist heute noch im stande, das gesamte Arbeitsfeld der griechischen Papyrographie, um mich dieses neuen Ausdrucks zu bedienen, auch nur einigermaßen zu übersehen, wie es sich seit anderthalb Jahrhunderten ausgebreitet hat?" ("Since who today is still capable of ignoring even to some degree the entire field of Greek papyrography—to use this new expression—since it has been expanding for a century and a half?") Goodspeed more commonly employs "palaeographer," as for example in reference to a conversation of 31 July 1899; see below in this chapter.

[64] Letter to Sarah, 7 April 1899 (Goodspeed box 48, folder 1); Goodspeed n.d., ch. II, pp. 6–8 (pp. 7 and 6, respectively, for the quotations), where (p. 6) he identifies Wessely as "Professor Franz Wessely"; cf. Goodspeed 1953, 108: "Franz Wessely," "chief interpreter" of the Rainer papyri. For Wessely (1860–1931), as a rule referred to as Carl in the literature, see Harrauer 2007; cf. Bierbrier 2012, 573: "*Carl* Franz Josef Wessely" (our stress). Note further Goodspeed's 4 May 1899 letter from Munich to President Harper (University of Chicago, Office of the President: Harper, Judson and Burton Administrations, records, box 46, folder 16): "At Vienna I met Karabaçek [*sic*], the Arabist, and called on Wessely, who shewed me the Rainer papyri, and insisted on taking me home to supper, and presenting me with a splendid lot of his printed articles." For Goodspeed's habitual use of archaic "shewed," see

(2) At Straßburg, as it was then spelled, he joined a small class for advanced students that Professor Theodor Nöldeke was holding in his home. One day as the group was waiting for the last student to arrive, "the old gentleman looked around on us and said, whimsically, 'Meine Herren, ich bin der einzige Deutscher!'"

It was true. He was the only German there. There were two Americans, one Englishman,

> one Welshman, one Greek; the only German in the class came in a moment later. The next day I went back to Noeldeke's class, and it was Ethiopic day. I had done some Ethiopic in Chicago, and it attracted me strangely that morning, a fact that was to influence me greatly a few weeks later, at the British Museum.[65]

(3) It was at Mainz, as he later thought, near the end of his circuit of Germany, that he received "a letter of great importance."

> It was from Mr. Joseph Bond of Chicago ... He very generously offered me five hundred dollars to enable me to visit Egypt and the Holy Land the following winter. Of course I welcomed the opportunity.[66]

There is no doubt that the source of the financial support was Mr. Bond, a Chicago businessman and University of Chicago trustee, but perhaps Goodspeed misremembered that the letter conveying the news came not from Bond himself, but from Shailer Mathews, soon-to-be "Junior Dean" of the Divinity School—either that or there were two letters, one from Bond, one from Mathews. It is certain in any case that "Dean Mathews" in his letter "suggested" that Edgar might use some

---

below in this chapter, n. 89. Karabacek et al. 1894 is an early, substantial, and magnificently illustrated survey of the Vienna collection as it stood in the first half of the 1890s (see p. XII for the 100,000 figure); a more recent history of the collection: *P.Rain.Cent.*, pp. 3–39 (by H. Loebenstein).

[65] Goodspeed n.d., ch. II, pp. 14–15; cf. Goodspeed 1953, 109. Nöldeke (1836–1930) was a leading Orientalist, especially influential for his earlier work dating the *suwar* (Surahs) of the Qur'an, a "fierce Prussian nationalist and racial bigot" and an "intimidating" presence according to Irwin 2008, 197–198, 214. He is known to ancient historians primarily for his translation of the Arabic *History* of al-Ṭabarī (Nöldeke 1879).

[66] Goodspeed 1953, 109; cf. Goodspeed n.d., ch. II, p. 20. Edgar hardly "welcomed the opportunity" when it first arose; writing to Father from Jerusalem (4 February continuation of 2 February 1900) and reflecting, he confessed—right after calling Mainz a "horrible town!"—"[T]he sheer certainty of having to add Palestine and Egypt to my itinerary had an abysmal effect on me. I knew then I was in for it you see!" Joseph Bond (1852–1902) was another early benefactor of the refounded University of Chicago, president of the American Radiator Company and soon to be (3 December 1901) Edgar's father-in-law (obituary in the *Chicago Tribune*, 9 August 1902, p. 8; Goodspeed 1953, 116–119). The chapel named for him is at 1050 East 59th Street. A "letter from Mr. Bond: enclosure 1040 mk." reached Edgar in London (letter to Father, 21 July 1899); the amount ($260; cf. "World's Currencies" 1899, 128–129) suggests that this was an installment, as does the fact that Edgar remained on the lookout for additional funds (cf. 26 November continuation of 20 November 1899 letter to Father, 6 February 1900 letter to Mother).

of the money toward purchasing papyri, a quarry he would pursue whenever the chance arose in the winter months ahead.[67]

❉ ❉ ❉ ❉

Following his German travels, Goodspeed would spend the summer of 1899 in England, coming first to London via Harwich, 16 June, and booking a room at 10 Bedford Place, "not very cheap and not very good" (the Ascot Races were in progress); nevertheless it became his residence of choice whenever he stayed in London (Fig. 3). He found his way "speedily into the manuscript room of the British Museum," and there met Frederic G. Kenyon, assistant keeper of manuscripts, already renowned editor of the Museum's Greek papyri. Kenyon proved to be "generosity itself," and Edgar, with typical rapidity, would number him among his "friends" in a mere nine days' acquaintance.[68] Two days after that declaration, on 27 June, after another audience with Kenyon, he reported to Charles:

> [T]hese chaps are not nearly so rich in them [papyri] as the Berlin men, in point of numbers : but Kenyon's luck in finding important literary pieces beggars all description, and puts him at the head of the whole bunch. He was very nice indeed, and spoke, incidentally, of my work in a surprisingly polite and appreciative way.- He has edited Mrs. Brownings' [sic] letters + I think Brownings poems; and is altogether

---

[67] Shailer Mathews (1863–1941), professor of New Testament history and interpretation, had joined Chicago's faculty in 1894. "Junior Dean": This appointment was approved and ratified by the Board of Trustees on 7 November 1899 (University of Chicago 1899, 244). Goodspeed's "Dean Mathews" on Goodspeed 1953, 109 and elsewhere, is therefore anachronistic. On a personal level, Mathews was responsible for introducing Edgar to his future wife, Elfleda Bond (Goodspeed 1953, 39, 94, etc.); see preceding note. He was an enthusiastic supporter of Goodspeed's later "manuscript hunting" (Goodspeed 1953, ch. XV). Mathews's "suggestion" to purchase papyri is mentioned in letters to Charles (21 February continuation of 20 February 1900) and to Father (21 [sic; 27] May continuation of 25 May 1900). In the latter of these, it is made clear that Mathews was thinking of the University's collection, but Edgar toys with the idea of keeping the papyri that he had purchased in Egypt (see below, Ch. 3, 27 May 1900)—"technically" permissible if Bond's grant was a "fellowship"—before proposing them as a gift to the University in Bond's name.

[68] Despite Kenyon's proverbial reserve, as documented by former colleagues (Kendrick et al. 1952). "[G]enerosity itself": thus Goodspeed n.d., ch. III, p. 1. Goodspeed n.d., ch. III, "Oh to be in England —," is a summary of the summer's events; cf. in great brevity Goodspeed 1953, 109–111. For Kenyon (1863–1952), editor of the Aristotelian *Constitution of Athens* and much more, see Bell 1952; cf. Pellé 2007. Goodspeed had already sent him an offprint of his 1898 article on the Ayer papyrus, to which Kenyon responded with detailed comments about both the hand and the text on 27 July 1898 (Goodspeed box 1, folder 22). A second letter, 24 August 1898, reveals that Edgar had asked to be sent the proofs for the parts of *P.Lond.* II relating "to the distribution of seed-corn," doubtless in connection with his work on the Karanis grain receipts. "[F]riends": 25 June continuation of a 23 June 1899 letter to Mother.

Figure 3: 10 Bedford Place, "where I hang out when in London."
Edgar J. Goodspeed photo; courtesy of the SCRC, University of Chicago.

a shining light and mighty nice young man as well. He has a bran˻(d?)˻ new book just out, which I must see.⁶⁹

Kenyon's generosity and kindness, however, did not extend to publishing the Museum's papyri; this was "reserved for the officers of the Museum," and thus Goodspeed wondered if he might "find something in his secondary line, Semitics."⁷⁰ In the event, he did, commencing work, 4 July, on two Ethiopic manuscripts, one from the fifteenth, the other from the eighteenth century, containing *The Acts of Thekla*, a popular and influential apocryphal account of a disciple of St. Paul.⁷¹ "Thekla" would become Edgar's principal academic occupation in London; indeed, it turned out to be a project that down to its completion ran parallel to—and at times won out over—his commitment to papyri.⁷²

Working on Thekla transferred Edgar from the Museum's reading room, with its "huge dimness," to the Oriental room, "quite an exclusive place [...] delightful [in its] light and comfortable [... with] skylights all along the ceiling, and big adjustable racks to hold the folios at any angle you please, and very few readers, and the best blotting pads I about ever saw."⁷³ It also brought him into the orbit

---

⁶⁹"[I]mportant literary pieces": e.g., Kenyon 1891a, 1891b, 1897b, any one of which would make a papyrological career; "my work": See previous note. Kenyon did edit the letters, verse, and prose of Elizabeth Barrett Browning (1897a, 1897c) but had not yet tackled Robert "Brownings poems"; his ten-volume centenary edition of these would appear in 1912 (Bell 1952, 280–281, with further discussion of his work concerning both Brownings). "[Y]oung man" seems odd as Kenyon was 36, Goodspeed not yet 28; cf., however, his characterization of Grenfell below. "[N]ew book": Kenyon 1899 ("just published" according to the *Guardian* of 8 February 1899, p. 16), which Goodspeed would see in Cairo on 20 December (letter to Father).

⁷⁰Goodspeed n.d., ch. III, p. 1.

⁷¹The Thekla project is first mentioned in a 4 July extension (dated "The Glorious Fourth") of a 1 July letter to Father, though Edgar may have discovered one of the manuscripts on 23 June (letter to Mother). Early on Goodspeed sought the counsel of and was encouraged in this work by Rendel Harris (cf. 5 July 1899 to Mother; for Harris, see below in this chapter, n. 104) and Nöldeke (cf. 10 July continuation of 7 July 1899 letter to Charles). A postcard from the Nöldeke (box 7, folder 6), postmarked "8.7.99" and addressed to 10 Bedford Place, Russell Square, is, after apology for delay, packed with much advice in limited space. For the *Acts of Thekla*, see, e.g., S. J. Davis 2001, 6–26.

⁷²Goodspeed 1901a and 1901b are his (identical) publications. A translation was included in a celebratory article in the *Sunday Chicago Tribune*, 24 February 1901, on the front page of section five: "First Translation of the Book of Thekla from the Ethiopic Made by Professor Edgar G. [sic] Goodspeed of the University of Chicago, Assisted by German and English Scholars" (Nöldeke and R. H. Charles [on whom see Chs. 2 and 3] are named). The *Tribune* overheatedly calls Goodspeed's work "one of the most important biblical discoveries of a decade" and gets much wrong, starting with the number of manuscripts (not one), their medium (not papyrus), and their date (not the fifth century).

⁷³"[D]imness": 19 July, 7 a.m., continuation of 17 July 1899 letter to Charles. The description of the Oriental room is drawn from letters of 1 July 1899 to Father (4 July continuation) and 5 July 1899 to Mother (6 July continuation). Goodspeed's emphasis on the rooms' lighting make us wonder if the eye problems that would plague him both later that summer (cf. 6 August continuation of 3 August 1899 to Mater) and later in life (see Epilogue below) were not already an issue, though good light is naturally a concern for anyone working with manuscripts.

CHICAGO BEGINNINGS AND AN AMERICAN ABROAD   25

of E. A. Wallis Budge, keeper of Egyptian and Assyrian antiquities.⁷⁴ Goodspeed approached Budge with "fear and trembling" (cf. 2 Cor. 7:15, Phil. 2:12), but like Kenyon he would turn out to be "most obliging."

> He occupies a room next the Mummies [...] I was admitted almost immediately and had a great talk with him. He thinks I ought to issue Thekla as a little book all by herself, and took a genuine and very helpful interest in my labors and problems in connection with her. He looks young for a man who has published so much; he is a stout man, with no gray hairs and with a stubby little moustache, and a rather small head. He told me he had lost 3 months or so from an operation on one of his eyes since coming back from Khartoum,- last winter I believe. He advised me about a lot of things on Thekla. Once speaking of Syriac he said, "of which we've all done h<u>ea</u>ps and t<u>on</u>s" in a most matter of fact way.⁷⁵

Despite his genuine enthusiasm for his new discovery, Edgar was scarcely averse to leisure and socializing. On 21 June, still during his first week in London, he went to Oxford "to see what it looked like on ˏwhat we callˏ Commencement Day" and caught sight of Cecil Rhodes and Lord Kitchener, "two great Englishmen," processing together into the Bodleian Library's Schools Quadrangle on the way to receive their honorary degrees in the Sheldonian Theatre.⁷⁶ In July, on the fifth, he took delight in attending the Henley Regatta,⁷⁷ and the following week was devoted to a cycling tour, a circuit from the capital extending as far west as Bristol and as far south as the Isle of Wight, with two friends. July 22 found him at the Queen's Club for an inter-collegiate track and field event—"The Prince [of Wales] was there, and also Walter Camp! I was more interested in the latter"⁷⁸—

---

⁷⁴For Budge (1857–1934), see the Prologue as well as Bierbrier 2012, 90–92.

⁷⁵"[M]ost obliging": Goodspeed 1953, 109. The remainder of the quoted material comes from the 26 July continuation of a 24 July 1899 letter to Mother. Goodspeed would end up publishing Thekla in both book and article form (see above, n. 72). Budge was in the Sudan in the autumn of 1897: Budge 1920, 152–153.

⁷⁶21 June continuation of 19 June 1899 to Father, Goodspeed 1953, 109–110, and Goodspeed n.d., ch. III, p. 1 (the last of these being the source of the quotations), showing no awareness of the controversy surrounding Rhodes's degree, stemming from his disgrace for instigating and planning the Jameson Raid (1895–1896), an attempted coup in the Transvaal; see Rotberg and Shore 1988, ch. 19 (516–550). Kitchener was freshly returned from his victory in the Sudan (cf. Neilson 2011). For the degree conferrals, see Rotberg and Shore 1988, 650–652; cf. Graves 1904 (illustrated) and Walter Duncan's lithograph of the ceremony in the *Graphic* of 1 July 1899, p. 17. Edgar's letter refers to the event as "Commemoration Day"; this is correct, but more technically it was Encænia Day within Commemoration Week. Goodspeed often seems to be sheepish or to offer excessive justification when describing non-academic endeavors, particularly to his father, for whom his time abroad represented a financial hardship. Here he begins, "I am a little in doubt as to whether I've been a fool today, or done a very clever thing."

⁷⁷See Goodspeed box 52, folder 1, for four photographs of the Regatta; "nice camera shots" are mentioned in his 5 July letter to Mother.

⁷⁸22 July continuation of 21 July 1899 to Father; for the event, see, e.g., "New England Loses," *Philadelphia Inquirer*, 23 July 1899, p. 15. Edgar was situated near the finishing tape and enclosed a piece of it

and throughout Edgar expended considerable time exploring London's sights, often but hardly exclusively in the company of a "stunning Buffalonian," Miss Granger.[79]

Clearly more important, though, was networking, or as Edgar called it, "lion hunting."[80] Having "bagged" Kenyon and Budge, he turned his attention to Flinders Petrie, boasting that he would catch him "like Proteus next Monday [24 July] when he emerges to look at his exhibition at University College."[81] On the appointed day, he and Fulton Coffin, "an old University friend,"[82] lay in wait amidst the displays, and when Petrie appeared, Edgar introduced the duo, and "we had a talk. He is a heavy set, dark, brisk man, in a flannel shirt and alpaca(?) coat. He rather proposed that I might drop into his camp at Abydos next winter, for a few days of excavating and modern Arabic,- an opening I took advantage of at once, you may be sure."[83]

Another such opportunity came into view a few days later, on 28 July, as Goodspeed was about to leave London for Oxford and the ninth summer meeting of

---

(not extant) and a program (tipped into the "Student Travel Letters") with his correspondence home. He had hoped (25 August continuation of 22 August to Charles) to appear in the "reproductions," i.e., photos, that were printed in the 5 August 1899 issue of *Harper's Weekly* (p. 799), but he seems not to be present. The "Student Travel Letters" illustrate Edgar's keen interest in athletics, especially the fortunes of the University of Chicago's teams. See also Ch. 3, n. 60. The Prince of Wales was the future Edward VII; for Walter Camp (1859–1925), the "father of American football," see, e.g., *New York Times*, 15 March 1925, p. 1.

[79] Miss Granger is probably Edna Granger (cf. *Buffalo Commercial*, 6 September 1899, p. 16), the future Edna Granger Dyett (1879–1965). An obituary has not been located, but a school of practical nursing at Buffalo's Millard Fillmore Hospital appears to have been named for her. In this period of his life Goodspeed seems to have preferred the company of women, but he also had numerous male companions and friends. The extrovert's desire for society, for companionship and association, trumped any gender considerations.

[80] "[L]ion hunting": 24 July 1899 to Mater, 4 November continuation of 3 November 1899 to Charles. Goodspeed's considerable ambition is almost jarringly evident throughout his relatively unguarded correspondence with his family.

[81] 21 July 1899 to Father. For William Matthew Flinders Petrie (1853–1942), pioneer archaeologist of Egypt and the Holy Land, see, in brief, Bierbrier 2012, 428–430; at length, Drower 1995. "Proteus": *Odyssey* 4.349–570. The exhibition catalogue: Petrie 1899; note also Drower 1995, 254.

[82] Coffin, a Canadian, was a fellow in the Department of Comparative Religion at Chicago, 1894–1898; he studied under Harper and George S. Goodspeed (Edgar's cousin), professor of comparative religion and ancient history and university recorder. The description here is retrospective, from Goodspeed 1953, 110. In a letter to Harper, 1 February 1897, Edgar writes jokingly of the "demolition" of Coffin's doctoral thesis on the day before (University of Chicago, Office of the President: Harper, Judson and Burton Administrations, records, box 46, folder 16).

[83] To Mater, 24 July 1899. Goodspeed 1953, 112, mentions the meeting only in passing, while Goodspeed n.d., ch. III, p. 3, reads, "Hearing that I might be in Egypt the coming season he proposed that I should visit him at his camp at Abydus, where he would be looking for the tomb of Osiris. I rather thought I might accept." For Petrie's work at Abydos, see Drower 1995, ch. 11 (249–273), "Most Ancient Egypt (1899–1903)."

the Delegacy for the Extension of University Teaching.[84] It was then that Kenyon "urged" him "to look up Grenfell and Hunt at Queen's College."[85]

Next day Goodspeed took the train from Paddington Station with Coffin, whom he had convinced to attend the Extension meeting, or at least part of it; Edgar had a room waiting at New College, but Fulton would need to rent private accommodation.[86] At last, on Monday morning, 31 July, Goodspeed called on Grenfell; Hunt was also there (his quarters at Queen's were just across the hall and on the same landing as Grenfell's). They received him "most graciously" in what must have been for Goodspeed a mind-spinning encounter.[87]

> [T]hey recalled my name at once, and before we sat down, had handed me the newest Berlin Urkunden and pointed out my 2 pieces signed in my own inimitable fist. As tho' this were not enough they spoke of having heard of my Homer note, and told me of a new big "5th book" piece they have.[88] They said they were going to excavate in the Fayoum in the winter, and said I must visit them there. They shewed me their papyri in the next room, tins and tins of them, gave me their views on Krebs, Wilcken, Wessely, Revillout, Mahaffy, and other palaeographers,[89] and said I must

---

[84] See Goodspeed's report in 1899b, 446–447. The meeting began on 31 July and was a three-week residential summer school for continuing education, including English literature and biblical studies. The sponsoring organization was the American Society for the Extension of University Teaching. Goodspeed's account of the event in the "Student Travel Letters" is unsurprisingly more critical and gossipy. One example: "The personnel of this Extension meeting, needless to say, bears absolutely no comparison with that of a Summer ¼ at the Univ. in any respect. The great audience last night was mostly girls, moreover: the men are ˌmostlyˌ either very young or "furriners"'" (30 July continuation of 27 July 1899 letter to Charles). Whatever his misgivings—and it should also be noted that Edgar was ill during this period—he saw fit to hold onto his meeting pass, which is preserved in Goodspeed box 57, folder 8. He had admired it on receipt: "It's a pretty little green-leather covered thing, that folds up like a book :- very neat affair, with the arms of the University on the outside in gilt" (to Father, 1 July 1899).

[85] To Charles, 30 July in continuation of 27 July 1899.

[86] "[P]art of it": Coffin returned to London on 10 August. A photo of Coffin in front of New College's Robinson Tower ("August 1899") is in Goodspeed box 52, folder 1. Coffin would stay with Mrs. Davis at 9 Museum Road. When Goodspeed tired of his college accommodation—he would move out on 15 August—he first sought to stay in the same house (14–15 August continuations of 11 August 1899 to Father). Goodspeed n.d., ch. III, p. 3, erroneously has Coffin in New College.

[87] "[M]ost graciously": Goodspeed n.d., ch. III, p. 5, which adds, "The greatest thing that happened to me in England was meeting them."

[88] Homer note: Goodspeed 1898b; new big "5th book" piece: P.Oxy. II 223 (Trismegistos 60897).

[89] This clause reappears almost verbatim in Goodspeed n.d., ch. III, p. 5, but "shewed" becomes "showed" and "palaeographers" becomes "other workers in the field," possibly alluding to, though not exactly quoting Matt. 9:37, Luke 10:2, and/or 1 Cor. 3:9. "[S]hewed": According to the OED, this form of "show," which Goodspeed uses consistently in his earlier writing, was obsolete outside of legal documents ca. 1850, but in our view ca. 1900 seems a more reasonable terminus. We also believe Goodspeed's preference for the archaism is consciously derived from biblical language; cf. KJV (1611), numerous examples, initially at Gen. 12:1, lastly at Rev. 22:8. That he was alert to finer points of KJV diction is clear from an anecdote related in Goodspeed 1953, 27, an instance when "wrastling" rather than "wrestling" proved to be the correct reading in the KJV's first printing. More substantially: The KJV lay at the base of Goodspeed's controversial but eventually vindicated "American Translation" of the

come to dinner at Queen's the next evening.

Back in Grenfell's quarters after next evening's dinner in the college's Common Room, Grenfell repeated the invitation to visit the site of the upcoming excavations in the Fayyūm—they were to be funded by University of California benefactress Phoebe Apperson Hearst.[90] He also broached—Grenfell must have talked this over with Hunt beforehand—Goodspeed's participation in publishing their anticipated finds: "They astutely stipulate that they be allowed to publish what they please of the stuff. But they think they will leave a lot and rather suggested proposing me, if I want the chance, as their candidate to get out the rest. Very kind, but I'm dubious."[91]

Throughout the remainder of the summer Grenfell took Goodspeed under wing. Indeed, Edgar would later recall him saying, after their 1 August dinner in the Queen's Common Room, "Look here, Goodspeed, aren't there some people in Oxford you'd like to meet? Come back to lunch with us Sunday, and I'll take you around to see them!"[92] These were probably not Grenfell's exact words, but he did show Edgar around and introduce him to Frederick Conybeare and Percy Gardner.[93] Goodspeed was also a lunch guest at Grenfell's family home, where he got to know Grenfell's mother, Alice Pyne Grenfell, "an Egyptologist, and clearly

---

New Testament (Goodspeed 1923; cf. Bademan 2006). His brother Charles recalls (C. T. B. Goodspeed 1932, 21) "the morning program" when he and Edgar were growing up in Morgan Park as consisting of prayers and readings from which "the boys gained ... a familiarity with the phraseology of the King James Version that has remained with them."

For Krebs and Wessely, see above. Bierbrier 2012 has brief treatments of Ulrich Wilcken (1862-1944; p. 577), (Charles) Eugène Revillout (1843-1913; p. 462), and John Pentland Mahaffy (1839-1919; p. 349); for Wilcken and the wide-ranging Mahaffy, see also Poethke 2007a and Stanford and McDowell 1971, respectively. Grenfell and Hunt's views unfortunately go unrecorded, but the former's "open and unvarnished" correspondence (thus Hickey 2017, 222) with J. Gilbart Smyly (see below, n. 96) reveals a competitive respect for Wilcken (cf., e.g., IE T(rinity) C(ollege) D(ublin) MS 4323, item 82), disdain for Revillout (cf., e.g., TCD MS 4323, item 54), and genuine affection for Mahaffy—though Smyly was clearly considered the better papyrologist (TCD MS 4323 *passim*; cf. also Hunt 1920, 219–220). Not in Goodspeed's list but also discussed, whether here or on another occasion, was Swiss "palaeographer" Jules Nicole, for whom see the concluding pages of this chapter.

[90] For Mrs. Hearst, see Hearst 2005 and Nickliss 2018.

[91] 1 August 1899 to Father. Goodspeed n.d., ch. III, p. 5, has Grenfell saying on this occasion, "We may not find anything, but if we do, you're the only American that has taken any active interest in this sort of thing, and you better come back here next summer and work on them with us, and what we don't publish we will nominate you to." If these words were in fact spoken—they do not appear in the extant "Student Travel Letters," but note Grenfell's 10 February 1900 letter transcribed below—they presumably were part of the 5 August conversation (below).

[92] Goodspeed n.d., ch. III, p. 5; cf. Goodspeed 1953, 110: "Grenfell also offered to take me about to call on anybody I wanted to meet in Oxford."

[93] 1 August 1899 to Father records only that Grenfell is "going to take me to see Conybeare + Professor Gardner Sunday afternoon." For Frederick Cornwallis Conybeare (1856–1924), biblical and Armenian scholar, see Margoliouth and Stearn 2015; for Percy Gardner (1846–1937), classical archaeologist and numismatist, Toynbee et al. 2004.

a strong minded woman."[94] The American thoroughly enjoyed the Oxford social scene with its lunches, teas, and dinners as described and toted up in a letter to cousin Sue.[95]

On 5 August, Grenfell again broached the subject of the Hearst papyri, fleshing out the earlier proposition and making a particular appeal to Goodspeed's American patriotism. As Edgar described the invitation to his mother,

> Grenfell yesterday proposed to me with some insistence that I come back to Oxford next year, the last of May, say, and work with them on their volume on the Mrs. Hearst, U. of Cal., papyri, which they are going to find(!) next winter. He proposes either joint authorship, or that I publish some of them separately. He says they have so much on hand and in view [of] that it would really be a favor to them, if I would do it. He held up to me the prospect that if I declined, the editor of them would not be an American, as an appeal, he said, to my patriotism. Hunt was cordial, too, but more cautious : said of course, they might find nothing : also the Californians might have someone in mind : but Bernard said no to this; the Californians had given him the privilege of publishing all he pleased : + if he wished to have assistance, it was his affair. Only, after the things had left England, he could not put them in my way, he feared [...] Grenfell further said they would try to get me into Queen's to live, if I would come. The idea will be to get out the complete + valuable pieces in "our"(!) volume, and send the rest unpublished to California. "The rest" would (but who can tell!) probably be stuff like my collection, non-literary fragments."[96]

---

[94] 7 August continuation of 3 August 1899 to Mother. Alice Pyne Grenfell (1842–1917) was, *inter alia*, a politically engaged suffragette; see further *Journal of Egyptian Archaeology* 4 (1917) 280. Grenfell's father, John Granville Grenfell (b. 1839), had died in Pisa on 24 March 1897 (*Guardian*, 31 March 1897, p. 13). In a 30 May 1904 letter to J. Gilbert Smyly, Grenfell reflected, "[T]he memory of my father's death in 1897 is still fresh" (TCD MS 4323, item 41).

[95] Dated 7–8 August: Goodspeed box 48, folder 1. Rather less appealing for the Baptist Goodspeed was the board at New College, where "beer is the drink, two meals a day" (14 August continuation of 11 August 1899 to Father). Note also his wry description of the refreshments at the home of New Testament scholar Kirsopp Lake (1872–1946; Grant 2004), who had just come from Mt. Athos: "It was whisky and "baccy" as they called it, at Lake's:- monastic fare, truly" (16 August continuation of 11 August 1899 to Father).

[96] Letter to Mother, 3 August 1899, in continuation on 7 August. In general, for Grenfell's inclination to action vs. Hunt's innate caution: E. G. Turner 2007, 23. The issue of a collaborator would first be broached with Mrs. Hearst some months later, when her agent Egyptologist George A. Reisner (1867–1942; Bierbrier 2012, 459–460) closed a letter to her, "Have you anyone at the University of California who can publish Greek papyri? Grenfell and Hunt have so much that they would like to turn over certain Ptolemaic papyri to some one else. They suggest Prof. Goodspeed of Chicago, who is now in Egypt" (17 February 1900; George and Phoebe Apperson Hearst Papers, BANC MSS 72/204c, The Bancroft Library, University of California, Berkeley [originals lost]). Ptolemaic papyri would in fact be turned over to J. Gilbert Smyly of Trinity College Dublin (1867–1948; Hickey 2017, 222, with refs.); he was invited by Grenfell to collaborate in their publication on 29 April 1900, shortly after Grenfell and Hunt returned to England from Egypt (cf. below, Ch. 3; Grenfell's letter: IE TCD MS 4323, item 95). For a remembrance of Smyly, perhaps skewed by its author's time in America (thus Brian McGing, pers. comm.), see Grene 2007, 67–69.

Years later, Edgar would call this a "really bewilderingly handsome" offer, though at the time its bewildering aspects probably dominated his thoughts.[97] He had to mull over the prospect of spending the next summer in Oxford to work on the project, adding to his time away from home—and presenting financial and scheduling problems.

> We talked of this off and on, all the afternoon, as we walked the lovely avenues of Oxford. The work would involve the whole summer, Grenfell said. Of course I explained my necessity of returning July first, but asked for time, to write to Burton and reflect.[98]

Writing home to his mother on 7 August, pining over the family's summer place on Plum Lake in far northern Wisconsin ("Every day of this month I am wishing I were on Plum Lake as of old"),[99] Edgar pondered:

> The Grenfell proposition (it is now 6 p.m.} ₐ- We've "done" Keble + a walk, +ₐ Coffin is again deep in Tom Brown -)[100] grows upon me : but on the other hand the prospect of protracting my stay abroad is insupportable. I wonder if the University would think it worth its while to have me stay, on salary? That would solve one problem. If I were a millionaire, and could come home in ~~May~~ April - and return for the 3 months in June, I should close with B.P. at once, the thing would so strengthen my position at home and abroad.

This same missive reveals that Edgar also wrote to Burton (that letter is not extant), "asking his judgment and preference," and probably querying the virtues of Thekla versus "palaeography," as well as, perhaps, the career implications of joint versus sole authorship (a concern that arises elsewhere).[101] The reply was slow in coming. Eventually, on 31 August, a Thursday, with mail fresh in hand and on his way from 99 High Street "just across from St Mary's Entry"—he had moved there

---

[97] Goodspeed n.d., ch. III, p. 5, though erroneously connected, probably (cf. above, n. 91) to the 1 August conversation. "[B]ewilderingly" is elided in Goodspeed 1953, 110–111: "a most handsome offer."

[98] This block quote occupies the ellipse ("he feared [...] Grenfell") in the preceding one. In the two subsequent paragraphs, Goodspeed outlines pros and cons, with the latter predominating; contrast Goodspeed n.d., ch. III, p. 5: "[O]f course I was eager to do it, if I could get my Chicago teaching postponed one quarter." Edgar had been scheduled to teach in Chicago's summer quarter, beginning 1 July. For Burton, above n. 9.

[99] Continuation of 3 August 1899. A full chapter is devoted to Plum Lake (ch. 5, 62–77) in Goodspeed 1953.

[100] Goodspeed had borrowed *Tom Brown at Oxford*, an 1861 novel by Thomas Hughes (it had earlier been serialized) and sequel to *Tom Brown's School Days*, "from the Head Porter, a fine old chap": Goodspeed n.d., ch. III, p. 8. Perhaps this same porter was the one who had recognized Edgar as "one of these paper hunters," explaining that his name had appeared "in Whittaker's [*sic*] among the papyrus people" (8 August to Charles). This was pretty close to the truth: See Whitaker 1899, 675, a factually challenged account of Goodspeed's Alexander papyri.

[101] The quoted material is again from the 7 August continuation of the 3 August 1899 letter to Mother. "[J]oint versus sole authorship": Cf., e.g., 15 September 1899 to Father.

before the Delegacy had ended—to his new lodgings at 9 Museum Road,[102] Goodspeed runs into Grenfell on the street. One of the unopened pieces of mail turns out to be a note from Grenfell inviting him to lunch the following week—"but wouldnt I come tomorrow?"[103] And so, Goodspeed writes to Charles, 1 September, "I lunched with Grenfell + Hunt in Hunt's room in Queens [...] They were just as nice as ever." But, one guesses from what follows, they also pressed him on the invitation to return to Oxford next summer to work on their new papyri.

Over the next two weeks Goodspeed had plenty of time to contemplate the invitation. He spent them away from Grenfell, partly in Birmingham, attending the end of the Friends' Summer School, 12–15 September, having secured an invitation through an exchange of letters with James Rendel Harris, Quaker activist, biblical scholar and fabulously successful manuscript collector; it was Grenfell who had brought the opportunity to his attention.[104] While in Birmingham Edgar, who had been corresponding with Harris for several years, found him in person to be "a most kindly, earnest, patient-looking, yet nervous man, whom it is easy and natural to make friends with."[105] Their interactions in Birmingham culminated in an invitation to Harris to visit and lecture in Chicago during his coming American tour.[106] Edgar wrote a report on the Summer School for *Biblical World*,[107] but of course he also continued to write home and the pressure caused by Grenfell's invitation—he had still not heard back from Burton—burst forth on 13 September in the course of a letter to brother Charles[108] in which a homesick Edgar, in staccato syntax and with a strange misspelling suggesting panic, entreats Charles "to come over for a little."

---

[102] For Goodspeed's move from New College, see above, n. 86. Location of accommodations: Goodspeed n.d., ch. III, p. 8, which, in addition to the phrase quoted above, indicates that the new ones were "the rooms of a Brasenose oar, and his trophies adorned the walls"; see also 31 August continuation of 30 August 1899 to Mother.

[103] 31 August continuation of 30 August 1899 to Mother.

[104] Biography of Harris (1852–1941): Falcetta 2018 (in which Goodspeed is not mentioned). Harris's invitation: letter to Mother, 21 August in continuation of 18 August 1899. Grenfell's suggestion: letter to Father, 16 August continuation of 11 August 1899.

[105] Goodspeed and Harris had been exchanging letters while Goodspeed was still in his graduate studies. Harris's side of the correspondence is in Goodspeed box 4, folder 17. This includes a letter of thanks from Harris, 6 February 1896, for Goodspeed's "account of the Syriac MSS," i.e., his B.D. thesis. Edgar's description of Harris, the invitation to Chicago: letter to Father, begun on 15 September, just after the Summer School's conclusion.

[106] Goodspeed would again connect with Harris in Cambridge on 19 September 1899. A letter to Mother written the same day details their meeting, which included the discussion about Grenfell mentioned in the next paragraph. Note also Goodspeed 1953, 111 ("I had a memorable hour with Rendel Harris at Cambridge"), and n.d., ch. III, p. 12 ("I had some splendid interviews with Rendel Harris"). They would meet again in Cambridge as luncheon guests on 4 August 1900 (see Epilogue) soon after Harris's return from America (for which tour see Falcetta 2018, 137–138).

[107] Goodspeed 1899b, 447–449, incorrectly reporting the School's end date as 16 September.

[108] Begun on 11, continued through 14 September; the passage quoted comes from the end of 13 September's installment.

[I]t would ease my mind wonderfully: If not the prospect staggers me. (You observe, I dont mature worth a cent). All this, if I am to undertake the task. We must also remember that I am by no means sure to su<u>ccee</u>d in the thing : I think B.P. [Grenfell] has overestimated my accomplishments. In case I must stay + you wont come, I'd come home almost any way, to get there, covering my retreat with Thekla and the chance of making something of her. I am rather anxious to hear from E.D.B. [i.e., Burton] on this business. He hasn't yet expressed himself on either Thekla or the Hurst [sic] papyri.

Two days later, 15 September, the anniversary of Edgar's departure from Chicago, he writes to Father: "The Grenfell matter, gratifying as it is, seems to me most precarious : and to stay over 5 months [more than planned] to ₄try to₄ do the work and not succeed, would be a bad set-back." Meanwhile he was being advised by Rendel Harris (with whom he had talked about Grenfell—details unknown), Nöldeke, and Budge to prefer his Thekla project to the papyri.[109] Then, on the 20th, the long-anticipated letter from Burton (this too has disappeared) arrives, "[a] fine letter from Burton who consents only too graciously to the Oxford experiment. I should have kept that matter secret, I begin to think."[110] On the 22nd he confesses to Charles, "My heart sinks, and I throw up my hands when I think of the expense of the next few months, and the prospect of continuing them till another September !— we shall all be ruined [...] I have not yet sufficiently recovered to answer Burton's letter, which as I probably wrote Mater, was ideally kind and cheering and encouraging."

But the die had been cast: Edgar was trapped. He must have replied in the affirmative with thanks to Burton (another lost letter), and confirmed the plans for next summer; it is not clear exactly when or on what terms—later letters suggest these had been left open and unresolved.[111] And as he prepared to depart England for another series of travels on the Continent, this time on a trajectory to Italy and thence to Egypt ("Alas, alas, how I dread turning my face eastward again!"), another worry intruded: the advisability and cost of a proposed "Nile trip to Assouan," perhaps going up by rail and down by boat, apparently at Grenfell's suggestion, to save money.[112] From the papyrological standpoint the most noteworthy event of this second set of travels in Europe occurred as Goodspeed closed in on Rome for the XII International Congress of Orientalists, meeting there 4–15

---

[109] For Nöldeke, see above, n. 65; for Budge, above, n. 74 and Prologue.

[110] Mother, 20 September continuation of 19 September. In the same continuation, before the arrival of Burton's letter is revealed, Edgar writes, "The Oxford prospect attracts me less and less. I am sorry it appeals to my Univ. advisers."

[111] See Ch. 2.

[112] "Alas, alas [...]": 21 September continuation of a letter to Mother begun on 19 September 1899. Nile trip: 22 September 1899 to Charles. The matter of advisability stemmed from Goodspeed's lack of interest in Egyptology: Would the excursion therefore be professionally worthwhile? Concerns over the cost are probably due to the fact that Mr. Bond's funds had not yet arrived in full; see above, n. 66.

October, where he would be one of the University of Chicago's delegates. He had reached Geneva at the very end of September with the intention of seeing the papyrus collection "at the Museum" and visiting the home of Jules Nicole, professor of Greek language and literature, a scholar who had been acquiring papyri both for himself and for Geneva's Bibliothèque Publique et Universitaire, initially through the agency of his friend, famed Egyptologist and fellow Genevan, Édouard Naville.[113] In mild amusement, Edgar described the occasion in a letter to Sarah (1 October 1899), written on stationery from the Hotel Le Richemond, a short walk from Lake Geneva. He had just moved,[114] so it was only

> [w]ith great difficulty [that] I found Nicoles' address, and hunted him up. Grenfell told me he was nice, and he is, awfully. He shewed me this most important Homer, and his Menander fragment, whereby hangs a ~~tail~~ tale![115] His wife was with us, and his niece who knows more English than I do French, at anyrate [sic]: so we managed to converse in a somewhat roundabout manner.[116]

A longer account, written to Mother, plays up the farcical elements of the occasion:[117]

> After frantic and repeated efforts I found Nicole's new address and looked him up. He was awfully pleasant : I staggered about in fearful French, while his niece helped out with some English, and his wife was generally charming. He shewed me the great and famous pieces he has : the Homer of the 2^d century B.C., full of extra verses, and apparently undivided into books, the Menander [...] the apocryphal bit;- and many more. They were very kind and jolly ; Mme. Nicole insisted on dusting the glasses with her handkerchief, and Nicole kept hauling them out at a most tremendous rate. She remarked how I kept the Homer fragment in my hands and kept coming back to it; but Nicole said approvingly "Ah, c'est une perle[!]" After bowing myself out in English, French, and the sign language, I came here.

The Homer to which Goodspeed refers is a Ptolemaic fragment with parts of *Iliad* 11 and 12; the Menander is from the comic poet's *Georgos* (*The Farmer*); the identity of "the apocryphal bit," however, is unclear.[118] The "tale," which he does

---

[113] For Nicole (1842–1921), a good point of departure is his memorial volume (Bernard 1922), which includes a brief reminiscence from Hunt. Goodspeed is not a contributor, but he did supply an article for an earlier volume in Nicole's honor (Goodspeed 1905). For the collections and their eventual merger: Martin 1940, Schubert 2000 and 2003. (Our thanks to Paul Schubert for his helpful advice concerning the Geneva collection.) For Naville (1844–1926): Bierbrier 2012, 398–400.

[114] To 10, Boulevard de la Tour, south of the Rhône, not far beyond the University, as we learn from a 7 November continuation of a 5 November 1899 letter to Charles.

[115] "[W]hereby hangs a tale": Shakespeare, *As You Like It* II.vii ("And thereby hangs a tale").

[116] Goodspeed box 48, folder 1.

[117] 1 October continuation of 29 September 1899.

[118] Homer, Menander: Trismegistos 61226, 61569, respectively. The "apocryphal bit" must be the "apocalypse apocryphe" mentioned by Nicole in his letter of 3 February 1894 published in Martin 1940, 24; this has probably been edited in Bagnoud 2016 (Paul Schubert, email 2 July 2021).

not spell out for Sarah, begins in 1897 when Nicole published the Menander as two separate pieces and continues with a review in which a distinguished classicist established that the two belonged together as a single codex leaf preserving a continuous text on recto and verso.[119] This prompted Grenfell and Hunt's immediate re-edition of Nicole's Menander with a full-page dedication printed as if for an honorific monument on stone.[120] (Fig. 4) As Edgar told the story to Mother in an *obiter dictum* that omits the reviewer's contribution to the discovery:

> By the way, did I tell you the Oxford fellows' story on Nicole? He thought he had two ˌseparateˌ fragments of a lost play of some Greek writer ˌ(Menander)ˌ; and reconstructed the plot of it on this assumption. Grenfell and Hunt however saw that the two fragments fitted <u>together</u>, came down here and got out a small book on the subject, which they had the audacity to dedicate to the miserable Nicole, whose cherished hypothesis they had so ruthlessly exploded! They told me this at Queen's, with much appreciation of its picturesqueness.[121]

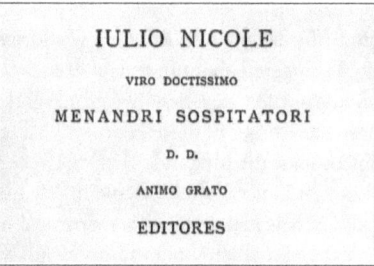

Figure 4: Grenfell and Hunt's dedication to Jules Nicole.
Public Domain.

---

[119]Nicole 1897 is the edition. The reviewer was Friedrich Blass (1843–1907); the review, Blass 1897. Goodspeed had met Blass at the University of Halle, the first university on his tour of German universities: Goodspeed 1953, 107, "First Halle, where I met and heard Friedrich Blass, whom Oxford rated the foremost classical scholar in Europe." Goodspeed's "Oxford" may be shorthand for "Grenfell and Hunt": The duo were close to Blass and probably knew of his discovery before it was published. When Blass's review did appear (18 December 1897), they were already in Egypt yet decided to take a detour to Geneva to autopsy the manuscript on their way home. Of course Blass could also have written to them in Egypt. Blass's obituary, in *Classical Philology* 2 (1907) 334, calls him "the chief adviser of Grenfell and Hunt in their publications for the Egypt Exploration Fund." Grenfell, cited in Lehnus 2007, 119 n. 3, called Blass "that great scholar and noblest and most chivalrous of characters."

[120]Grenfell and Hunt 1898. In translation from the Latin: "To Jules Nicole, most learned man, Menander's savior, the editors have gratefully dedicated [this volume]."

[121]30 September continuation of 29 September 1899. Perhaps this entered into the scholarly assessments of 31 July 1899, for which see above, with n. 89.

Chapter 2

Egypt, a "Lost" Epic, and "the Treasure of Leviathan"

Maior in externas fit qui descendit harenas.
– Petronius Arbiter[1]

Goodspeed's attendance at the Congress of Orientalists, mentioned near the end of the preceding chapter, was followed by sightseeing in Italy, including a visit to the ruins of Herculaneum, 6 November 1899,[2] and ending in Naples, whence on 8 November he sailed for Alexandria on the *Umberto Primo*.[3] A letter to cousin Sue[4] the day before departure details an itinerary that for various reasons did not work out as planned:

> I have an ambitious schedule : a week in Cairo, 3 on the Nile, going to Assouan and returning to Cairo : a week at Grenfell's Camp - and one at Petrie's, - if that opening proves open! Then on to Palestine, if quarantine is off Alexandria,[5] and up to Judaea for Christmas! Imagine! The associations! - <u>and</u> the pilgrims. Isn't it a great prospect![6]

---

[1] Poem 79, ed. Baehrens (the text current in Goodspeed's day): "Whoever disembarks on foreign sands becomes a larger person."

[2] Goodspeed was shown "a little section of the edge of the town, that was by the sea, which is opened to the air and light : perhaps 2 or 3 houses. In one of these - that of "Aristides",- my guide assured me the papyri were found. He even pointed out the rooms, 2 little ones, 9 feet square. They must have been "stack" rooms indeed, if they held 3000 rolls, but they may have been partly in the floor above. This part of town seems to have been covered with densely packed ashes, not so hard to remove as lava of course. Any way, I could crumble it with my fingers, and could have scooped a hole in it with my hands" (7 November continuation of 5 November 1899 to Charles). The Casa di Aristides was in fact the structure through which Bourbon diggers carried finds from the nearby Villa dei Papiri (Pirozzi 2003, 50). "[S]tack": punning on the bibliothetic, i.e., library-shelving sense; see *OED*, s.v., 1.d.

[3] Goodspeed's mostly serene voyage to Alexandria may be contrasted with the one undertaken, on the same Italian vessel and from the same port of departure, by the Presbyterian evangelist J. Wilbur Chapman during the following year: Ottman 1920, 91–92, "This very name [*Umberto Primo*] causes members of the 1900 Pilgrimage to shudder."

[4] Ch. 1, n. 23.

[5] For the 1899 outbreak of plague at Alexandria and the public health response to it, see Echenberg 2007, 83–106.

[6] Goodspeed box 48, folder 1.

On ship he was traveling and bunking with one of the University of Chicago's representatives to the recent Congress, Clarke Eugene Crandall, Yale Ph.D., instructor in Semitic languages and Goodspeed's companion for his planned journeys in Egypt and Palestine.[7] Also aboard is an Oxford man, a relative of Petrie's who is headed for Abydos to build the dig house in advance of Petrie's own arrival: "His name is Mace." This was Arthur Cruttenden Mace, who was already an experienced Egypt man, having been with Petrie at Dendera (1897–1898) and Hu (1898–1899).[8] He is therefore able to give the greenhorn Goodspeed welcome advice. They spend time together—at tea, at dinner, on deck, in the saloon. Mace advises Goodspeed on his prospective travels in Egypt "and seems quite to expect me at Abydos."[9]

From Alexandria, having arrived there on 12 November after some rough waves on the 11th, Goodspeed moved quickly to Cairo (13 November), haggling for a rate of $2 a day and registering with Crandall at the Hotel Bristol, "a smaller place," whose "proprietor" was "a wily Greek gentleman." While he found his accommodations pleasant, he was less content with the inhabitants of his new environment. "[H]ere I cant live too differently from the natives to suit me. The mere realization that they are about at all is most depressing."[10] Meanwhile, Edgar's new friend Mace was staying at the Hôtel du Nil, "off the "Mouski" in the native quarter."[11] Grenfell and Hunt were also in town—at the Villa Victoria.[12]

[7] Cf. the last paragraph of Goodspeed's letter to President Harper from Rome, 15 October 1899, at the close of the Congress (University of Chicago, Office of the President: Harper, Judson and Burton Administrations, records, box 46, folder 16): "Crandall now seems likely to make the Egypt-Palestine tour with me. I hope we may see Petrie's Abydos camp; and I am to put in a week at Grenfell's in the Fayoum. Grenfell made it very pleasant at Oxford: he is a splendid fellow." For Crandall (1857–1929), see the obituary in *The Sabbath Recorder* 108 (1930) 63–64, wherein it is noted that "his health demanded a change [from lecturing at the University of Chicago]. He then spent several months in research work in Egypt and Palestine, but his health did not admit his return for further work at the university."

[8] For the Tasmanian-born Mace (1874–1928), later (1922–1924) an assistant to Howard Carter in clearing the tomb of Tutankhamun, but famous for many other Egyptological accomplishments: Bierbrier 2012, 346–347.

[9] The foregoing description of Edgar's journey on the *Umberto Primo* is derived from a letter to Mother, 9–12 November 1899.

[10] 13 November 1899 to Charles. For the Bristol, cf. *Egypt and How to See It* 1907, 22 ("more economical but quite comfortable") and 157 ("near the Ezbekiek [sic] gardens"), and Humphreys 2011, 160–162, which includes Evelyn Waugh's unfavorable impression from his 1929 stay.

[11] "Mouski": Cairo's busiest commercial street "which derives its name from a bridge built over the Great Canal by one Mouski, a relation of the great Saladin who died in the year 1188" (thus Margoliouth 1912, 278). Lively physical description of the Mouski and its traffic congestion: Marden 1912, 45–46. Mace's selection should not surprise: His cousin Petrie favored the same hotel, initially "recommended to him as clean and reasonable," whenever in Cairo: Drower 1995, 35. Flaubert and Du Camp had stayed there for two months in 1849/1850: Humphreys 2011, 50.

[12] "Shâriʿa el-Manâkh 13, a quiet house pleasantly situated near the Place de l'Opéra": Baedeker 1902, 24. Its peaceful environment suited H. M. Stanley, who had written *In Darkest Africa* (1890) there: Humphreys 2011, 161.

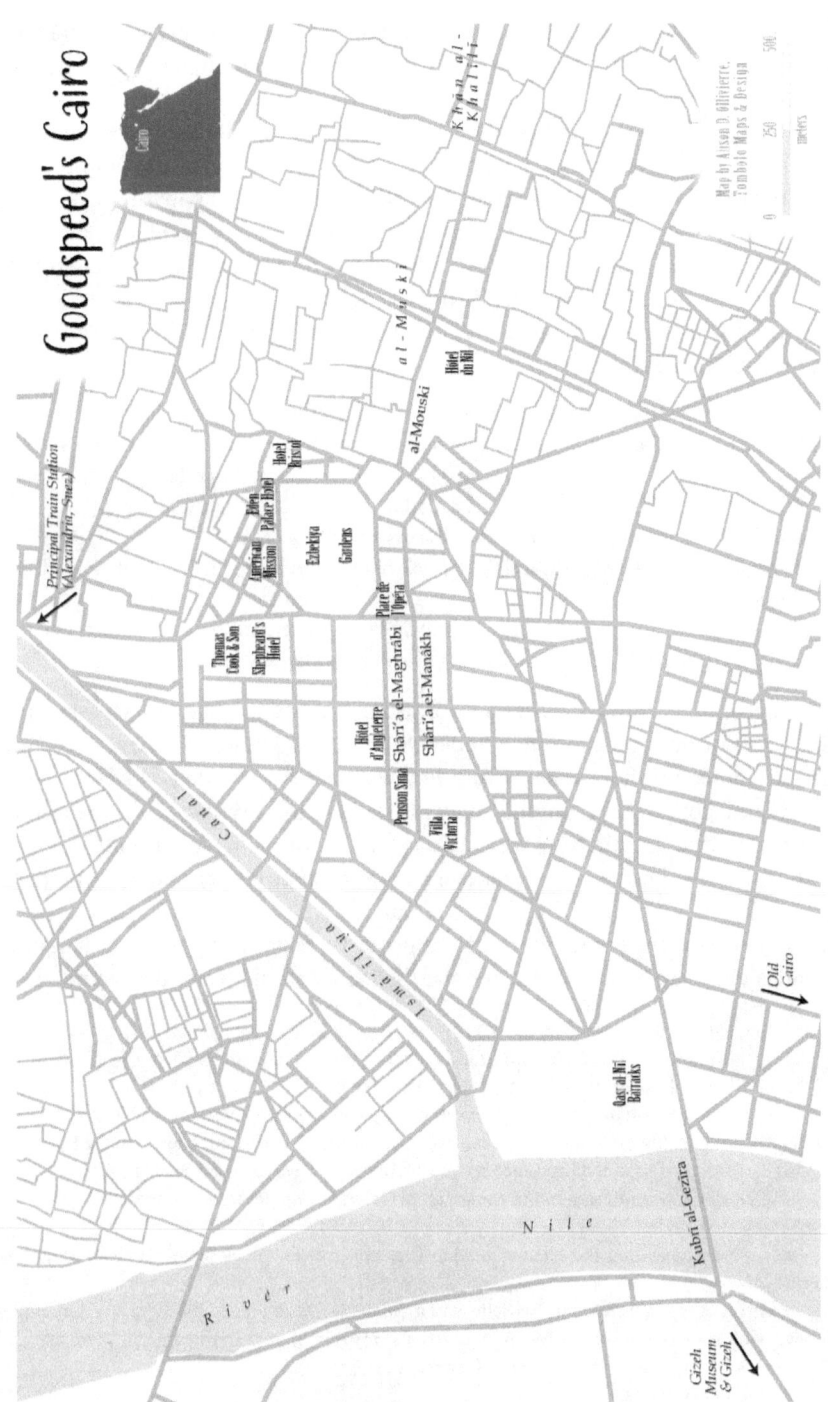

"Their presence + Mace's," Edgar tells Charles,[13] "gives Cairo a personal attraction and significance, as you can guess, such as the place would not have ₐmerelyₐ, as a curious and historic town."

Next day, 14 November, is a huge success—in its first half. Following a leisurely morning at the Bristol, Goodspeed and Crandall head toward Mace's hotel with a picnic lunch. They find him on the Mouski, "talking with a papyrus dealer, who was anxiously inquiring for "Howâga" (i.e., Stranger, foreigner) Grenfell." They then accompany Mace on some errands, after which the threesome, taking the "electric car" down to Old Cairo and crossing the Nile by ferry over to Gizeh,[14] "turned north along the river to the Museum, in the great Khedivial Palace, with its magnificent grounds."

> Here we had adventures : encouraged by Mace, I sent up my card to ₐBrugsch, while he sent hisₐ to Maspero.[15] Brugsch Bey received me kindly : and went off at once with my request to Maspero : ₐthen he came back + took me into M's office.ₐ in his office I found Mace : Maspero at once consented to my labors on their Greek papyri: and sent me back to Brugsch to be shewn the documents + go to work. With Brugsch I now found Hunt + Grenfell, and they shook hands with me cordially. Brugsch introduced me to a 4th man there[16] and asked me to come in tomorrow for business. All these meetings and movements took only about 5 minutes, and I rejoined Crandall in the waiting room, after the tallest bit of lion hunting I had ever done.[17]

Goodspeed then tours the Museum, finishing 30 rooms, Budge's guidebook in hand,[18] before stopping to lunch under the statue of Mariette.[19] Later, as he "was making notes on the "make" of big Egyptian papyri, Grenfell and Hunt came along, and stopped for a minute. They assured me they wanted to see me tomorrow and talk about things, so we shall meet at the Museum work room."[20]

But the day, begun so well, takes a testy turn after dinner and an "unsatisfying" talk with Crandall. "I find myself out of sympathy with my fellow traveller on nearly every point." Brooding afterwards, Edgar complained at length to Charles about an earlier slight, one that he feared would jeopardize some of the

---

[13] Letter begun on 13 November.

[14] For Cairo's tram service at this time, see *The Railway Official Gazette*, August 1899, p. 119.

[15] Emil Charles Adalbert Brugsch (1842–1930) was keeper of the Museum; Gaston Camille Charles Maspero (1846–1916) had only recently (1 November 1899) been reappointed as director general of the Antiquities Service: Bierbrier 2012, 83–84 and 359–361. Maspero has been mentioned in the Prologue.

[16] The identity of this individual is not revealed; it may well have been von Bissing (n. 43).

[17] The block quote and those in the paragraph preceding it: 14 November continuation of 13 November 1899 to Charles.

[18] Edgar was consulting the relevant section (pp. 149–219) of Budge 1898 or an earlier edition thereof.

[19] François Auguste Ferdinand Mariette Pasha (1821–1881), founder of the Egyptian Antiquities Service, who achieved first fame for his excavations, 1850–1854, at the Serapeum in Memphis and discovery of the galleries of the Apis bulls: Bierbrier 2012, 355–357.

[20] Quotation: See n. 17.

"lion hunting" that he had accomplished in London regarding his plans to visit Abydos. Crandall's

> letter to Petrie, written at Breasted's hasty and ill considered suggestion, did as much to queer the whole Petrie deal as anything well could. I hope to guard the Grenfell invitation with relentless exclusiveness. Crandall attempted the thing I had accomplished, by throwing to the winds every principle I have made all my progress with these men on : i.e. instead—but I forbear. It's simply disgusting. He doesn't "want to poke around Cairo 2 weeks, alone" : I felt like telling him some things.- Now don't give me away on this, please. I wanted company, and now I've got it; or its [sic] got me. If I succeed in pulling out the Grenfell visit, I'll be satisfied, tho' Ive not given up Petrie yet.[21]

The next two days, 15–16 November, bring more suffering, as Edgar describes this to Father: A toothache afflicts him on the 15th, a moth flies into his ear on the 16th, the appointment with Grenfell and Hunt and backup plans to meet up with them fall through. There is one bright spot: Volume II of *The Oxyrhynchus Papyri*, which he had ordered from London, has arrived—reading material for the imminent Nile excursion. Next day, 17 November, things get even better.

> To day [sic] I spent at the Museum. I found G. + H. alone in a splendid great glass domed hall, floored with marble and tiny flower beds-The Winter garden of the Palace! They helped me to everything! I read one fine papyrus today. Brugsch came along + shook hands : then Maspero, who remembered me + asked [if] I had what I wanted. We "young people" ate our lunches together at a table in the immense balcony, and were jolly in English and German. At 5 we, ₌C + I₌ went to tea at G's hotel, + met Quibell,[22] and saw a dealer (in native clothes) squatting by G. + [H.] with 2 tins of Coptic papyri to sell. Then G. + H. shewed us their new purchases !!![23]

The 18th of November finds Goodspeed on the Nile aboard Cook's steamer the *Cleopatra*.[24] (In a reversal of the earlier recommendation, he and Crandall are going upriver by boat; they will return by train, partly to economize, partly for flexibility on the downward leg.) The trip takes him and his traveling companions south to Aswan in exactly a week (25 November). During that week, writing to Mother, Edgar expresses misgivings about the whole trip: The time would much

---

[21] Quotations: n. 17. Crandall's letter is first mentioned in the 8 November continuation of 5 November 1899 to Charles: "Crandall had a letter from Petrie, which may affect things somewhat. C. must have written a rather stupid letter."

[22] For James Edward Quibell (1867–1935), the recently appointed (1 November 1899) inspector general of the Antiquities Service for the Delta and Middle Egypt, see Bierbrier 2012, 450–451.

[23] 17 November continuation of 15 November 1899 to Father. For the importance of the papyrus trade to Grenfell and Hunt's "economy," cf. Hickey and Keenan 2016, 372–373.

[24] The *Cleopatra* was one of several boats offering the "Cheap Express Service" intended for "travelers who wanted to spend less time and money on seeing the Nile": Humphreys 2015, 95. For a drawing of the vessel, see http://grandhotelsegypt.com/wp-content/uploads/2016/10/Thomas-Cook_boat_Hatasoo.jpg (accessed 21 November 2018).

better have been spent at the Museum because of the opportunities there "so generously opened up by Grenfell."[25] Meanwhile he has been "working into Grenfell's new volume" (note the omission of co-author Hunt),

> which is a magnificent thing, and makes me surer than ever that I cant fill the summer's bill. - You may see me walking in upon you some fine day five months hence, yet! But if I can possibly do that work with them, I must do it.[26]

To Charles, 20 November, he describes the *shāwadīf* (shadufs) and dura fields along the Nile—the latter look like Illinois cornfields. He has copied one of his Gizeh papyri, which "will delight your soul as a bit of legal paper as prolix and repetitious as any you are capable of."[27] The trip about whose value he had earlier been dubious has now become the greatest of his life's great experiences, though justifications are necessary on receiving a letter from Father criticizing its extravagance.[28] On 25 November, after disembarking and settling in at Aswan, he sailed over to Elephantine and

> entered the village on the island, and met a lot of women with antiques to sell. They had some Coptic ostraka _ i.e. potsherds with inscriptions _ and I rashly bought a Greek one : the woman asked one piastre : I gave her ½ that - i.e. 2½ cents![29]

Later in the day he writes a letter to Grenfell.[30]

On the return trip, Goodspeed spends extra time touring Luxor and the Theban region, 28 November–4 December, searching also for papyri on offer. He is unimpressed at the "most important antiquities shop" in Luxor, that of Mohammed Mohasseb, exclaiming that his papyri are "poor stuff,"[31] but elsewhere his funds are insufficient. One dealer in town, identified only as an "old codger," wants 15 pounds apiece for "some fair Greek rolls, not literary," which prompts Goodspeed to note that his papyri at home would be worth a fortune at that rate. "Unless I can get something very good and very cheap," he reassures Father, "of course I dont dream of buying, preferring ostraka at ½ a piastre each, or printing

---

[25] 18 November 1899 to Mother.

[26] 19 November continuation of 18 November 1899 to Mother.

[27] The future *P.Cair.Goodsp.* 13 (or its duplicate), which will recur below.

[28] Goodspeed effuses over his experience at the beginning of his 23 November 1899 letter to Father. Father's critical missive, written on 1 November 1899, was awaiting him in Aswan; see Edgar's 25 November continuation, which includes his apologia.

[29] 25 November continuation of 20 November letter to Father. Goodspeed mentions this sherd and another "picked up among the ruins of Philae" in Goodspeed 1904a, 45, but to our knowledge it has not been published by Goodspeed or anyone else.

[30] The main topic of this lost letter must have been the proposed visit to Grenfell's Fayyūm excavation site. For Grenfell's reply, see below.

[31] 28 November letter to Father. For the dealer, see Bierbrier 2012, 376–377, and Hagen and Ryholt 2016, 245–247. The former employs Goodspeed's spelling ("Muhassib"; Goodspeed seems later to have added a second, superscript "u" to clarify his own handwriting); the latter echoes his assertion of prominence.

Museum papyri, or my own!"[32]

During his stay at the Luxor Hotel,[33] Goodspeed, on 29 November, found waiting for him

> a card from Petrie, saying I may come from Dec. 5 to the 10th or 15th. This rather confounds Crandall, whose letter from Petrie gave him the impression that I was utterly clean gone forgotten by our friend. This card indicates that I have recovered practically all the ground lost me by the Breasted-Crandall bungle (I hope this is not too severe,) and to my surprise it seems to have a rather depressing effect on Crandall, who took my indirect discomfiture at Naples rather cheerfully. I mean the reply he got from Petrie, when he applied for permission to live with him a week, + Petrie said he "hadn't the pleasure" of my acquaintance."[34] Now please treat this a[s?] confidential : I am a little ashamed of writing it : and shan't spend over a day or 2 with Petrie in any case, for I want to get to Gizeh + to work.

As matters developed, Goodspeed did spend two full days and, at both ends, parts of two others "in the trenches with Petrie" at Abydos, 4–7 December.[35] When he arrived back in Cairo on 8 December, he found five letters awaiting him at Cook's travel agency next to Shepheard's Hotel: from Florence,[36] Sarah, "Pater," "Mater," and brother Charles. On the morning of the same day he notes in a letter to Charles receipt of a "nice letter from Grenfell." This letter, dated 5 December and sent to him at the Hotel Bristol, provides precise instructions for his anticipated visit to the dig in the Fayyūm and initial impressions of the site itself:

---

[32] 29 November, 9 p.m., continuation of 28 November letter to Father. "[O]straka at ½ a piastre each": a reference to his purchase at Aswan. At the bottom of the page, Goodspeed reports that the "codger" dropped his prices on the following day "with no pressing at all," but the papyri were still too dear.

[33] See Humphreys 2011, 176–177, for this first "Cook and Son" hotel. Goodspeed used "Cook's coupons" to pay, but in his day it was owned by Cook's former agent Ferdinand Pagnon.

[34] The final quotation mark, after "acquaintance," may be cancelled.

[35] The visit to Abydos is described in detail in a 4 December letter to Mother and illustrated by dated archival photographs (box 51, folder 3). Goodspeed is mentioned in passing in a letter of Hilda Petrie; see Drower 2004, 161. That letter is erroneously given a 1900 date, perhaps because Petrie had repurposed the December 1900 pages of a pocket diary for 1899. The diary in question records "Goodspeed + Crandall came" under 4 December and "Goodspeed left" under 7 December (a day after Crandall). Nothing should be made of Petrie's brevity, which characterizes his pocket diaries. Petrie also notes the visit of the pair in his 1899–1900 journal, under Saturday, 9 December (archive.griffith.ox.ac.uk, Petrie MSS 1.18, p. 10). We thank Alice Stevenson for sending scans of the relevant pocket diary pages and will address Goodspeed and Petrie in a future article.

[36] Probably the wife of his cousin George S. Goodspeed (cf. Ch. 1, n. 82), "my beautiful cousin Florence Mills": Goodspeed 1953, 32–33. George (1860–1905) and Florence (1861–1952) were married in 1884: Goodspeed 1953, 47. They had one son, botanist Thomas Harper Goodspeed (1887–1966). Edgar lived with them during his year at Yale (Goodspeed 1953, 55) while George was completing his Ph.D. George's obituary: *Biblical World* 25 (1905) 169–172. He died of pneumonia at age 45 while Florence lived to be 90, serving as director of Noyes Hall, a women's gymnasium and social center at the University of Chicago.

We left Cairo on Nov. 25 and I only got your letter and card last Saturday.[37] We are digging an ancient town called Umm el Baragât, about 1½ hours E of Gharak, on the edge of the desert. We shall be very pleased to see you any time you like. I should suggest you stayed 2 nights, for it takes a very long time to get to us. Saturday is our off day so I should prefer if you would arrive or leave on that day, as I have heaps of men at my disposal. To reach us in one day leave Cairo at 8. a.m. for Medinet el Fayoum which you will reach about 12.[38] Lunch at the 'Hotel Karoon', an Italian inn 3 minutes from the station.[39] Take the light railway train (station adjoins the main station at Medinet) which leaves at 4.15 p.m. from Medinet for <u>Sheikh Nour</u>, the last station but one before Gharak; ˏwhichˏ you will reach it at 5.46 p.m.ˏ[40] All the officials on the line talk English and ~~go~~ they will tell you when to get out. At Abu Nour you will find 2 donkeys, one for yourself & the other for your luggage, and one of my men who will conduct you to our camp, which is 1½ hours from Abu Nour.

<u>Bring as many blankets and wraps as you can lay hold on</u>, for the nights are very cold and we have no extra mattresses and your bed will be hard anyhow. In returning, if you go direct to Medinet by donkey from here (3½ hours) you can by leaving here at 9.30 a.m. reach Cairo at 8.20 p.m. Otherwise you must sleep at Medinet[.]

If you like, you can leave Cairo at 3 p.m., sleep at Medinet and come on by the train leaving Medinet at 10.15 a.m. ˏandˏ reaching ~~Medinet~~ ˏAbu Nourˏ at 11.46 a.m. Let us know at which ~~way~~ ˏtimeˏ you ~~want~~ intend to come ˏto Abu Nourˏ and remember we send to Gharak for letters on Wednesdays & Saturdays and you must post by 1.00 p.m. on Mondays and Thursdays to make sure of the letter reaching us.

We began digging this place yesterday.[41] It seems rather promising, being larger than most Fayoum sites & not dug previously. Papyri seem pretty plentiful. We have already identified the site as ~~Tep~~Teptunis in the μερίς of Polemo. Have you ever come across the name? As I have no copy of O.P. II here, I cannot say anything about

---

[37] The letter must be the one Goodspeed wrote from Aswan on 25 November (see above). "[L]ast Saturday": 2 December.

[38] For the journey from Cairo to Madīnet al-Fayyūm by train, cf. Baedeker 1898, 147.

[39] For the Karoon, cf. Baedeker 1902, 176, and *Egypt and How to See It* 1907, 62 ("the best hotel in Medina … clean and not uncomfortable for a short stay"). Recently built, it was recommended by Grenfell as a place to stay ("one does not need to bring insect powder") to Danish Egyptologist Hans Ostenfeldt Lange (1863–1943; Bierbrier 2012, 308); Lange was not impressed: Hagen and Ryholt 2016, 101. Nor was Emma Andrews (n.d., 2:3): "[T]he Greek Inn at Medina is impossible."

[40] The end of this sentence is difficult. It appears that Grenfell started his interlinear addition with the relative pronoun "which," but then changed the construction to a main clause by canceling the relative (admittedly not very well), adding "it" (clearly a later addition) and transforming his comma into a semicolon with the addition of a point. For the train to Shaykh Abū Nūr (on the Fayoum Light Railway), cf. Baedeker 1902, 177.

[41] The date of the letter implies that this was 4 December. Grenfell and Hunt 1900, 600, ibid. 1901, 376, and App. B all give the start date as 3 December. A 22 June 1899 letter to Mrs. Hearst from George Reisner reveals, in any case, that this was later than originally intended: "They wish to begin November 15th and desire us to apply for the <u>Gharaq</u> basin (S.W. of the Fayum) with <u>Umm-el-Baragât</u> and <u>Medinet Maʿdi</u>" (the ancient Narmouthis, not excavated by Grenfell and Hunt; George and Phoebe Apperson Hearst Papers, BANC MSS 72/204c, box 43, The Bancroft Library, University of California, Berkeley).

your suggestion on p. 253, but as you have the plate, no doubt it is right.[42] I hope you got the letter I left for you at the museum with Von Bissing.[43]

The letter left with von Bissing was picked up by Goodspeed the following day, as he reports in a continuation of his 8 December letter to Charles:

> At the Museum I met Quibell and Brugsch and Van [sic] Bissing, who shewed me the letter Grenfell left for me.[44] Grenfell leaves a list of a lot of papyri he and Hunt propose to edit; and says of the rest : "all the others are at your service as far as we are concerned; and the more you can edit the better because noone [sic] else is likely to do them."[45] He also recalls the summer plans on which I have been rather waiting for him to speak first: + reopens the matter in the same tone as at Oxford, saying he "hopes the scheme will come off." I am anxious to know just what he wishes to do : I hardly think they would take me into partnership, with full honors: I think B.P.G. thinks rather of giving me a certain lot of papyri to publish myself. This would of course have its advantages, if Mrs. H. stands the publishing.- We'll see.

✻ ✻ ✻ ✻

Over the next two weeks, until departing for the Holy Land on 24 December, Goodspeed worked assiduously transcribing papyri at the Gizeh Museum, hoping for results that would lead to publications. "I have a rich mine here: and am planning a contribution to the Am. Journal of Archaeology : in deed [sic] in my wilder moments, a series of contributions!" he enthuses to Charles on the evening of 9 December. "I pulled out one fine papyrus to day [sic]; and find my former facility in cursive, the fruit of labors on my big accounts papyrus - coming rapidly back."[46] On the 11th he receives from Charles at Cook's an Ethiopic grammar—an aid for his continuing work on Thekla.[47] But it is the next day, 12 December, that initiates

---

[42] O.P. = P.Oxy. The page reference corresponds to the Greek text of P.Oxy. II 270, "indemnification of a surety"; a plate is on the facing page. For Goodspeed's correction, see P.Oxy. IV, p. 263.

[43] Goodspeed box 4, folder 9. For Friedrich Wilhelm *Freiherr von* Bissing (1873–1956), see Bierbrier 2012, 60–61. Emma Andrews (n.d., 2:40) described him as "very clever - nervous, interesting - talks a great deal - has the clearest and keenest eyes I have ever seen." He had a rich archaeological, but controversial political career (propagandist in German-occupied Belgium in World War I; Nazi party member starting in 1925, subsequently expelled), for which see Gertzen 2012, a popular treatment that makes reference to more scholarly literature. During our period he was serving on the Comité of the *Catalogue général*—he would end up preparing the volumes for *Metallgefässe* (1901), *Fayencegefässe* (1902), and *Steingefässe* (1904–1907)—and excavating Abū Jirāb (Abu Gurob) with Ludwig Borchardt, for whom see below with n. 59.

[44] Grenfell's letter is present in the Chicago archive (Goodspeed box 4, folder 9).

[45] For Goodspeed's publication of these Museum texts, see *P.Cair.Goodsp.*; note also Goodspeed 1903c. Grenfell and Hunt permitted him to consult *P.Cair.Cat.* in manuscript (see *P.Cair.Goodsp.*, p. 3).

[46] In continuation of 8 December. Goodspeed would not publish any Cairo papyri in the journal mentioned. "[B]ig accounts papyrus": See Ch. 1, n. 51.

[47] While in Naples, 7 November (in continuation of 5 November 1899), Edgar had asked Charles

the most important subplot in the Goodspeed-in-Gizeh story. That day, writing to Father,[48] Edgar describes what had happened:

> As I was working away in the Winter Garden at the Museum this morning, Quibell came in and told me the Museum was just about to purchase a Greek <u>poetical</u> fragment, and Maspero had designated me as a suitable person to entrust its publication to. This rather took my breath away, I must say. I think I see Grenfell's hand in it. Quibell took me to see it in Brugssch's [sic] private room: and after lunch I got Brugsch's permission to take it into the Winter Garden, to transcribe. It's a beautiful literary uncial : I think the finest I ever saw, and plain as ABC. There's a good deal of it, too, and it's brand new, and in the only kind of Greek verse I know,- dactylic hexameters! Some people <u>do</u> have greatness thrust upon them dont they? Still, I'm not out of the woods yet, though my transcription is practically ready; and the entire lack of books here in Cairo makes me sober. Laundry or fullers' accounts on the back indicate that it is earlier than the first year of the emperor Claudius Tacitus.[49] Altogether it's the finest papyrus I ever got my hands on, and while it is hardly classical but probably some Alexandrian imitation - it's all about Helen and Castor + Pollux and Agamemnon and Menelaos and so on. I feel much elated at having a chance I've so hopelessly hoped for. Of course there are slips possible yet; but all the men seem to feel very generously toward me, and that is worth much. I shall try to push it this week.

After lunch with "two jolly German archaeologists" and Quibell,[50] he "kept an appointment with a dealer opposite the American Mission" who showed him "a £70 lot of Greek + Coptic papyri.[51] It seemed poor stuff after that poem [... M]y mind reverts constantly to the new papyrus. As Uncle Henry says, predestination is a true doctrine!"[52]

---

about possibly sending his "little Ethiopic grammar over," specifying "[t]he blue one." August Dillmann's *Grammatik der äthiopischen Sprache* (1857; new ed. in 1899, but published after Goodspeed had left Chicago) comes immediately to mind, but "small" seems an inaccurate description of a book nearly 500 pages long. Praetorius's slimmer *Äthiopische Grammatik* (1886) is another option, but Dillmann's *Grammatik* is later referenced as essential to Edgar's completion of Thekla (Ch. 3 with n. 109).

[48] 12 December continuation of 11 December.

[49] "[G]reatness thrust upon them": "If this fall into thy hand, revolve. In my stars I am above thee; but be not afraid of greatness: some are born great, some achieve greatness and some have greatness thrust upon 'em." – Shakespeare, *Twelfth Night* II.v. The accounts (Trismegistos 97877) on the back of this literary papyrus have not yet been published in full. They are on a fragment that has obvious associations with Trismegistos 9131 (*BGU* I 9, IV 1087, and XIII 2280); it is the largest and best preserved of the group.

[50] "[A]rchaeologists": presumably von Bissing (n. 43) and Schäfer (n. 57 below), both still needing to be "introduced" to Father.

[51] The location suggests the dealer may have been Michel Casira/Kasira, whose shop was "across from the American Mission" according to Hagen and Ryholt 2016, 72, 206. There Goodspeed would later (21 February 1900) buy the fragments that would become his "Andromeda" (see the beginning of Ch. 3).

[52] "Uncle Henry": Captain Henry S. Goodspeed, Civil War veteran, one of Thomas Wakefield

On the 13th,⁵³ he continues work on the poetic fragment, making corrections and a few conjectural supplements. He thinks the hand is not earlier than AD 200. Quibell responds favorably to a request for a facsimile. "I also had a long talk with the young German archaeologist von Bissing, a Basel + Berlin man, who has some good ideas" (sc. about the text).⁵⁴ But access to books remains a problem: He spends an afternoon hour in the shops "trying to get wind of some books to work on in connection with this papyrus," and he discovers for himself that Quibell's description of the Museum library as "a poor, poor affair" is accurate. Grenfell's counsel is of course sought, the approval of his "results" by both von Bissing and Quibell providing insufficient reassurance.

Next day,⁵⁵ Edgar reports that while en route to the Museum on foot (as habitual—and a good way to study "Arab life," as he would put it a week later),⁵⁶ he was overtaken by the Egyptologist Heinrich Schäfer:⁵⁷

> As I was crossing the big bridge,⁵⁸ Schäfer and another German passed in an open cab: they hailed me and made me get in: the "other" introduced himself as Borchardt,- Pater will recall him as the "earliest fixed Egyptian date" discoverer.⁵⁹ I was glad to meet him at the museum[.] I had a long talk with Von Bissing (who is I believe a German baron): he read me a long letter from Grenfell, who has already found 40 Greek papyri + 20 Demotic, in 1 week's digging!

Upon arriving at the Museum, Goodspeed continues:

Goodspeed's four older brothers, and his financial benefactor (C. T. B. Goodspeed 1932, *passim*).

⁵³Continuation of 11 December letter to Father.

⁵⁴Basel is probably a mistake for Bonn, where von Bissing had studied classical philology and archaeology and then Egyptology and art history between 1892 and 1896; in 1895 he was in Berlin receiving training from Adolf Erman (cf. Bierbrier 2012, 60–61, with 180–181 [on Erman]).

⁵⁵14 December letter to Mother.

⁵⁶20 December letter to Father, in continuation on 21 December.

⁵⁷For (Johann) Heinrich Schäfer (1868–1957), see Bierbrier 2012, 490–491. The prior winter he had made his first visit to Egypt, working with von Bissing and Ludwig Borchardt (n. 59 below) at Abū Jirāb (where he would continue to be involved through 1901) and with Ulrich Wilcken at Herakleopolis. On 26 October 1899, he had also joined von Bissing on the Comité of the *Catalogue général*; see Garstin 1900, 312.

⁵⁸The Kubrī el-Gezīra bridge, predecessor to today's Qaṣr al-Nīl bridge.

⁵⁹For Ludwig Borchardt (1863–1938), see Bierbrier 2012, 68–69. A key figure (alongside Maspero) in the creation of the *Catalogue général*, he had been replaced on its Comité by Schäfer. He was the leading agent for the purchase of antiquities for German collections (Hagen and Ryholt 2016, 42–43 and *passim*), as Goodspeed will soon learn to his dismay. Later notoriety came from his role in "the Nefertiti affair": D. M. Reid 2015, 81, 87–93, 154–155, 273, 356. His late-life travails as a Jew with German citizenship led in a complicated series of events to the creation of the Swiss Institute in Cairo (Schweizerisches Institut für Ägyptische Bauforschung und Altertumskunde): ibid., 273–278. "[E]arliest fixed Egyptian date" is a reference to Borchardt's paper at the 1899 Rome Congress of Orientalists (also attended, as we have seen in Ch. 1, by Goodspeed, who informed his father of the discovery); cf. Urquhart 1901. Borchardt 1899 is his publication of this research.

> Brugsch called me into his room + turned over to me a sheaf of uncatalogued papyri to do what I could with. After lunch, in the grounds, a dealer approached us, and Schäfer and Von Bissing turned him over to me, so I went with him to his large uncomfortable house overlooking the Nile, and saw a couple of hundred of his nearly 900 pieces, while he plied me with little cups of coffee, brought in by one of his younger sons, whom he had summoned by a loud hand clap. I asked if his son knew Greek. He replied with scorn, "No! he knows not any thing!" They were both finely dressed in Arab garb, not a bit Europeanized. Old Sheikh Farag must be rich. He offered me the whole outfit of papyri, Greek, Coptic, (many parchments, too) Arabic, Demotic + Hebrew for ..₤.100.- I wouldn't have the whole of them for anything! He is the same man who sold Mr. Ayer the Ayer papyrus; + he inquired anxiously about Mr. Ayer.[60]

But these are only interludes amid his obsession over the fragment. On 15 December, still writing to Mother, a new problem has emerged:

> I have had a quiet day at the Museum. The Epic fragment hangs fire badly from lack of books, but most painfully from the contumacy of the dealer, awful beast, who demands ₤10, while the Museum has offered but ₤2 and will not go above ₤5.[61] This is inside information. Still Maspero is interested, and Quibell committed to the purchase. Moreover I shall be through with the papyrus tomorrow, and it may go back to the dealer for a time, if it likes. I still hope, and rather hopefully. It promises to make a rousing piece of work, and even the fuller's accounts on the back may prove important, if, as now appears, they are the only dated papyrus from the reign

---

[60] For Ayer, see Ch. 1 and App. A. "Old Sheikh Farag": Farag Ismaïn, a famous and physically imposing Bedouin dealer, born c. 1830 (obviously a guess) and still active in the 1900s; cf. Hagen and Ryholt 2016, 214–215, as well as 166, which reproduces Lange's account of his visit on 28 November 1899, i.e., roughly two weeks before Goodspeed. As Egyptologist Francesco Ballerini (1877–1910; Bierbrier 2012, 37) describes him in a letter of 21 January 1903, "È un vecchio tipo di Beduino tutto avvolto nei suoi ampi vestimenti greve e cerimonioso come un patriarca dell'antico testamento" ("He's a typical old Bedouin, completely wrapped in his flowing robes, as stern and formal as an Old Testament patriarch"): Pintaudi 2016, 385. The price that Goodspeed mentions would seem to corroborate the report (Hagen and Ryholt, 215) that Farag was in debt at the time and thus selling at a discount. He lived in the Bedouin village Kafr al-Haram in the shadow of the pyramids. Goodspeed's reference to a "house overlooking the Nile" becomes sensible when one remembers that the nearby plain flooded during the winter.

Many years later, Goodspeed (n.d., ch. IV, pp. 12–13) would refer to the seller of the Ayer papyrus simply as Ali. This is presumably just a slip, though Farag Ismaïn may have had a son named Ali Farag (Hagen and Ryholt 2016, 195, 214). Breccia 1935 seems to have made a similar mistake, also years after the fact, when he confused Farag Ismaïn with Farag Ali (Hagen and Ryholt 2016, 214–215, n. 821). Farag Ali cannot have been the dealer whom Goodspeed visited: At the time, this Farag was "a good-looking young man" (ibid., 57), and his shop was just "a little hole" conveniently located near the Ezbekīyah Gardens (i.e., not overlooking the Nile), but only reached through "the most horrible alleys" in an Arab neighborhood (ibid., 213, quoting Lange's wife, Jonna).

[61] "[H]angs fire": "is delayed." The idiom is taken from the realm of firearms, especially flintlock musketry, referring to an unexpected delay between the sparking of the flint and actual discharge of the weapon.

of Tacitus.

The morning was marked by another "talk with von Bissing"—Edgar describes it as a "long" one—"about the difficulties in the papyrus." In the late afternoon, he spends another unsuccessful hour in the shops searching for helpful books.

On the next day, writing at 9 p.m., still to Mother, and obviously exhausted, he broaches the subject with pessimism:

> I came back from the Museum much disgusted with the world, and my own labors. I am haunted by the idea these months in Berlin and Cairo spent on papyri no one will publish, are wasted.

He wonders whether next summer will also be a waste of time; nevertheless, he had begun work that afternoon on a fresh papyrus, a Christian prayer,[62] and he is eminently satisfied with working conditions at the Museum.

> My relations at the Museum are entirely pleasant and cordial with every one, and I feel very much at home there. There's not in the wide world a better room to read papyri in ˬthan mine,ˬ the entire ceiling being a dome of glass.

His new friendship with von Bissing develops.[63]

> My friend the Baron begins his lunch with 4 raw eggs, a lá [sic] weasel. He brought Kenyon's "Palaeography" out today for me to look at.[64] Yesterday [19 December] he picked me up, and took me the last part of the way in his carriage - i.e. cab, but as they're open and have 2 horses, they seem like carriages.

Ominously (to us, but not yet to Goodspeed), he learns that the epic had "been sent up to Maspero, at Keneh, + he is to dicker with the dealer."[65]

As the trip to the Holy Land nears its start, Edgar describes to his father his long day of Museum work, 20 December from 10:00 a.m. until 4:00 p.m., including getting his hands on one or two new papyri:

> The first one I undertook is now in practically finished shape, - not a difficulty, gap or doubtful reading in it, though it is 300 words long. It will delight Charles' heart, being legal phraseology of the most stunning description. I am thinking of

---

[62] *P.Cair.Cat.* 10263: Trismegistos 64558; published in Jacoby 1900, with Grenfell's assistance acknowledged on p. 31. This identification is confirmed in the 8 February continuation of a 6 February 1900 letter to Mother: "I put in the morning at the Museum, working on that 5th century prayer. It is addressed to Christ; was found with a mummy, and was evidently meant partly to avert evil spirits :- a strange bit." Grenfell informed Goodspeed of Jacoby's publication, which he describes as "very bad," by postcard from Kawm Aushīm (ancient Karanis), 25 December 1900; see Goodspeed box 4, folder 9.

[63] 20 December to Father.

[64] "Kenyon's 'Palaeography'": Kenyon 1899.

[65] "Keneh" or Qinā (Qena), from the Greek Kaine, is in Upper Egypt on the Nile's East Bank, about 350 miles south of Cairo.

undertaking a translation of it.[66]

He briefly remarks, "A card from Grenfell reached me today, and I have just written him a rather long letter."

❋ ❋ ❋ ❋

Grenfell's postcard, dated 15 December but postmarked "19.xii.99, Gharac-Fayoum," was addressed to "E.J. Goodspeed c/o Dr. F. von Bissing, Ghizeh Museum, Ghizeh." Grenfell is puzzled about Goodspeed's silence in the aftermath of his letter of 5 December:

> Nothing heard from you, I am afraid you have not got the letter which I wrote some time ago to you at the Hotel Bristol, saying we should be very pleased to see you any time. We are digging a town called Umm el Baragât, 1½ hours E of Gharak. I gave details in my letter how to reach us. If you come, let us know beforehand[.][67]

As noted above, Goodspeed had asked for Grenfell's counsel on the epic, and the letter bearing that request, sent on the 13th at the latest,[68] would surely have addressed his visit; presumably it had not arrived at the camp before Grenfell posted his card.[69] Whatever the exact details, Grenfell's 5 December letter had clearly not been forgotten, for a missive to Sarah, 18–19 December, states, "I'm thinking of paying him a visit at his excavating camp in Fayyûm (Gherac) where he has made every arrangement to receive me."[70] The longer term was also on his mind, specifically whether he could get a leave of absence for the quarter beginning 1 July, and whether he would be on salary or not "in case Grenfell makes a suitable proposition."[71]

Nonetheless, the epic fragment continues to dominate his thoughts and aspirations:

> Maspero writes Quibell that he will buy the Epic for the Museum if £6 will do it.

---

[66] No doubt the future *P.Cair.Goodsp.* 13, which is the right length and has a very clean text full of legal verbiage; a translation accompanied his edition, and he later published one separately (1903c). Translating documents as a component of their editions was not the norm at this time. Grenfell and Hunt introduced the practice in 1897 "at the request of several subscribers to the Graeco-Roman branch" of the Egypt Exploration Fund (*P.Oxy.* I, p. [v]), but the practice did not catch on quickly or everywhere.

[67] Goodspeed box 4, folder 9.

[68] The 13 December, 9 p.m., continuation of 11 December to Father speaks of this communication in the past tense.

[69] The information in Grenfell's 5 December letter, quoted in full above, suggests that his card would have reached Gharak on 16 December, the same day that a letter from Goodspeed sent on the 13th would have arrived there.

[70] Goodspeed box 48, folder 1.

[71] 21 December continuation of 20 December to Father.

When Quibell told me this, I remarked upon the price : + he paralyzed me by saying, he had recommended its purchase at that figure, chiefly on the judgment of von Bissing (the Baron) and myself. This amused me. - But I think the Keneh dealer will take £6, and things seem to be coming my way again. The epic will make a beautiful piece of work - a short article, only, of course; but an important one. And I think the fragment will be conceded one of the finest uncials known. My plan is to try it on the Journal of Hellenic Studies, or the (English) Journal of Philology.[72]

Having made progress on his Christian prayer, he considers prospects for its publication, hoping in all to produce "three or 4 little things to print from this Gizeh experience."[73] The practice reading has been good preparation for next summer, and he values the acquaintances he has made since coming to Cairo, mentioning Maspero, Brugsch, Quibell, von Bissing, Schäfer, and Lange by name and in that order. All this should justify the faith placed in him by his financial backers—Father and Mr. Bond. Thekla is on a back burner for now, but he is nevertheless working on Ethiopic vocabularies to advance this project as well. Meantime, brother Charles has evidently expressed doubts about Edgar's "manuscript work," which, Edgar tells Father,

> find echoes in my own breast: still, if I can get literary pieces to do now and then, it is all right for they carry me at once into history and criticism . - And its [sic] all Greek, of course. As to next summer, I feel that if G.+H. take me in on the level, the gain in prestige and reputation will be of great value. If they don't, I hardly care to stay, I think. This is precisely your view, if I remember: and I should think it would certainly be Charles': He must mean that they won't take me on on an equality, + so it wont be worth while. – We'll see what Grenfell says.[74] I have written him frankly, writing a proposition.[75]

The last two days before leaving for the Holy Land he spends fruitfully at the Museum, "reading some jolly little Ptolemaic pieces, which will certainly print,"[76] and making out a few more words in the Christian prayer on the 22nd,[77] discovering "a nice little Odyssey fragment" on the 23rd.[78] The latter prompts him to ask Father to see if Charles back home could "gently extract from my little "Odyssey" (which, being all to pieces, is.- or was .- tied up in a white paper among my books-) the leaves containing Bk. XV (Fifteen) lines 215 to 254, and would send them to me at once care Thos Cook + Son, Cairo." He bids a "fond adieu" to "the men at the

---

[72] Again, 21 December continuation of 20 December to Father. "(English)": to distinguish this *Journal of Philology* (founded 1868) from the *American Journal of Philology* (founded 1880).

[73] For the prayer's publication, not by Goodspeed, see n. 62.

[74] "We'll" could equally be "Will."

[75] It would obviously be useful to have Charles's letter to Edgar and Goodspeed's frank epistolary proposition to Grenfell; both are lost.

[76] These presumably are among those that end up in *P.Cair.Goodsp.*; see n. 101.

[77] 22 December continuation of 20 December to Father.

[78] The future *P.Cair.Goodsp.* 1.

Museum – Brugsch + von Bissing [...] They are very nice. von B. is really a very attractive young fellow. Everyone at the Museum has shown me great kindness, and I am in deep clover there."[79] On the contrary, he cannot resist a parting shot at Crandall, who will be accompanying him to the Holy Land.

❉ ❉ ❉ ❉

As we have seen from his letter to Sue, quoted at the start of this chapter, Goodspeed had been aiming to spend Christmas in Jerusalem, but these plans were later modified. On 23 December he purchased tickets to Port Said and thence to Beirut by the Khedivial Line.[80] He departed just before noon on Christmas Eve, a Sunday, reaching the Suez Canal later that day. Quarantine problems in Ottoman ports delayed his departure from Port Said until 26 December. New Year's Day found him in Damascus. From there he visited in turn Haifa, Sidon, and Tyre; took a horseback tour of Palestine; and saw Nazareth and the Sea of Galilee before spending a month in Jerusalem.[81]

Grenfell wrote again on 3 January. He refers to the coveted poetic fragment, describes the early results of the Hearst excavations, outlines work plans for the coming summer, and ends jokingly in Greek:

> The epic fragment is as you say about A.D. 200, late second or early 3rd cent. It isnt an uncommon sort of uncial. By all means of course publish it. We make no claims upon it, even if we had any to make. It is an interesting little piece and should be facsimiled seeing that there is a date on the verso. I have no doubt I could ~~get~~ arrange for its publication with a plate in the Journal of Hellenic Studies, and, if you like, I will write about it to Kenyon who is on the editorial Committee.
>
> Though just at present things are rather quiet, this site has proved distinctly good. We began by finding the temple enclosure in which the houses of the priests produced a good number of Greek and demotic papyri[.] Since then in other parts of the site we have done well, and Hunt has now flattened out about 600 Greek pieces, of which 1 in 5 approximately is worth publishing.[82] As usual they are mostly 1–3rd cent AD. [*sic*] with a sprinkling of Ptolemaic. The miscellaneous anticas too

---

[79] This quote and the one preceding it are from the 23 December continuation of 20 December to Father.

[80] "Khedivial Line": a reference to the British-flagged steamboats of the Khedivial Mail Steamship and Graving Dock Company, Limited.

[81] For the itinerary we have consulted Goodspeed 1953, 113–114, Goodspeed n.d., ch. V ("Those Holy Fields"), and the "Student Travel Letters." See also Goodspeed 1900a.

[82] For Hunt's methods, as he described them later on, i.e., 20 October 1920, see *P.Oxy.* L, p. vi: "The Damping Out and Flattening of Papyri." These 600 would have been substantial pieces; significantly more fragments had been found. Grenfell's figure may be compared with the 735 town papyri that received "T(ebtunis)-numbers." For Grenfell and Hunt's T-numbers (which, it may be added, were applied in the field), see Ryholt 2013. *P.Tebt.* II, the volume dedicated to the pieces found in the town as opposed to the cemeteries, contains 160 papyri with full editions and 265 *descripta*.

have been above the average in interest, including some hoards of coins,[83] inscribed statuettes and a few gold & silver ornaments.[84] Just now we are engaged in clearing two Coptic churches, (a good part of the site is late[85]), one of which has curious and interesting pictures.[86] Next week we shall begin the tombs which are close by. There ought to be some good ones, but I much fear they will be affected by damp & of no use as far as papyri are concerned.

I am very glad to hear you are likely to be able to help us in publishing the next volume. We can give you plenty to do. Probably it will be best for you to pay us a visit here when we can talk things over fully. But in the meantime this is what we propose (subject to unforeseen events). We have so much to do next summer with our volume for the Fund, and Lord Amherst's papyri,[87] that unless anything very startling turns up, we dont think of working at the papyri we find this winter until next year. But if you could come to Oxford this summer, you could have the whole collection to work at. Probably you could make rough copies of all the interesting ones: at the end of the summer we could decide which papyri you would edit and which we, and during the next year you could in America prepare the MS of your part. We intend to send the whole MS to the press by Nov. 1901, so that the volume (which would be under our joint names) would come out in 1902, I hope by June.

I dont know what your plans are for the next 4 months. We arent likely to be back in England till the middle of April. If you like, you could take the papyri we have found now to Gizeh and work at them till we arrive in Cairo some time in March. I dont anticipate to do more than double the amount we have now got, even if we do that. But of course it is vain to prophesy.

We have got a spare mattress now, but bring as many blankets as you can. We shall be very pleased to see you any time except for a week at Bairam, i.e. from about Jan 30–Feb 5, when we have a friend coming.[88] As letters take some time to reach us, please write a week before you propose to come.

          Yours very sincerely

          Bernard P. Grenfell

ἐγράφη ἀπὸ κώμης Τεβτύνεως τῆς Πολέμωνος μερίδος[89]

---

[83] Cf. Milne 1935.

[84] "[I]nscribed statuettes": Cf., e.g., Lutz 1930, 10–11 with pl. 15.

[85] Grenfell's parenthetical addition is interesting in light of the account of *sebhakīn* activity in Gallazzi and Hadji-Minaglou 2000, 9–10.

[86] Cf. Walters 1989, Boutros 2005, 120, 126–127. The reference to a *second* church is new and important.

[87] "[V]olume for the [Egypt Exploration] Fund": Grenfell has in mind *P.Oxy.* III, published in 1903, but subscribers would end up receiving *P.Tebt.* I before it, in 1902. "Lord Amherst's papyri": the documents intended for *P.Amh.* II (1901).

[88] "Bairam": the *Īd al-Fiṭr*. "[A] friend": as yet unidentified. During Grenfell and Hunt's 1903/1904 Oxyrhynchus season, J. A. R. Munro (1864–1944; see further Gill 2011, 367–368) visited; in an 18 January 1904 letter to J. Gilbart Smyly, he is described as an "Oxford friend": TCD MS 4323, item 51.

[89] "Written from the village of Tebtunis of the district of Polemon." The letter is in Goodspeed box 4, folder 9. Note here the spelling with *beta* as opposed to Grenfell's letter of 5 December with its apparently hesitant use of the less common, and generally later, spelling with *pi* in the transliteration Teptunis.

Remarkably, this letter reached Goodspeed in Jerusalem because on 12 January he writes from there to Mother:[90]

> My letter from Grenfell I must abstract for you. It is about as follows: "Dear Goodspeed: The Epic fragment is as you say about A.D. 200"...."It isnt an uncommon sort of uncial. By all means of course publish it. We make no claims upon it even if we had any to make. It is an interesting little piece and should be facsimiled" (etc)[.] He then offers to write Kenyon about getting it into the Journal of Hellenic Studies. They have found 600 Greek papyri over 100 of which they think worth publishing. "I am very glad to hear you are likely to be able to help us in publishing this next volume. We can give you plenty to do. Probably it will be betterst for you to pay us a visit here when we can talk things over fully. But in the meantime this is what we propose." "We have" - but I must condense - he offers to let me have the papyri already found, to work on in Gizeh if I like; also to work in Oxford this summer (i.e. from April 15 on) making rough copies of the lot. Then we can decide in September which ones I shall edit, I preparing my MS in America by Nov. 1901, + they theirs in Oxford: "The volume (which would bear under our joint names) would come out in 1902 I hope by June"....."We have a spare mattress" etc. This plunges me into new problems, gratifying as it is.

At the end of his Holy Land pilgrimage, Edgar wrote to his father from Jerusalem in final summation of the experience:[91]

> Between ourselves, and now that it's all over, my heart broke within me when I got Shailer's letter in Mainz - horrible town![92] I was sick, and the sheer certainty of having to add Palestine and Egypt to my itinerary had an abysmal effect on me. I knew then I was in for it you see! Shocking confession, isn't it? But when I fam about to plunge again into the unknown, I feel gloomy and confidential. Hinc illae lacrimae.[93] [...] I see now that Palestine was more important for me than any other land I've seen; or perhaps than all.

Back in Cairo on 6 February, he reports to his mother his going to Cook's and finding a "heap of mail." The next day, however, brought a jolt, whose source (in Goodspeed's understanding, at least) was that German stranger whom he had met not quite two months ago while crossing the Nile on "the big bridge":

> At the museum Quibell met me with a body blow. The Epic has taken flight. Borchardt outbid Quibell, and got it for the Berlin Museum at 10 pounds. So the world wags. It is a big disappointment, but there are other fish in the sea. It's a good thing I wasn't here : I fear I should have discounted the Bond money, + plunged on

---

[90] In continuation of 10 January.
[91] 4 February continuation of 2 February.
[92] For the letter received in Mainz, with its guarantee of money for Goodspeed's travels beyond Europe, see Ch. 1 with n. 66.
[93] Terence, *Andria* 126, which became a proverbial explanation: "Hence those tears."

it. Therefore, let us rejoice.[94]

But this was putting a brave face, and the disappointment would linger. On the following day he continued to his mother:

> I had a little interview with Brugsch, saw Quibell + von Bissing as usual. And now let me again remark what a fool I was to go off and leave the Epic matter unsettled : the chance of a lifetime is irretrievably gone. The thing would have made me as a classicist : 3 or 4 periods would have done the business : and I let it slip from me[95] simply by the grossest carelessness. This comes of having nobody along to direct you: this will disappoint you all, I fear: as for me I am tremendously ashamed of myself.[96]

He nevertheless continues his "present humbler labors,"[97] expressing most enthusiasm about the *Odyssey* fragment he had discovered in the Museum last December. But time is running out, and as he writes to Charles on 10 February, he finds himself, as in Berlin a year ago, hustling to "finish some little pieces of papyrus : history repeats itself." He witnesses "the opening of the mummy case of Merneptah in the presence of Maspero ₄alias "the great man"₄, Brugsch ₄alias "the old boy"₄, Quibell, von Bissing etc etc."[98] Afterwards, Maspero stops by his work table:

> I thanked him for remembering me about the Epic : He thinks as I do that its [*sic*] not really classical but some Alexandrian imitation : He pleased me by saying there were some new Greek papyri from Ashmunên, locked up in his boat;[99] and if I liked, he would have them brought over and I might have a look at them : so he's going to do it.[100]

---

[94] To Mother on 7 February, 9:20 p.m., in continuation of 6 February. The "Epic," more precisely a fragment of the Hesiodic *Catalogus mulierum*, is Trismegistos 60062. Its *editio princeps*, which explicitly indicates the involvement in the acquisition of only von Bissing, not Borchardt, is Wilamowitz-Moellendorff 1900. (Von Bissing had sent Wilamowitz a transcription.) For earlier speculation regarding its identity, see Meliadò 2008, 14–15; the correct solution to this *piccolo giallo* ["little mystery"] eluded him because he was aware only of Grenfell's letters to Goodspeed. For the "Bond money," see Ch. 1. "Therefore, let us rejoice": *Gaudeamus igitur*; cf. Ps. 118:24.

[95] The reading of "me" is difficult but makes most sense given the small space between "from" and "simply."

[96] And he would still feel the sting for another half century or more: See Goodspeed n.d., ch. VII, p. 3's remembrance of his "gloom over the loss of the literary papyrus to the rapacious Germans." Whether he ever identified von Bissing, "the most amiable youth in the world" (Ch. 3), as the villain is unknown.

[97] 9 February continuation of 6 February to Mother.

[98] Cf. Maspero 1902, 317–326, esp. 326, which discusses the event mentioned by Goodspeed, though misdating it to March, and indicates that Schäfer, Borchardt, Daressy (Bierbrier 2012, 142–143), and Groff (Bierbrier 2012, 230) were among the "et ceteri." We are grateful to Christina Riggs for her guidance on this issue. For a newspaper account, see the German-language *Westliche Post* (St. Louis), 27 March 1900, p. 4.

[99] Presumably the *dhahabīyah* belonging to the Antiquities Service (cf. Orsenigo 2010, 147), but T. Davis et al. 1907, xxvi, write, perhaps loosely, of Maspero's "dahabeah."

[100] "Ashmunên": ancient Hermopolis Magna. Nothing would result from Maspero's gesture:

"Meantime," Goodspeed continues,

> my work moves on. I have had Brugsch photograph the Odyssey fragment : he shewed me the plate today : it's amazingly good. Brugsch has a great reputation as a photographer. My idea is to offer a series of a dozen or 20 papyri with introductions to the Amer. Jour. of Archaeology, say; leading off with the Odyssey piece: and a plate of it. I own the negative, + shall send that along. This morning I read Ptolemaic bits chiefly. There is one complete letter; only I cant yet be sure what it means![101]

That same day, 10 February, Grenfell writes a letter to Goodspeed, which he receives on 12 February.[102] Preparations for the visit to Tebtunis are the main concern, in anticipation of Goodspeed's arrival a week hence. It starts with precise directions, revised from his 5 December letter, and continues with a list of things to buy and bring before offering condolences over the epic fragment's loss and addressing the delay of final Californian approval of Goodspeed's participation in publishing the papyri they have been finding.

> We shall be very pleased to see you next Saturday the 17th. Please get out at Damian the station after Abu Nour. It is somewhat nearer to us than Abu Nour. You will find there a couple of my men with a donkey for your luggage. If you want a donkey for yourself, please write as soon as you receive this. Damian is 1¼ hours walk from us; local donkeys are inferior. We have a spare mattress here, so dont bring that, but bring as many wraps as you can. The tent you will be in lets in a good deal of air and the nights are still cold.
>
> You would be doing us a favor and conferring a benefit on yourself, if you could bring us some vegetables. Salad, cauliflower, carrots and 'badingan' are what we lack most.[103] You might entrust a man with 25 piastres to expend. Also a plum cake would be acceptable.[104] We will repay you of course.
>
> Very sorry the epic fragment has taken wings. It is very rough luck on you, and

---

Edgar's 13 February continuation to Charles describes these papyri as "a heterogeneous mass of Greek, Coptic + Arabic fragments - a hopeless lot." Goodspeed n.d., ch. VII, p. 3, erroneously reports, "[S]everal of them I afterwards published in my "Greek Papyri in the Cairo Museum.""

[101] The fruition of this work was not in the *American Journal of Archaeology* but in *P.Cair.Goodsp.*, where the *Odyssey* papyrus would lead off, but without plate. It contains 15 papyri from Gizeh; seven (nos. 3–9) are Ptolemaic. Two of these, *P.Cair.Goodsp.* 3 and 4, are letters; the latter is virtually complete and must be the one referred to here.

[102] The date of receipt is established by Goodspeed's quotations of the letter in his own letter to Charles written later on the same day, 12 February, 10 p.m. (in continuation of 10 February). See n. 107 for the relevant text.

[103] '[B]adingan': eggplant (aubergine); cf. Michell 1877, 60. For the word's Persian roots, see Mutzafi 2014, 59–60. It endures in the modern Persian bademjan (Michael Zellmann-Rohrer).

[104] Suggestive of the British fondness for plum cake: Frederic Manning's 1929 war novel *The Middle Parts of Fortune* (Manning 1990), 185, 199. In *The Curse in the Colophon* (Goodspeed 1935), 193, the American consul in Trebizond suggests that the hero ingratiate himself with the monastery's "agoumenos" by "a present of fish, vegetables, and perhaps a nice plum cake."

I had written to Kenyon who sent me the enclosed for you.[105] We have been doing very well during the last month, but I dont anticipate much more now from the tombs.

I have at length heard from Reisner who has written to California about you.[106] Till we I hear from there I dont suppose we can make a definite arrangement, but I trust things will go all right for you. We shall decline having any inexperienced person mixed up with our papyri, and so far as I know you are the only American who has worked at the subject. However we will talk about this when you come.[107]

Goodspeed would publish two descriptions of his visit to Tebtunis. The better known of these is the article "Papyrus Digging with Grenfell and Hunt" (with four photographs),[108] which appeared in the 10 November 1904 issue of *The Independent*, a weekly magazine of current events, culture, and reviews published in New

---

[105] Kenyon's enclosure is not extant in the Goodspeed archive. Cf. also Meliadò 2008, 15 n. 11.

[106] Reisner in fact did not write to Mrs. Hearst until 17 February: Ch. 1, n. 96.

[107] Goodspeed box 4, folder 9. The content of this letter—specifically, Grenfell's echoing of Goodspeed's "The Epic has taken flight" (cf. the 7 February letter to Mother) and the fixing of a date for Goodspeed's arrival at Tebtunis—indicates that a letter from Goodspeed is missing from the sequence. A letter posted in Cairo by 1 p.m. on Thursday, 8 February, would have reached Grenfell on Saturday the 10th (cf. Grenfell's letter of 5 December 1899). Grenfell must have responded to Goodspeed's letter the evening that he received it.

Here is Goodspeed's account of Grenfell's 10 February letter (cf. n. 102): "Pouring over my pile of letters ½ hour later, I struck an unopened one from Grenfell : very amusing. After telling me to bring plenty of wraps, he says: You would be doing us a favour as well as conferring a benefit upon yourself, if you could bring us some vegetables. Salad, Cauliflower, Carrots + "Badingan"(?!) are what we lack most. You might entrust a man with 25 piastres to expend. Also a plum cake would be acceptable. We will repay you of course.- Very sorry the Epic fragment has taken wings" etc. He encloses a nice letter from Kenyon, to whom he had kindly written ; Kenyon's letter, which is to me, offers every encouragement to me about putting it in the Hellenic Studies' Journal, etc. etc. A long and most kind letter. Alas! -They are now sounding the California people on my proposed collaboration ! I rather think there'll be excitement out there : B.P.G. "trusts all things will go well for" me + stoutly adds "We shall decline having any inexperienced person mixed up with our papyri, + so far as I can hear [sic] you are the only American who has worked at the subject." This consulting the Cal. officials is not an afterthought : we took it into account in our Oxford talks."

Goodspeed also excerpts Grenfell's 10 February letter, but much more succinctly, in Goodspeed n.d., ch. VII, p. 4. In a letter to Father on 14 February, he reports buying Grenfell's plum cake after tea.

[108] The photographs are captioned as follows: "Dr. Hunt and Dr. Grenfell in Camp," "Ruins of Arsinoe," "An Egyptian Train," and "Dr. Grenfell in the Field." The last three of these were taken by Goodspeed himself, and, with the exception of "Ruins of Arsinoe," are preserved in the Goodspeed Papers; cf. Figs. 8 and 9. (The photograph published as "Dr. Grenfell in the Field" was first labeled "Grenfell and Arab diggers"; this was then crossed out, and "Mr. Grenfell in the Field" was added.) "Dr. Hunt and Dr. Grenfell in Camp," a famous portrait of the duo, was sent to Goodspeed by the Englishmen. It is referred to in Grenfell's postcard of 25 December 1900, which was written at Kawm Aushīm (the ancient Karanis); see Goodspeed box 4, folder 9.

York City.[109] Almost exactly two years before this, he had prepared a more popular account—the change in tone and emphasis is noticeable—for the *Chicago Daily Tribune* (with three halftone illustrations).[110] Both articles draw heavily for their details on a six-page letter he had written to his mother, beginning Saturday, 17 February, and finishing Tuesday, 20 February, the morning after his late-night return to Cairo from the Fayyūm. The journey is further illustrated by photographs beyond those employed for the articles and now also preserved in the Goodspeed Papers.[111]

According to his letter,[112] Goodspeed left Cairo by train early in the morning of Saturday, 17 February, a day that was "cool and fine," passing pyramids and fields "beautifully green, with occasional spaces of yellow blossoms like mustard." He arrives at "Wasta, or el-Wastah" two hours later. From there, at about 10 a.m., he catches the train to "Medinet-el-Fayoum." He and his "huge basket of vegetables" occupy a second-class compartment, "large, and comfortable, but pretty dirty." At 12:15 p.m. he is in "Medinet el Fayoum […] enjoying coffee and pastry at the Hotel Karoun Café" to the sound of "creaking water wheels."[113] (Fig. 5) The provincial capital strikes him as "an unusual place, with the swift current of [the] Bahr Yusuf running right through the town. One mud brick bridge is a veritable rialto with shops along each side of it!"[114] (Fig. 6) By 2:15 p.m., he is "seated on the dirt on top of Kûm FARIS, the highest rubbish mound of Arsinoe."[115] (Fig. 7) At 4:15 p.m. he is "[s]eated in the 3rd class carriage of the narrow gauge line […] waiting for the little train to start. As I hastened to the station," he writes, "after a long ramble in the ruins of Arsinoe, a man accosted me- a tall native, a fellah: barefooted, dressed in a long blue garment, + wearing a white turban.[116] [Fig. 8] He handed me a twisted

---

[109] No. 2919, in vol. 57 (July–December 1904), pp. 1066–1070.

[110] "How Ancient Records Are Dug Out Of The Sands Of Egypt," 16 November 1902, no. 320, vol. LXI, p. 42. The halftones captioned "The Camp at Umm-El-Baraghat" and "A Bridge of Shops + Medinet" represent known photographs (cf. Figs. 10, 6). "Mr. Grenfell in the Field," however, varies significantly from the photograph in the Goodspeed Papers with that label and probably represents another, now lost, image. Note below, at the start of Ch. 3, Goodspeed's reference to the "shots [plural] at Grenfell."

[111] See Goodspeed box 48, folder 1, tipped into the manuscript; box 51, folder 3; and box 57, folder 4.

[112] For the full text of the letter, including additional annotations and documentation of Goodspeed's self-corrections, etc., see App. B. Here we present a clean-text narrative in chronological order derived from the more complicated account in the letter. For Goodspeed's own summary of the events: Goodspeed n.d., ch. VII, pp. 6–11.

[113] "[W]ater wheels": Cf. Oliphant 1882, 8–11.

[114] Emma Andrews (n.d., 2:4), visiting in December 1898, noted that the Baḥr Yūsuf's "many branches flowing through the town, and the numerous bridges […] gave many novel features - making a kind of Egyptian Venice or Amsterdam." Cf. also Macmillan & Co. 1905, 91–92: "one of the most picturesque towns in Egypt, owing partly to the unusual fact of its having a stream running through it. The bazaar, which is more than a mile long, is very interesting and pretty, passing over several canals. But unfortunately the picturesque old bridges have been replaced by modern iron ones."

[115] "Kûm FARIS": Cf. Baedeker 1898, 150–151.

[116] "[F]ellah": "tiller of the soil," Egyptian peasant. "[L]ong […] garment": i.e., *jalābīyah*.

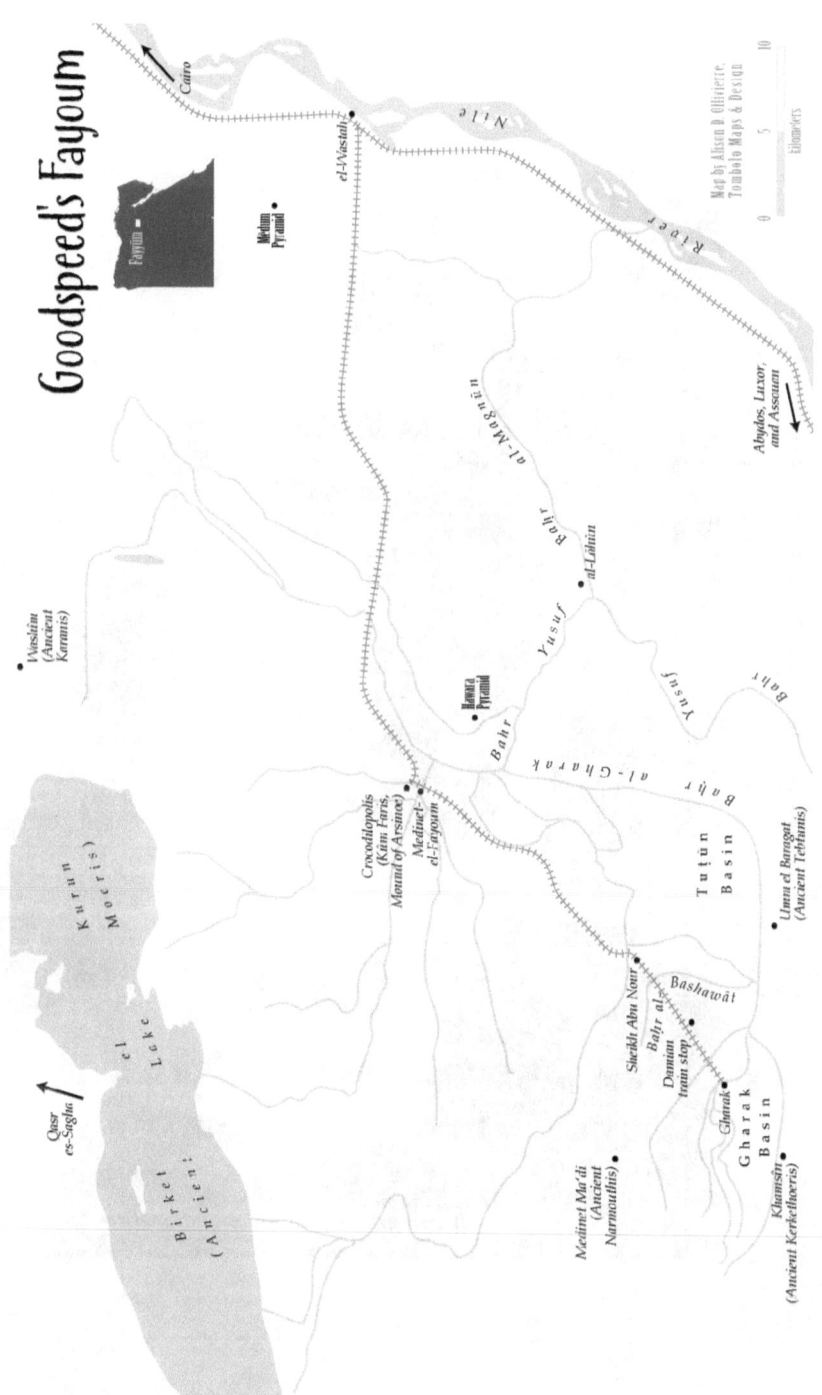

Figure 5: The Hotel Karoon with waterwheels in the foreground, ca. 1900. Photographer unknown; photographic print owned by T. M. Hickey.

Figure 6: "An Egyptian rialto."
Edgar J. Goodspeed photo; courtesy of the SCRC, University of Chicago.

Figure 7: "Sebbakhin at mound of Arsinoe."
Easton T. Kelsey photo, 1920; courtesy of the Bentley Historical Library,
University of Michigan.

Figure 8: "An Egyptian train (and Mohammed Mansour?)."
Edgar J. Goodspeed photo; courtesy of the SCRC, University of Chicago.

scrap of paper. I read "Dear Goodspeed : The bearer of this, Mohammed Mansour, has come in to Medinet to buy planks + will return to Damian in the same train as you. There will be a camel waiting which will take your luggage.""[117]

Goodspeed does not arrive at the excavation site from Damian until 7:30 p.m., "after a rapid walk of an hour from the train, escorted by [not just Mansour but] 3 of Grenfell's most trusted men. They carried me over canals on their shoulders, led me by the hand when it was very rough, and closed in a solid group about me when the dogs of each village or hamlet rushed upon us![118] [...] Grenfell came out to meet us, and then Hunt with a lamp in his hand. They made me welcome, + I washed up in Grenfell's tent. After which we had a mighty good dinner [...] We had cold turkey, tomato sauce, potatoes, boiled rice; a blanc-monge [sic] with prunes;[119] coffee; and everything was nice [...] Hunt retired early; I talked till 10 30 with BPG."[120]

Goodspeed is "awakened Sunday morning by hearing the swift steps of passing Arabs on the hard sand outside [... These are] Grenfell's men gathering from the adjacent villages. Mahmoud brought me some water and I joined G. + H. in Grenfell's tent for a fine breakfast at 7.20.[121] We had oatmeal, eggs and bacon, bread, jam and tea : all first class [...] I walked out with Hunt after breakfast to the town mounds, where he shewed me the ruins of their Coptic church with its pictures of

---

[117] The "twisted scrap of paper" is not extant in the Goodspeed Papers. Its bearer is no doubt the Mohammed Mansur—"'one-eyed and split-nosed,' a cheerful fellow who never grumbled" (Drower 1995, 188)—who worked for Petrie. For a request by Grenfell for some of Petrie's workers, including "Muhd Mansur," see Quirke 2010, 136; note also the presence of the brother of Petrie's headman 'Ali in App. B. Grenfell's earlier correspondence mentions only donkeys as beasts of burden.

[118] "[D]ogs": Cf. Maspero 1892, 334.

[119] "[B]lanc-monge": Goodspeed's spelling (the "o" is certain) is not unknown (cf., e.g., Ragan 1922, 11), perhaps influenced by the sound of this French word to the English-language ear, especially one untrained in French, like Goodspeed's (see the end of Ch. 1). Dictionaries define it as a sweet, gelatinous, opaque dessert made of cornstarch and milk.

[120] According to his much later recollection (Goodspeed n.d., ch. VII, pp. 7–8), the night's conversation ("It was a memorable and even a historic talk") included Grenfell's telling "the now famous tale of the mummied crocodiles," namely how a month earlier one workman in frustration used his mattock to crack one open and found it to have been wrapped and stuffed with papyri. *As I Remember* (Goodspeed 1953, 114) attributes the telling to both Grenfell and Hunt ("they told me"). The story, which has achieved legendary status, graces the preface to *P.Tebt.* I at p. vi and has been retold many times since, but its veracity is suspect. Goodspeed does not mention it in his "Student Travel Letters," nor does it appear in any of Grenfell and Hunt's writing about the excavation before the publication of *P.Tebt.* I. For further discussion, see App. C, n. 45.

[121] A "Mahm(oud) Mabruk" is listed with thirteen others on the back of p. 1 of Crum Notebook 67 (Crum MSS., Griffith Institute, Ashmolean Museum, University of Oxford). This notebook, originally Hunt's, largely concerns the Tebtunis excavations, though its initial pages document work during the preceding season, 1898/1899, at Euhemereia and Theadelpheia. Goodspeed, moreover, may be referring to the Mahmoud Mansoor who is mentioned later in his letter (but see n. 130 below) or even the brother of Petrie's famous headman 'Ali (see App. B, n. 48).

S[t]. George and the dragon, etc, and its 2 pretty columns.[122]

"Then I walked on alone to the barren level desert which Grenfells men have pitted with thousands of little holes:- The Ptolemaic cemetery [... where] they have found more Ptolemaic papyri than anyone ever found before! [...] You see," Edgar explains to his mother, "in this cemetery, they found a lot of crocodile mummies, wrapped in cloths stiffened with big pieces of papyrus: also a good many human mummies finished in the same way. They are now figuring on three volumes from this years digging.[123] They thus wish me more than ever to come to Oxford to work on the first one, which will be devoted to a selection from the 700 Roman papyri [they have already found[124] ...] While it might be more flattering to be taken on for the Ptolemaic ones, I am on the whole well pleased with the Roman field, as it covers my period, and I've had experience in Roman papyri[125] [...] I spent the morning, following Grenfell from pit to pit among his men: he is rather short and walks briskly about,[126] his surveyor's staff in his hand, a broad white felt hat pulled over his eyes, and the invariable cigarette in his teeth.-[127] I photographed him [Fig. 9], I hope successfully. The afternoon I spent with Hunt till tea: when [...] we all three went out to the excavations, 10 minutes walk from the tents [...]

"After dinner, we sat about the little table in Grenfell's tent and talked till nearly 10. The tent is full, with G's bed and the dining table, chairs and a few boxes, besides piles of clay lamps, Ptolemaic vases and little bronzes, etc.[128] The moon was up when I sought my tent: also a wind which shook the tents all night.- At sunrise [Monday] I got up, and again we were together for breakfast in Grenfell's tent.

---

[122] "Coptic church": See above n. 86, and note that Walters questions the identification of St. George.

[123] Three volumes would in fact be produced through the agency of Grenfell and Hunt. The third volume, however, which presents material recovered from the human mummies, proved a difficult labor. Its first part appeared only in 1933, after Grenfell's death in 1926; it was published by Hunt and J. G. Smyly, "with assistance from B. P. Grenfell, E. Lobel, and M. Rostovtzeff." Hunt would be the posthumous editor of part two, 1938, alongside Smyly and C. C. Edgar. For Smyly, see Ch. 1, nn. 89, 96.

[124] Cf. above n. 82.

[125] "[E]xperience in Roman papyri": Certainly true, though at this moment of writing, in addition to BGU III 810–811, only Goodspeed 1898a and Goodspeed 1898b had appeared in print.

[126] "[R]ather short" seems an exaggeration: A 1920 photo of Grenfell and Francis W. Kelsey (Pedley 2012, 272) suggests that the former was only slightly shorter than the latter. Kelsey's passport application, contemporary with the photo, indicates a height of 5'10" (National Archives and Records Administration, Roll 805: 19 Jun 1919–20 Jun 1919, Certificate 89781), the very same height that Goodspeed's 1898 passport application states (National Archives and Records Administration, Roll 514: 1 Sep 1898–30 Sep 1898, certificate not stated). Years later his actual passport (no. 391145, issued 17 May 1927) listed him at 5'9" (box 57, folder 8, "Travel documents, 1899–1927").

[127] Some of Grenfell's cigarette tins were reused for packing papyri and are preserved in the collection of the Center for the Tebtunis Papyri, University of California, Berkeley. Cf. Imaging Papyri Project 1998.

[128] For the Tebtunis pottery, see the inventory, "Tebtunis pots," in Crum Notebook 67, p. 15, and O'Connell 2007, 819–820. Note also Hunt's 11 July 1926 letter to G. Caton-Thompson (Griffith Institute, Ashmolean Museum, University of Oxford; reproduced in full in App. F), which mentions "small bronze objects" that were sent to the Cairo Museum.

Figure 9: "Mr. Grenfell in the Field."
Edgar J. Goodspeed photo; courtesy of the SCRC, University of Chicago.

I walked with him to the work: he is a fast walker : and the wind cool and dust laden was against us. I spent an hour and a half with G. among the men: then said goodbye, and joined Hunt in the tents where he was separating papyri from the wrapping of those Ptolemaic crocodiles! - damping them out and laying them away in sheets of paper.¹²⁹

"[A]t 11.05 [I] left those hospitable tents [with their piles of pots and mummies], and struck off on foot with Mahmoud Mansoor,¹³⁰ for the railroad. We reached it in 1 hr. 40 mins. good walking;- along a rapid little canal first, then across the desert and past a town or two [...]¹³¹ When we reached the railway, there was no station; I really dont see how Mahmoud knew it would stop there :-¹³² he spread out his wrap on the dust for me to sit on;- and I proceeded to demolish a substantial lunch of chicken, duck and native bread, which G. had sent with me in a sand proof box.- This, with a bottle of mineral water and my bag, Mahmoud had carried in that same big outer garment, slung from his neck, all the way from the tents. When we reached the railway, and he took it off, he uttered an explosive "alhamdu lillah."-"Praise God"- for which I couldnt blame him. He waited till my train came at 1.15 + saw me on board[.]"

Goodspeed catches the train for Madīnet al-Fayyūm; he then takes the train from Madīnet at about 4:00, expecting to arrive in al-Wāstah at 5:30. He arrives late in Cairo and finds himself "hunting a place to sleep," eventually settling at the

---

¹²⁹This division of labor, Grenfell in the field with the men and Hunt in his tent "processing" papyri, was typical; cf. Rathbone 2007, 220.

¹³⁰Is this the Mahmoud mentioned with no surname earlier in the narrative, or did Goodspeed intend Mohammed Mansour, the individual who picked him up in Damian? Or is Mahmoud Mansoor a relation (brother?) of Mohammed Mansour? Curiously, "Muh(ammed) Mabruk" precedes "Mahm(oud) Mabruk" in Crum Notebook 67; cf. above, n. 121.

¹³¹"1 hr. 40 mins. good walking": much longer than the one hour's walk inbound, but that was at "a killing pace" (App. B) and even short of Grenfell's estimate of an hour and a quarter (letter of 10 February, reproduced above). "[R]apid little canal": probably two adjoining canals, a stretch of the Bahr al-Gharak and then the Bahr al-Bashawāt, for which Abdel Azim and Ayyad 1948, 237, mention a strong current, albeit at a time of the year when the water was higher. "[T]he desert": the stony ridge (*gebel*) separating the Gharak and Tutūn basins. We thank Dominic Rathbone for discussing these issues with us. "[A] town or two": presumably including Dānyāl el-Bahari, the northern (as the Arabic indicates) of the "twin" villages named Dānyāl. See further next note.

¹³²The lack of a station, and even an indication of a train stop noticeable to Goodspeed, suggests that he caught the return train at "Damian" (Arabic Damyān, which Brendan Haug suggests to us is the colloquial Egyptian equivalent of Dānyāl). The isolated "Damyān Halt" was located about half a kilometer north of Dānyāl el-Bahari (n. 131), the village that gave the stop its name; see further Egyptian Ministry of Finance 1914, though also indicating two *Dānyāl* stops north of *Damian*. One of Grenfell's letters (5 December 1899, reproduced above) estimates that the stop before Damian, Abu Nour, was one and half hours distant from the camp, but it lay adjacent to a major canal, the Bahr al-Nezla, that presumably would have merited Edgar's mention, and Grenfell was renowned for fast walking; note Goodspeed's earlier remark ("he is a fast walker"), confirmed concretely by the anecdote recorded near the end of the full transcription of this letter in App. B.

Eden Palace Hotel,[133] running into a former traveling companion in the hallway, taking tea at 11:30, and finally going to bed about midnight. Before retiring, he offered his mother a brief assessment of his adventure:

> So ends my visit to Grenfell's camp. I could have seen little more by remaining longer. I feel that it was emphatically the thing to do, coming out here, 2 hard days of travel, for two nights and a day at Grenfell's camp. I shall have no more memorable day of Egypt to look back upon. I wish you could have seen the little cluster of tents there in the blowing desert! [Figs. 10 & 11]

---

[133] For the Eden Palace, cf. *Egypt and How to See It* 1907, 22 ("more economical, but quite comfortable") and 157 ("opposite the Esbekieh gardens"). When Edgar stayed there it was a new building, erected in 1899; see further Humphreys 2011, 160–161.

Figure 10: "Grenfell and Hunt's camp."
Edgar J. Goodspeed photo; courtesy of the SCRC, University of Chicago.

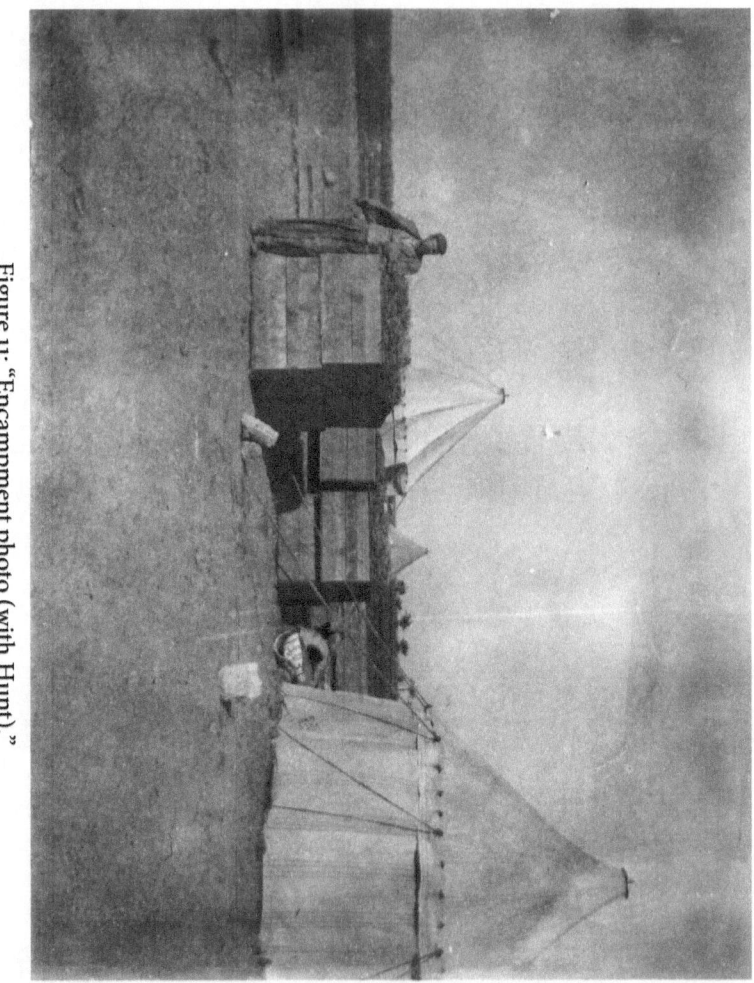

Figure 11: "Encampment photo (with Hunt)."
Edgar J. Goodspeed photo; courtesy of the SCRC, University of Chicago.

Chapter 3

An Oxford Summer

> And that sweet City with her dreaming spires,
>   She needs not June for beauty's heightening,
> Lovely all times she lies, lovely to-night!
>   – Matthew Arnold[1]

On the morning after his return to Cairo, Goodspeed closed his letter to his mother with a perpendicular addition to the right margin, ending cryptically with the words, "I fear I cant finish today." That same day, a Tuesday, 20 February, he began a letter to his brother Charles in which he would mention his Tebtunis photos—"two of the Medinet pictures are beauties [Figs. 12 and 13]: but the shots at Grenfell were not very successful, I fear" —and express his anxiety that there might be opposition from California to his participation in the publication of the Tebtunis papyri.[2] That afternoon, he walked out to Gizeh "and saw Ali el-Arabi's papyri. I saw only one I wanted : he asked 7 pounds : I was prepared to give but one, so after some coffee, I left."[3] He also checked out the wares at Kasira's shop in Cairo,[4] finding "some extensive scraps of a Homer ˏamong much rubbish.ˏ"[5] As he later wrote in their publication,

---

[1] Cf. Goodspeed 1899b, 446: "That sweet city with her dreaming spires." He reports reading Arnold's "Thyrsis" in a 16 August continuation of an 11 August 1899 letter to Father, sent from Oxford. Note also Epilogue (12 August).

[2] His remarks about the photographs appear in the continuation of 21 February; his worries that there will be resistance to his involvement, in the continuation of 23 February. As we have seen (Ch. 1, n. 96, Ch. 2, n. 106), Reisner wrote to Mrs. Hearst about this issue only on 17 February.

[3] The dealer's full name (Hagen and Ryholt 2016, 192–195) was "Ali Abd el-Haj el-Gabri" (c. 1840–1932), called, briefly as here, "Ali el-Arabi," or simply "Ali in Giza."

[4] "Kasira": Michel Kasira, or Casira (d. 1911), whose shop was located across from the American Mission, just around the corner from Shepheard's Hotel (Hagen and Ryholt 2016, 72, 206). According to Goodspeed 1903a, 237, he was "one of the most trustworthy of the local dealers."

[5] Goodspeed states that these fragments were in the hands of "a Greek." Whether he means Kasira himself or someone "consigning" to Kasira is unclear. The former on its face seems more likely, but as we will soon see, Goodspeed refers to Kasira's reopening of "the "Greek" deal," and Goodspeed 1903a, 237, can be read as indicating only that the fragments were acquired "through" Kasira.

Figure 12: "Medinet el-Fayum."
Edgar J. Goodspeed photo; courtesy of the SCRC, University of Chicago.

Figure 13: "Medinet."
Edgar J. Goodspeed photo; courtesy of the SCRC, University of Chicago.

They had to be sorted out from a mass of miscellaneous fragments, with which they had probably been found. The shop was rather dark, and the pieces had not been cleaned; but the hand was clearly literary, and the few words I made out in sorting them over, led me to think that they were, like most literary papyri, Homeric.[6]

Goodspeed offered one pound, but Kasira's asking price was five. The prospective buyer demurred, thinking, "Another old chap is going to bring me his new pieces tomorrow to see."[7] Nevertheless, early next morning, 21 February, on his way back from Cook's, Kasira "hailed me, and reopened the "Greek" deal. Result, I bought a lot of rather good Homer for $6."[8] Goodspeed soon "had a ˌflatˌ tin box made for my little new papyrus, which I really believe was quite a bargain."[9]

The goal of this last-minute quest for papyri of a literary character was, as he later admitted, to compensate for "the Berlin disaster."[10] The Kasira acquisition was apparently insufficient for this end, for after breakfast on the 21st, the search continued.

I went with old Farrag the Gizeh dealer, to a fine old house clear off in the Arab quarter : and here in a charming European furnished office, I looked over his papyri for 2 hours.[11] They weren't much: but the room with its carved stone, and dark wood ceiling, and huge old Chinese vases ,- was a dream. I didn't buy, but may buy one piece.- You know, papyri are high! worth many times their weight in gold, the most ordinary pieces! Tho' the dealers dont know good from bad, of course. This evening, 2 called + shewed me a lot of poor papyri. I didnt want any of them.

After an hour's work at the Museum that afternoon Goodspeed saw "Baron von Bissing, who was as effusively cordial as ever." On the 22nd, he spent most of the day at the Museum, going in the afternoon to another (unnamed) dealer:

---

[6] Goodspeed 1903a, 237. In fact only one of the thirteen fragments purchased was Homeric (*P.Chic.*, p. 2). After this quotation we return for details to the letter to Charles.

[7] "[O]ld chap": probably Farag, whom, as we shall see, Goodspeed meets on the following day.

[8] "[A] lot of rather good Homer for $6": For the actual "Homer" in the purchase, see n. 6. In Egyptian pounds the price paid would have been a bit under 1.25.

[9] The box: 23 February continuation of 20 February to Charles.

[10] Cf. Goodspeed's later description of events, Goodspeed n.d., ch. VII, p. 11: "I still yearned to get a papyrus for my own collection from Cairo, ˌespecially after the Berlin disaster,ˌ and went over Ali's stuff in Gizeh, and Kasira's in Cairo, with great hopes. And before I leaft [sic], C̶a̶i̶r̶o̶,̶ ̶h̶o̶w̶e̶v̶e̶r̶,̶ I picked up from the bottom of a tin box at Kasira's shop, a number of scraps which struck me as literary and all in the same hand." "Berlin disaster": Ch. 2.

[11] "[O]ld Farrag": presumably the "Old Sheikh Farag" whom Goodspeed had visited on 14 December (Ch. 2), here explicitly identified as the Gizeh "Farag," i.e., Hagen and Ryholt's Farag Ismaïn: Hagen and Ryholt 2016, 214–215. Although "[h]e spoke little English" (Hagen and Ryholt, 215), Goodspeed does not mention any trouble communicating with him. It is tempting, in any case, to associate the "office" Edgar visited with Farag Ali (Hagen and Ryholt, 213), whose "shop" was located in an "Arabic neighborhood conveniently located a few minutes away from the Ezbekiya Gardens"—this could explain some of the confusion between the two Farags, conceivably relatives—but Goodspeed's description of the premises is markedly different from Jonna Lange's. See further Ch. 2, n. 60.

"[H]e had nothing worth considering." On the 23rd, he spent "an hour or two at the Museum" finishing up. On departure he left "cards for the great men,[12] wrung the hand of Baron von Bissing, the most amiable youth in the world,[13] and descended the oil clothed staircase a prey to varied emotions":[14] regret at leaving the Gizeh Museum after more than three months' pleasant work and camaraderie; relief at last to be turning homeward ("In 6 months, I mean to sail for home! Think of that!"); uncertainty whether the California people would be "obdurate" against his participation in the Tebtunis project (he would not weep if the decision went against him); and trepidation at the approach of what, a month later, he would refer to as his "Oxford bondage."[15]

❧ ❧ ❧ ❧

It would be nearly twelve weeks, after yet a third itinerary on the European continent, before Goodspeed would reach the "City of Dreaming Spires"—and the summer spent in Oxford would turn out to be an enigmatic one. It is omitted altogether from *As I Remember,* whose account jumps from the invitation to Oxford to his return to the States after "two solid years abroad."[16] Even in "Abroad in the Nineties" it is only briefly, in the two final pages, chapter VII, pp. 13–14, the latter torn all along its left edge, bearing both handwritten insertions and final coda, that Goodspeed, seemingly having run out of steam, addresses his Oxford summer. Nevertheless, these pages begin with a significant summation of the papyrological side of his routine in Oxford and his working arrangement with Grenfell and Hunt:

> It was no small privilege that summer to work away much of the day copying Tebtunis papyri as best I could, and then after an hour on the river, going around to Queen's to submit them to my chiefs and get their suggestions. It was a most agreeable business, for they were most considerate.

Fortunately, the "Student Travel Letters vol. 2" fill the gap left in the memoirs and, in so doing, illuminate and perhaps even explain Goodspeed's later silence on his Oxford summer. They provide bases for a depiction, more complicated, less regular, and surely less "agreeable," both of his workdays and his relationship with his "chiefs"—Grenfell, especially. But they also document that in Oxford

---

[12] Presumably first and foremost Maspero, earlier called "the great man" (see Ch. 2).

[13] "[Y]outh": Von Bissing (b. 22 April 1873) was only a year and a half younger than Goodspeed (b. 23 October 1871).

[14] "[O]il clothed": denoting a type of floor covering used as a substitute for carpet, also known as "floorcloth" (Cooper and Hersey 1997, 11).

[15] 28 March, in continuation of 27 March to Mother, from Rome. Otherwise all the foregoing is drawn from the 20 February letter to Charles and its continuations.

[16] Goodspeed 1953, 114–115.

Goodspeed's scholarly attention, in a hurried and one-pointed ambition to get into print as much and as soon as possible, thereby both satisfying his own inner drive and justifying the faith placed in him by his supporters in Chicago, was divided, even scattered, among several different projects.[17] These centered on his personal collection of papyri, including his long account roll (Chapter 1); the British Museum manuscripts of the Ethiopic *Acts of Thekla* (Chapter 1); the papyri he had selected in Egypt for his "Gizeh study" (Chapter 2);[18] the fragments purchased in Cairo, especially the hexameters and a fragment of *Iliad* 5 (the present chapter); and the Tebtunis papyri (also the present chapter), the ostensible reason for his being in Oxford in the summer of 1900 in the first place.

❦ ❦ ❦ ❦

A letter to Father, begun 26 February, finds Edgar on the *Queen Olga* off the south coast of Crete.[19] Next day he arrives in Athens. He tours Greece for three weeks (Athens, Corinth, Corfu, Pyrgos, Olympia). Sailing from Naplia (Nafplio), he arrives in Rome on 17 March. Here he meets the Tunnicliffs from Macomb, Illinois—an "exceedingly pleasant" reunion.[20] In particular,

> Miss T. is a most enterprising and intelligent sightseer, and I have really had a busy time of it seeing things under her instructions. On the galleryies and churches she is rather an expert; and as for company none could possibly be jollier. We shall meet again, I hope, in Florence.[21]

---

[17] He himself will later (28 June continuation of 27 June 1900 letter to Mother) count as exactly six the number of projects underway: "6 going at once was mildly distracting." See also 2 June to Charles, naming 5 projects, and 18 June to Mother, 5 articles and Tebtunis papyri; both are quoted below.

[18] The future *P.Cair.Goodsp.*, though, as mentioned in Ch. 2 (n. 101), only 15 of the 30 pieces there published derive from papyri Goodspeed had selected and worked on at Gizeh.

[19] The Scottish-built *Koroleva Olga*, in the service of the Russian Steam Navigation and Trading Company. See Lyon 1976, 488–489.

[20] "Tunnifcliffs": Damon George Tunnicliff (1829–1901), a lawyer and (briefly) a judge on the Illinois Supreme Court, and his wife, Sarah Alice Tunnicliff née Bacon (1846–1936), had three daughters, one of whom, Helen Honor Tunnicliff (1870–1933), was married (1896) to Goodspeed's friend, Ralph Charles Henry Catterall, whose visit with Edgar in Oxford is covered in the Epilogue. Helen's younger sisters were Sarah Bacon Tunnicliff (1872–1957) and Ruth May Tunnicliff (1876–1946), M.D., Rush Medical College, 1903. For the contemporary University of Chicago affiliations of all three women, cf., e.g., University of Chicago 1898, 6, 23 (as well as the next n. for Sarah). Hallwas 2011 is a "hometown" account of these extraordinary siblings. Present in Rome were Helen and Sarah, as well as Ralph and Helen's son Ralph.

[21] "Miss T.": Sarah Tunnicliff. She would later be known for her air-pollution abatement efforts in Chicago (Gilman and Gilman 1927, 238), but at the time of Edgar's letter she was still nominally employed as a mathematics instructor at the University of Chicago-affiliated Kenwood Institute (University of Chicago 1899–1900, 139). A later photograph is printed in the *Chicago Tribune* of 18 March 1921, p. 23. "Miss T." is absent from Goodspeed 1953, while she and her traveling companions become "some delightful American friends" in Goodspeed n.d., ch. VII, p. 12. The quotes here come from the 28 March continuation of 27 March to Mother.

And meet in Florence they would, but not before Edgar, still in Rome on the 27th, received a pair of letters, one from Charles and "one stupid one but doubtless well meant from Breasted, requesting m̶y̶e̶ at Erman's suggestion, not to print anything on the Keneh papyrus.²² This first enraged, th̶a̶en amused me." He writes immediately to both Breasted and Erman.²³ Anxious to get back to his Thekla project, he is "half inclined to go to Strassburg to finish Thekla under the wing of Nöldeke," but not until "after Florence and Venice and a few days in Switzerland": "[T]o leave the thing untouched until Oxford would be fatal."²⁴

After a little over two weeks in Rome, Goodspeed moves on in Italy, to Florence, Bologna, Venice, and Verona. Most of the last twelve days in April he spends in Switzerland, moving from Lugano to Lucerne, Brünig, Berne, Lausanne, Zurich, Konstanz, and Basel. At St. Gallen, on 25 April, he visits "the famous old convent library," about which he had been hearing since his "first palaeographical studies with Gregory."²⁵ The Librarian Adolf Fäh was out,²⁶ but thanks to "an amiable German woman," Edgar was still able to view its treasures—"everything"— including "24 papyrus leaves of Isidore of Seville(?), Latin, nicely mounted by my Berlin friends."²⁷ While in Lucerne on the morning of 26 April, he writes Grenfell, advising him that he "should be a day or two late at Oxford."²⁸ The half inclination to make a detour to Strassburg has been forgotten. He is in Paris on 30 April and writes from Bruges to Father on 1 May. The night of 1–2 May Edgar ships from Bruges via Dover to London, there once again taking up temporary residence at 10 Bedford Place in Bloomsbury. Waiting for him at the bank on 3 May were half a dozen letters from home and one from Grenfell, written at sea from the S.S. *Bohemia* on 24 April:²⁹

---

²²I.e., the epic fragment bought by the Germans; see Ch. 2. Goodspeed n.d., ch. VII, p. 2, recollects, "I was amused later to receive by way of Breasted a message from Berlin pleading with me not to publish my transcription of the papyrus! A thing which had of course never ͵even͵ occurred to me. But it had occurred to them, naturally enough, having got the papyrus as they had. Of course a man like Krebs [Ch. 1] would have acted very differently. And yet this is the sort of backstage work that sometimes goes on even in learning, and one must learn to take it with calm."

²³Letter to Mother, 27 March. "Erman": Jean Pierre Adolphe (Adolf) Erman (1854–1937), Egyptologist and professor ordinarius at Berlin (1892–1923), an influential educator and patron in his field (Bierbrier 2012, 180–181).

²⁴Mother, 28 March continuation of 27 March.

²⁵For Gregory, see Ch. 1, n. 10; he will become more than a memory in the summer ahead.

²⁶Fäh (1858–1932): Dora 2005.

²⁷Trismegistos 61324: Indeed Isidore, but also homilies from the collection attributed to Eusebius Gallicanus. "Berlin friends": See Ch. 1; Hugo Ibscher (1874–1943; Bierbrier 2012, 273) surely did this work. The quotations here and in the preceding sentence come from a 25 April letter to Mother, written in Konstanz.

²⁸To Mother, begun 25 April, continued on the 26th.

²⁹Grenfell's reference to the *Bohemia* is anachronistic; the ship had been purchased by the Italian firm Lavarello and rechristened the *Pompei* [sic] in November 1899. See Kludas 1986, 96.

I wrote a postcard to you at Florence in answer to yours, but doubt whether it has reached you. As soon as we got back to Cairo Hunt caught the influenza from which he has not yet recovered completely, and I was hardly at all at the Museum, so you must forgive us if most of your queries remain unanswered.

I paid Reisner a brief visit & we arranged that our papyri should be published at Oxford independently of the [Egypt Exploration] Fund volumes.[30] It will be a tough job for us and we shall be only too glad to let you do as much as you can on the Roman papyri (Reisner consents to this). So we ~~have~~ are bringing back a few for you to begin on; the boxes will (inshallah) arrive about the middle or end of May. So if you like to come to Oxford in the 2nd week of May, ma'alêsh. We found a number of things after you left, chiefly ancient Egyptian or Roman portraits;[31] also a few more mummy cases in a cemetery 6 miles off.[32]

---

[30] Reisner mentions the visit in a letter to Mrs. Hearst from Keft (Qift, the ancient Coptos) dated 17 April:

I enclose list of objects found by Grenfell and Hunt in the Fayum. Grenfell has been here for two days on business connected with the work and the publication of the results. I will write you a detailed account of his proposals in a few days.

Grenfell says he never expects to have such another year. It is the first big find of Ptolemaic papyri. Among the antiquities I have starred the more important objects. Notice especially the 12 portraits, the toilette boxes, the mummies, and the jewelry.

Despite Grenfell's assertion, the Fund would end up being affiliated with the first and third Tebtunis volumes; cf. *P.Tebt.* I, p. ix:

Since there was no prospect of our being able to edit them adequately for some years if we could devote to them only the scanty remainder of time available after finishing our annual volumes for the Egypt Exploration Fund, we proposed to Mrs. Hearst and the Committee of the Fund that the publication of this volume should be undertaken jointly by them, so that copies might be supplied to subscribers of the Graeco-Roman Branch of the Fund, who would, we thought, have every reason to be satisfied with obtaining this important selection of texts. The scheme was approved by both parties, and in consequence this book is at once the first of the Graeco-Roman Archaeological series in the publications of the University of California and the annual volume of the Graeco-Roman Branch for 1900–1901, and also (on account of its exceptional length) for 1901–1902. This circumstance will explain the existence of two title-pages in the copies sent to the subscribers to the Graeco-Roman Branch.

The "scheme" was broached to Mrs. Hearst by Reisner in a letter from Keft dated 16 August 1900; it speaks of the proposal as having already been "accepted by the Fund." A letter from Grenfell to Smyly (IE TCD MS 4323, item 46) indicates, however, that the arrangement was still a matter of contention on 5 May 1901. The Reisner letters: George and Phoebe Apperson Hearst Papers, BANC MSS 72/204c, The Bancroft Library, University of California, Berkeley (originals lost).

[31] The Tebtunis portraits have attracted significant scholarly interest; refs. in O'Connell 2007, 810 n. 11.

[32] Here Grenfell is referring to Kawm al-Khamsīnī (sometimes called "Khamsin"; the ancient Kerkethoeris). The connection of Khamsīnī to the Tebtunis excavations is made explicit in, e.g., his 12 March 1902 letter to Smyly from al-Lāhūn; see Hickey 2017, 231. Note also Grenfell and Hunt 1901–1902, 3–4, where the link to Kerkethoeris is proposed in print for the first time. In the card-file inventory of the Hearst Museum, the second excavation site is misidentified as Gharak. The source of this confusion is uncertain, but it may have been Grenfell and Hunt themselves: We observe that *O.Tebt.* 4,

We hope to reach England on the 27th. We don't think of producing a Tebtunis volume till 1902 or 1903.³³

Goodspeed took the parenthesis on Reisner's consent as indicating full "California" consent.

Next day, 4 May, he began working again at the British Museum on Thekla, stopping in to see Kenyon,

> who knew about the collaboration with G. and H. and rather felicitated me on it. He said Wilamowitz had made the first announcement of the Hesiodic papyrus at a meeting of the Hellenic Society or something : also that B.P.G. was in London yesterday.³⁴

That evening Goodspeed would hear from Grenfell directly, through a postcard written and sent from Oxford earlier in the day:

> It is fortunate in some ways you stayed in London for the papyri are with Hunt (Romford Hall, Romford 20 min. from Liverpool St G.E.R.).³⁵ He is recovering and hopes to come up at the end of next week. If however you want the papyri at once, go down to Romford to fetch them, or else arrange with Hunt to have them brought up to his brother's city office.³⁶ An account of our dig will appear in next week's

---

identified as coming from "Khamsîn" in *P.Tebt.* II, has "Gharak" written on it in ink. Note also Milne 1935, 216 ("an exploratory excavation in the town at Gharak"; source: Grenfell and Hunt's records?), as well as the heading of the list of objects sent by Reisner to Mrs. Hearst (App. C, n. 20), but in this case, the reference must be regional: "Objects found by Grenfell and Hunt at Gharek-el-Fayum, 1899–1900"; cf. also Ch. 2, n. 41.

³³ Goodspeed box 4, folder 9. The first Tebtunis volume in fact appeared in 1902.

³⁴ 4 May in continuation of 1 May to Father. "Hesiodic papyrus": Goodspeed's lost epic fragment; this appears to be the first indication that he is aware of its attribution. Wilamowitz would produce the *editio princeps*; see further Ch. 2, n. 94. But in a letter written around this time (to Mother, 7 May continuation of 5 May), Edgar reports, perhaps based on information from Hunt, that "Diels of Berlin ₐa very important manₐ is to bring out that so called Hesiod. We figure that since Wilamowitz calls it Hesiodic, Blass [Ch. 1, n. 119] will consider it post-classical - as I did." The Third General Meeting of the Society for the Promotion of Hellenic Studies took place on 3 May, but the published proceedings (Society for the Promotion of Hellenic Studies 1900, xxxiv–xxxv) make no mention of an announcement from Wilamowitz. He was made an honorary member of the Hellenic Society during 1899/1900 (p. xl). Grenfell could have been in attendance on 3 May. For Hermann Alexander Diels (1848–1922), professor ordinarius in Berlin, see https://dbcs.rutgers.edu/european-scholars/9345-diels-hermann-alexander (22 June 2020).

³⁵ "Romford": Hunt's birthplace; cf. Bell and Simpson 2004. For the town in general, see Powell 1978. Romford Hall was "a large red-brick building which survived *c.* 1914 but was later demolished": Powell 1978, 72. "G.E.R.": Great Eastern Railroad.

³⁶ Hunt's younger brother, Francis John Hunt (1873–1935), a solicitor in his father's firm, A(lfred) H(enry) Hunt and Co. (A. H. Hunt died 28 November 1893.) Contemporary periodicals like the *Commercial Gazette* (e.g., 17 July 1895) and the *Times* (e.g., 7 July 1900) reveal that the firm's London address during this period was 17 St. Swithin's Lane, E.C.

'Athenaeum' probably.[37] I have also written an account for the N.Y. 'Journal'.[38]
P.S. Just heard from Hunt who suggests you should go to Romford Monday.

Upon this suggestion first mediated through Grenfell, but confirmed by Hunt's invitation to lunch, received on the morning of the event, Monday, 7 May, Goodspeed travelled to Romford.[39] He describes the day's events in detail to Mother. First Thekla, "proving quite different from any known version, which tells both for and against it,"[40] got two hours at the Museum; then

> I took the 11.51 from Liverpool St. Hunt had given me directions for finding the house, and also drawn a map shewing its relation to the station : he crowned all this by meeting me just outside the station. At lunch I met his brother (he has 2 others) and 2 sisters, and his mother : a pleasant, brisk little English woman, who seemed surprisingly young, and wore a white muslin cap.[41] After lunch in the big dining room, we walked about the big lawn and gardens, saw the cow pasture and hothouse, got acquainted with the dogs, and enjoyed ourselves generally. Hunt is a charming fellow, quiet and considerate. Later at the station I met another -a married-sister and rode part way in to London with her - 3rd of course. The[y] are all very nice jolly, straightforward people, and seem to live in great comfort. The big brick house was very spacious, and ˏveryˏ nicely furnished. The extent of the grounds surprised me, for the house seemed when I entered it, quite in the midst of the town.[42]

[37] It did in fact appear: Grenfell and Hunt 1900.
[38] The *New York Journal* was a fitting venue given that it was owned by Mrs. Hearst's son William Randolph. Grenfell and Hunt's article appeared on 10 June 1900; they are somewhat loosely identified as "Directors of the Phoebe A. Hearst Exploring Expedition." Since the article is unknown to the scholarly world and the pertinent issue of the *Journal* is difficult to obtain, we provide a full transcript in App. C. Approximately two weeks before the *Journal* article, on 26 May, an unsigned summary of the *Athenæum* piece titled "The Newest Papyri" appeared in the *New York Times Saturday Review of Books and Art*. An independent account of the Tebtunis finds was published earlier: The *Times* of London reported on them on 24 April 1900 ("Archaeological Discoveries in Egypt, 1899–1900," attributed to "our own correspondent" and dated 15 April), and this story was picked up by American papers like the *Times-Picayune* in New Orleans ("A Year's Discoveries in Egypt," 16 May 1900, with the subhead "Good Work by University of California Explorers, Who Find an Unknown Town and a Great Many Papyri") and the small-market *Leavenworth Times* ("Discoveries in Egypt," 15 May 1900) and *Marion Daily Star* ("Discoveries in Egypt," 12 May 1900, with multiple subheads highlighting the California excavation, including "Manuscripts Stuffed in Crocodiles").
[39] Hunt's invitation is not preserved in the Goodspeed Papers.
[40] 6 May continuation of 5 May to Mother.
[41] The 1901 census records the family members at Romford Hall as follows: Mary A(nn) E(llen) Hunt, head of household, 54; Francis J., son, single, solicitor, 28; Sydney, son, single, articled clerk, 23; Alfred E., son, single, 21; and Emmeline, daughter, single, 18. Mrs. Hunt (1843–1926) was the daughter of James and Mary Ellen Pertwee; Surridge, A. S. Hunt's middle name, appears to have been given in honor of the solicitor to whom his father had been articled, eventually his business partner (cf. A. H. Hunt's obituary in the *Essex Newsman*, 2 December 1893, p. 3). Hunt's other sisters were Ethel M. (the eldest, married in 1895 at age 26; not counted by Goodspeed initially but met later at the station) and Mabel (the middle sister, born 1876, the teacher mentioned later in the letter).
[42] The 1901 census gives the address as 31 South Street.

The purpose of all this [as we know but as he now tells his mother] was to bring in some papyri Hunt brought back in advance of the boxes, for me to begin on. So there lies near me a little packet, unopened, which Hunt had once sent in ˄to Kenyon˄ for me, (in vain:- K. was away) and was on the point of mailing to me. You see they are not at all slow in letting me get at them. Hunt is at home, getting his muscle back after the influenza he caught in Cairo. He saw me to the train, and we may meet Friday or Saturday in Oxford. His eldest (unmarried) sister is a very pleasant lively girl indeed; she teaches somewhere near London, and was going to leave home later in the day for her post. Hunt was going "to shoot rooks."-[43] Well, it was an interesting glimpse of an English house of the most delightful kind.

At Romford, besides turning the papyri over to Goodspeed, Hunt informed him that his Berlin mentor Krebs had died, and the news hit him hard: "Hunt shocked me with the news of Krebs death."[44] Still in London on 14 May, writing to Father, he grumbles about the cold and the natives' practice of fortifying "themselves with strong waters : one old bloke this afternoon I had to move away from, in order to breathe." But by 17 May, after claiming to have finished the Thekla translation,[45] he is in Oxford, strolling down the High Street, visiting his landlords of the previous summer at no. 99, going out past Queen's and Magdalen across the Cherwell to his new accommodations at the "Isis" Boarding Establishment on the Iffley Road in a high room looking toward the Christ Church cricket ground.[46] It proves to be "a most popular house."[47] (Figs. 14 & 15) "One of my dearest possessions," Edgar tells his mother, "is a battered little blue glaze lion, I picked up at Grenfell's last February."[48] Soon, by 20 May, a picture of "Pater" will also grace his room.

❈ ❈ ❈ ❈

Thus started what, for Goodspeed, will turn out to be a trying summer during which he became less confident in his own papyrological abilities and almost immediately overwhelmed by the pressures of dealing with Grenfell. The letters to

---

[43] "May 8 ... the traditional time for controlling the numbers of rooks by thinning the young birds [also known as 'branchers'] just before they begin to fly": James 1963.

[44] This quote and the preceding one come from the 7 May continuation of 5 May to Mother. Krebs's exact cause of death is unknown. Marius Gerhardt reminds us (email, 5 September 2018) that Wilcken's obituary (Wilcken 1901) merely mentions an "unheilbares Leiden," i.e., an "incurable disease."

[45] 16 May continuation of 14 May to Father. The project was far from finished, though, as we shall see throughout this chapter and in the Epilogue. His next step was to "find some man to read my Thekla to, - some Ethiop, of course."

[46] Letter to Mother, 17 May. In the 18 May continuation, he writes of looking "out over the tree tops at the Christ Church tennis players, on the grass." The Christ Church Sports Ground is still located on the Iffley Road and has both lawn tennis courts and a cricket pitch in season (Trinity Term).

[47] As declared in a [15 June] letter to Father.

[48] Letter to Mother, 18 May, in continuation of 17 May.

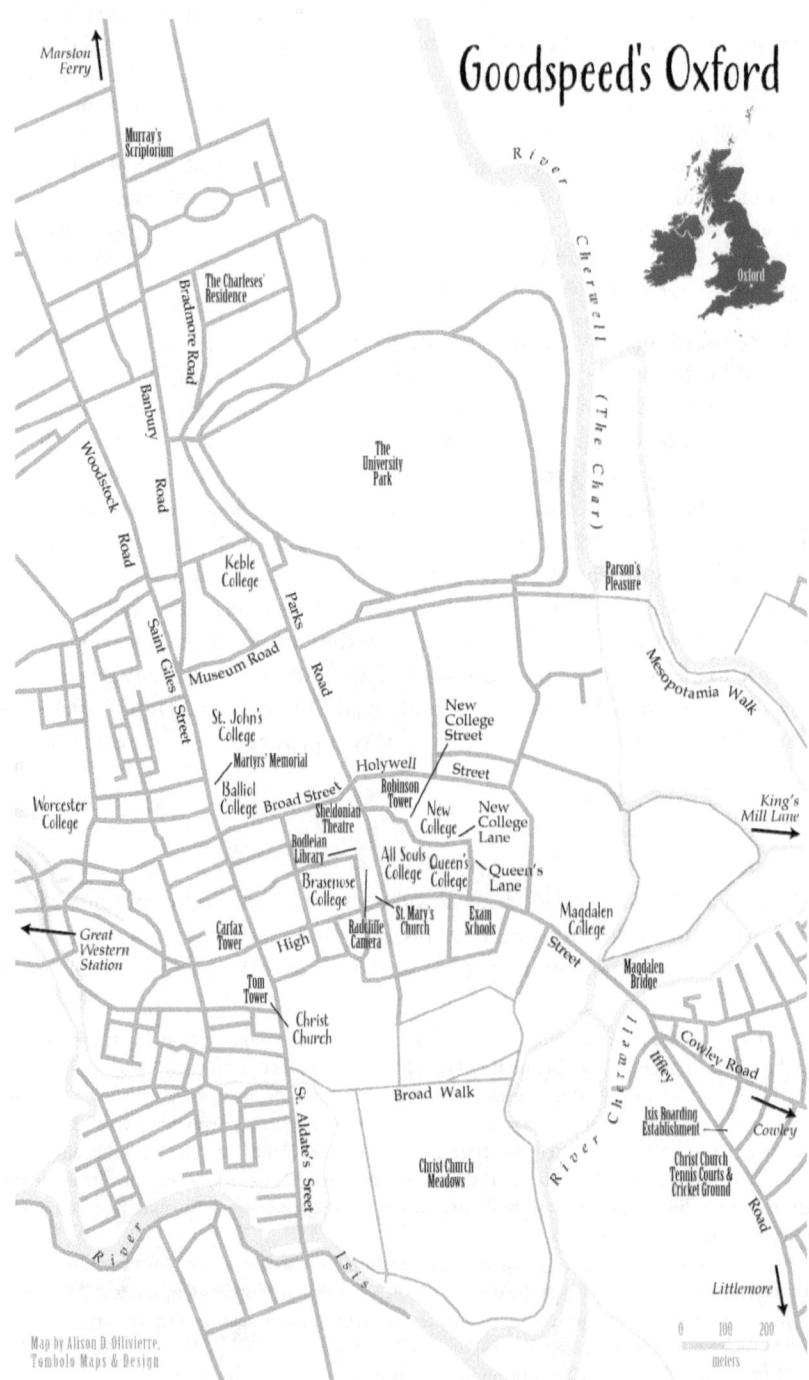

The "Isis" Boarding Establishment,
49, 51, & 53, IFFLEY ROAD,
OXFORD,

Opposite Christ Church Cricket Ground, and Five Minutes
from Magdalen College and Examination Schools.
Close to the Trams.

TERMS :—
**From £1 5s. to £2 10s. weekly; and from
5s. to 7s. 6d. daily.**

TABLE D'HOTE AT 6.30.
Mrs. ALFRED JEFFERY, Proprietress.

Figure 14: An advertisement for the "Isis" Boarding Establishment, 1900.
Public domain; sourced from *Alden's Oxford Guide* (personal copy of T. M. Hickey).

his family from this period read like a diary, a format that we replicate here.[49] They open a window not only onto Goodspeed's scholarly and leisurely pursuits but also his emotional oscillations during his three months in Oxford.

18 May, Friday, he began work on the Tebtunis papyri, but, despite his previous claim of completion, still "put an hour on Thekla" that evening. Afterwards, a call to "G. & H.," working at Queen's on "the beautiful Lord Amherst thing [...] and their book on the Cities of the Fayûm,"[50] yielded an urgent request "to come in again soon: - "tomorrow" Grenfell said."

19 May, Saturday, Charles's birthday. Edgar seems not to have heeded Grenfell's request, perhaps because Oxford is rejoicing over the lifting of the siege of Mafeking (now Mahikeng) from a seven-months-long envelopment after a final Boer assault. Edgar gets caught up in the "dissipation," hanging a small silk Union Jack from his window and later marching "with a torch light procession from Cowley Road up the High to Carfax," and from there visiting various bonfires, Balliol's in the Broad Street, one by the Martyrs' Memorial, a Victorian monument commemorating three Protestant bishops burned at the stake, and then the "municipal one" down on St. Giles. After helping convey an effigy of "Oom Paul" on a gallows to the tune of "Rule Britannia" and hearing a short speech, made by

---

[49] In fact, the "Student Travel Letters" can be read as a diary throughout. When Edgar (22 December 1899 to Father, in continuation of 20 December) speaks of the "diary habit having become fixed on me," he here is referring to the letters, not to a separate diary.

[50] *P.Amh.* and *P.Fay.*, respectively. Goodspeed is presumably referring to the first volume of *P.Amh.*, which consisted of religious texts and appeared in mid-September of that year (cf. *London Evening Standard*, 17 September); he mentions its "numerous facsimiles."

Figure 15: Postcard for the "Isis" Boarding Establishment, ca. 1900.
Public domain; courtesy of its owner, Stephanie Jenkins.

popular demand, from the half-brother of Baden-Powell,[51] he came back down the High, finding

> an impromptu fire blazing by the Exam Schools; and B.P.G. looking on. We beheld 6 undergraduates heave upon their shoulders the portly Cronshaw, Chaplain of Queen's[52] [...] and gyrate about the fire with him.

Edgar himself would become the object of attention at some point during the festivities, an "undergraduate who seemed to be indulging" calling him a "bloody fool" when he feigned not knowing the reason for the celebration.[53] Still he thought "no place, not even Venice, lovelier than Oxford," but B.P.G.'s fireside request for a Sunday morning meeting felt something of an imposition. Nonetheless this time, on 20 May,[54] he dutifully appeared, though

> somewhat apprehensively. There wasn't much to talk over, really. Grenfell loaned me a new book of Nicole's and gave me a note of admission to Queen's Chapel for this evening.[55] ˏI didn't ask for either, of course.ˏ He also asked me to dinner for Friday next - Alas! I wish he weren't quite so resourceful.[56]

Goodspeed spent most of the day on Thekla ("Papyri have had a rest today"), comparing his text and translation and preparing an abstract of the story. "I think it's no ordinary martyrological piece." He confesses, "I haven't succeeded in getting to church, though I started twice."

21 May, Monday:[57] "After a day of diligent, joyous and resultful time on what Grenfell affectionately calls "ˏtheˏ papyruses," I went around to S[t]. Cross Cottage, and saw Miss Lake."[58] In addition: "I purchased a 2ᵈ hand duodecimo Iliad

---

[51]"Oom Paul": "Uncle Paul," i.e., Stephanus Johannes Paulus Krueger (1825–1904), president of the South African Republic. "Baden-Powell": Colonel Robert Stephenson Smyth Baden-Powell (1857–1941), the commander of the garrison at Mafeking, later founder of the Scouting Association. His half-brother (Goodspeed simply calls him "the Col.'s brother"): Baden Henry Baden-Powell (1841–1901), residing at Forlys Lodge, 29 Banbury Road.

[52]The Reverend George Bernard Cronshaw (1872–1928), later the executor of Grenfell's will.

[53]Compare (Galsworthy 1995, 524) the crowd that Soames Forsyte encounters in London on Regent Street ("a shrieking, whistling, dancing, jostling, grotesque and formidably jovial crowd, with false noses and mouth-organs, penny whistles and long feathers, every appanage of idiocy, as it seemed to him. Mafeking! Of course, it had been relieved!") and the affronts to his dignity that follow: "His face was tickled, his ears whistled into. Girls cried: 'Keep your hair on, stucco!' A youth so knocked off his top-hat that he recovered it with difficulty."

[54]Still to Mother, in continuation of 17 May, at 10:00 p.m.

[55]Jules Nicole, for whom see Ch. 1 with n. 113. The book in question was probably the second fascicle of *P.Gen.* I.

[56]"Friday next": 25 May.

[57]To Charles, continuing through 24 May.

[58]A reference to Isabel Monica Strong Lake (b. 1876), the younger sister of the New Testament scholar Kirsopp Lake. For Isabel, later an Anglican nun, see *Census Returns of England and Wales, 1901* (Kew, 1901), class RG13, piece 1384, folio 137, p. 7; and *Census Returns of England and Wales, 1911* (Kew, 1911), class RG14, piece 13585 (folio and page not specified). For Kirsopp, who was curate of St. Mary

today, (Greek, complete) for TUPPENCE!⁵⁹ It will be of great use in a couple of Iliad papyri I am doing."

22 May, Tuesday, Edgar adds: "I am really getting hold of this "Roman" cursive, which is the worst Greek to read, ever written." Nonetheless, had the weather been good, he reports that he would have abandoned his papyri and gone to see the great cricketer W. G. Grace take on the University eleven.⁶⁰

23 May, Wednesday, at 10 p.m.:

> I find my little fragment (Bond papyri) is an interesting section of 17 lines from Iliad V, with accents and long vowels marked : a rare feature. It will print swimmingly.⁶¹ But the big thing I bought for a Homer is a puzzler.⁶² Neither Homer nor Hesiod. It will be no snap, but seems clearly to be a prize. We'll see. - The afternoon has been Tebtunis papyri, interrupted by tea.

The progress of his work has been slow, but Oxford agrees with him "beautifully," and he is pleased that the "eternal change and globe trotting" are over.

24 May, Thursday (correctly recorded, by later insertion, as the Queen's birthday), he spends an evening hour at the Radcliffe Camera on his Gizeh study. "The thing seems nearly ready: but it always seems so." Earlier he had worked on papyri, perhaps Tebtunis papyri or maybe his own, in his room. Then, after a social call to the biblical scholar Thomas Kelly Cheyne (1841–1915): "Coming back down the

---

the Virgin on the High Street from 1897 until 1904, see Grant 2004.

⁵⁹The size of the volume(s), if Goodspeed is reporting it accurately, limits the possibilities significantly. Our best guess is August Cartelier's *Iliade: Texte revu avec des notes en français*, Paris 1877. In collating his own fragment of *Iliad* 5 for publication (Goodspeed 1900b; see below), he will rely instead on Walter Leaf's edition (presumably the first, 1886, unless the first volume of the second edition had just become available).

⁶⁰Grace (1848–1915) was then in the autumn of his playing days, and on the day in question he did not bat due to an injured thumb; the University would win by an innings and 330 runs (*Buckingham Express*, 26 May 1900, p. 7). The centenary of Grace's death occasioned the publication of three biographies, the most substantial being Tomlinson 2015; for a concise treatment, see Howat 2011. We have perhaps been remiss in not giving enough emphasis to Goodspeed's passion for sports (though cf. already Ch. 1 with nn. 77, 78), especially American football, at which Chicago under Amos Alonzo Stagg (1862–1965; coach 1892–1932) was an early powerhouse. Edgar's father was an early and ardent supporter of the team (C. T. B. Goodspeed 1932, 57–58).

⁶¹"Bond papyri": Goodspeed begins to use this designation for the papyri that he purchased from Kasira (Casira) in Cairo, 21 February 1900 (see above). As we shall see, in the "Student Travel Letters" the name will in the end come to be used only of the *Iliad* papyrus mentioned here. Its *editio princeps*: Goodspeed 1900b, later *P.Chic.* 6. For Mr. Bond, see Ch. 1, n. 66.

⁶²It begins to dawn on Goodspeed that eleven (cf. *P.Chic.*, p. 2) of the hexameter fragments he had bought from Kasira in Cairo were not Homeric (or Hesiodic), but belonged to a single work of "Alexandrian" (post-Homeric) vintage. As he wrote at the beginning of their *editio princeps* (Goodspeed 1903a, 237), "It was not until some months later, in Oxford, that a more leisurely inspection of them revealed their unusual character, and convinced me of their true importance, as the fragments, unfortunately meagre, of some Alexandrian hexameter poem, no longer extant." The fragments were republished as *P.Chic.* 2; the documentary recto of the roll remains unpublished.

High, I met my Oxonians: and when I left them, B.P.G. had arranged that I should come around at 4 tomorrow and they would get me into the Queen's [College] barge to see the races."

25 May, Friday.[63] Morning and afternoon are devoted to papyri. At 4:00 p.m. he calls on Grenfell.

> Going down to the barge, B.P.G. said perhaps I better put my post Homeric hexameters into the Journal of Hellenic studies ⸢as they would make a facsimile⸣! And tonight I shewed it to them, and they told me it ought to console me for losing that so called Hesiod! Isn't that gratifying? B.P. said I should get Blass to help me (on restorations, as they do) : and he said the thing should be facsimiled. This seems most encouraging. – Isn't it really wonderful, how my Oxford days grow in richness and interest?

Dinner at Queen's ("We sat at a table on a low platform at ⸢the⸣ end of the hall: after dinner a long responsive Latin grace was said") is followed by adjournment to the Senior Common Room and "a most interesting and informing talk chiefly about candates [sic] for the Chichele professorship of History."[64]

In the days ahead Goodspeed would enjoy the afternoon boat races, the "Summer Eights"—great entertainment with lots of pretty "girls" on the scene, as was typical for that week.

26 May, Saturday: He spent the morning and one afternoon hour working on the post-Homeric hexameters. "There are few complete lines but there must be fragments of 200 or more. I think I must take B.P.G's advice," he writes, "and send a copy to Blass for suggestions .-You know what a genius he is for making emendations and restorations. Grenfell always falls back on him." At night, "I have been polishing off that Gizeh study and piecing to gether [sic] an immense Tebtunis Iliad."[65]

27 May, Sunday, he seeks his father's advice and help:

> Coming back [from services at Christ Church Cathedral], I dropped in at Queen's, and recovered from the toilers a bit (a whole column!) of my new Epic, so amazingly bestowed by Providence to console me for the Gizeh tragedy. I did not sit down, hurrying here to write [...]

---

[63] To Father, continuing through 27 May.

[64] "Latin grace": a statutory requirement in Oxford (and Cambridge) colleges; see R. H. Adams 2013. The Chichele Professor of Modern History at that time was naval historian Montagu Burrows, who would hold the post until his death on 10 July 1905. The discussion in which Goodspeed was involved concerned the appointment of a deputy professor since Burrows was no longer lecturing due to difficulties with his hearing. This position would go to medieval and military historian Charles Oman, one of the two candidates discussed (classicist and historian J. B. Bury was the other). See Johnson and Slee 2004 and Griffith 2009.

[65] "[I]mmense Tebtunis Iliad": The text that would be published as P.Tebt. II 265. It appears (as [T-]547) on the list of papyri assigned to Goodspeed in Grenfell's letter of 5 November 1902. This letter is transcribed in full as App. D.

About my new Epic, which is very queer, and a much bigger thing than the so called "Hesiod," - all about Andromeda and the "loathsome sea monster,"- please advise me. Mathews in his Mainz letter suggested that I might buy a few papyri for the University out of the Bond money : or rather that if I did, "Mr. B. might be pleased." I bought these 2 [i.e., the Andromeda and *Iliad* 5 fragment] with this in mind, tho' if the thing's a fellowship, I suppose I could, technically, keep them.[66] But my idea, between the faculty and ourselves, is this. If the Epic proves good, publish it (, after consulting Mathews) as the Bond papyrus, and explain that I purchased it in Egypt for Mr. B. or through his generosity, and it has been presented by him to the University. You see the drift. This would be a legitimate acknowledgement, I think, of his great kindness. If you like, sound Mathews: I don't think Mr. B. should be asked.- One other point : if the Journal of Hellenic Studies will accept it, hadn't it better appear in England? This will be best for me; and as long as an American edits and an American Univ. owns it, my patriotic feelings will be satisfied: You see, I am just offering both Wright and Gildersleeve contributions; and don't wish to crowd them.[67]

28–30 May, Monday to Wednesday,[68] are in fractions devoted to work on his new epic, to "patching together the pieces of the big Tebtunis Iliad" and spending time on other fragments from the excavation, and to checking at the Bodleian on some points regarding Thekla. On the evening of 28 May he pays a social call to the Charleses, during which R. H. Charles offers to help with Thekla in two weeks' time.[69] On the 30th, his principal diversion for much of the past week, the "Summer Eights," ends, to his great regret.

31 May, Thursday,[70] after a day divided between Gizeh and Tebtunis pieces, he resumes a discussion about Grenfell with brother Charles:

---

[66] For background, see Ch. 1, with nn. 66 and 67.

[67] The idea of naming the papyri for Bond never came to fruition in print, although *P.Chic.* was "Loyally Inscribed to MRS. JOSEPH BOND" (Mr. Bond had died in 1902). A 13 June letter from Father, not preserved but mentioned in the 23 June continuation of a 21 June letter to Charles, informed Edgar that Mathews was in favor of the plan. "Journal of Hellenic Studies": a British journal, which did accept Goodspeed's "Andromeda" (Goodspeed 1903a; text republished as *P.Chic.* 2). "Wright": John Henry Wright (1852–1908) of Harvard, editor of the *American Journal of Archaeology*, 1897–1906. Goodspeed intended his Gizeh study for *AJA* (cf. 2 June to Charles, quoted below), but the eventual *P.Cair.Goodsp.* ended up being published in Chicago's Decennial Publications in 1902. "Gildersleeve": Basil Lanneau Gildersleeve (1831–1924), editor at the Johns Hopkins University of the *American Journal of Philology*, which had published the Ayer papyrus (Goodspeed 1898a; later *P.Chic.* 3) and would also publish the edition of his "Iliad V" fragment, which he must be referring to here (Goodspeed 1900b; later *P.Chic.* 6).

[68] Letter to Mother.

[69] "Charleses": The biblical scholar Robert Henry Charles (1855–1931), then professor of biblical Greek at Trinity College Dublin, but resident at 17 Bradmore Road, Oxford, and his wife Mary (née Lilias). See further Law 2004. Charles is probably best known to ancient historians for his translation of the chronicle of John, bishop of Nikiu (Charles 1916).

[70] To Charles, and continuing through 3 June.

B.P.G. is in London today I think. Your remarks on his interest in me seem just.[71] I am becoming aware that here as at Gizeh, there are men looking to him for the chance he really thrust upon me, and looking in vain. It is all rather mysterious : but, sink or swim, it will be an education. The Charleses both cried out that he was such a wonderful man ; and there's no doubt of it. To have done (with Hunt's help and without,) 6 volumes[72] of first class importance by the time one's 31,[73] is a staggering record. I only hope I can maintain an understanding with him. I am sure you will be interested ˬinˬ + gratified by my reception at Oxford. Grenfell certainly doesn't do things by halves.

Before signing off for the night, he writes:

Well, Big Tom has just told (or tolled) his curfew of 101 strokes,[74] and I have a beautiful column of Andromeda uncial to decipher. Rather rich my getting so much better a thing than the Dutch did, for about 1/10 their price, was n't [sic] it? This thing has parts of some 200 lines : that, had 35 pretty complete ones.[75]

1 June, Friday, after an hour spent on "Andromeda," as Edgar's hexameter fragments will henceforth be called, and the rest of the day on Tebtunis papyri:

On the street after tea, I met my principals. B.P.G. again expressed his confident belief that "Hellenic Studies" would be glad to print Andromeda.[76] He also said their boxes had come, so I shall now be overwhelmed with papyri. Both beamed. - The day is cold.

2 June, Saturday: Before 11 a.m., he works on his Gizeh study, afterwards on a 900-word Tebtunis lease, stating that he has "a really good transcription."[77]

---

[71]We have been unable to locate the letter with the remarks in question. Charles clearly had some reservations about Grenfell's influence on Edgar.

[72]"[W]ith Hunt's help": *P.Grenf.* II (1897), *P.Oxy.* I (1898), II (1899), and presumably *P.Amh.* I (mid-September 1900; cf. n. 50 above) but not *P.Fay.* (later in 1900). "[W]ithout": *P.Grenf.* I and *P.Rev.*, both published in 1896.

[73]Grenfell, born 16 December 1869, was still 30.

[74]"Big Tom": the bell in Tom Tower, a Christopher Wren design, built 1681–1682, at the entrance to Christ Church on St. Aldate's, obviously resonant enough to be heard from the Isis 1 km. by air eastward. "[C]urfew": traditionally 9:05 p.m. Greenwich Mean Time = 9:00 p.m. "Oxford time." "101": representing Christ Church's original 100 students + 1 added by special bequest in 1663. For details: Trevor-Roper 1973, 16–18, and chch.ox.ac.uk/visiting-christ-church/tom-quad (accessed 21 July 2020).

[75]Goodspeed's line counts are more or less accurate, but the "Dutch" (a derisory label; Mencken 1977, 369–371) got a much less fragmentary manuscript. *P.Chic.* 2 (i.e., "Andromeda") presents 220 lines of Greek text, though all but a handful of these are incomplete, and some contain but a single letter. The Hesiodic *Catalogue* papyrus, as published in Wilamowitz-Moellendorff 1900, has 50 lines, 60% of which are complete or restorable.

[76]"Andromeda": As indicated above (n. 67), Grenfell's confidence about the locus of publication proved sound. Meliadò 2008 is an excellent monographic treatment of these hexameters, actually an anthology; note also Perale 2020, 393–421. The nonchalance on display in their *editio princeps*, in Goodspeed 1903a, 237, stands in contrast to the emotional twists and turns of the "Student Travel Letters."

[77]The identity of this papyrus, mentioned already on 22 May in correspondence to Charles that

A letter received from Nöldeke (in response to one from Goodspeed from the end of May) solves some of the "soluble" Thekla problems. Perhaps Nöldeke can solve more problems, thereby lessening the burden Goodspeed will place on R. H. Charles. On this day Goodspeed pauses to assess the current state of his labors:

> [M]y time [abroad] is now so gloriously short! These next 10 weeks - once 20 dolorous months - are all too short for the work that I should like to have done when I sail. I am anxious to have a clean sheet when I begin my new labors. I never began to have so delightful and fruitful a series of tasks well under way (weigh?) as I have now. Thekla. Tebtunis, Andromeda, the Bond Iliad, - these are successively the apple of my eye. Just now the Gizeh Study is most conspicuous, as being nearest ready. Unless Wright trims it - which Heaven forfend!- it will be my longest article yet.

3 June, Sunday: A day off from Tebtunis, "but I have looked over my everlasting Gizeh Study a good deal, and see only points to ask the "firm" [Grenfell and Hunt, presumably] about."

4 June, Monday,[78] though a bank holiday, consists of work on Tebtunis papyri and participation in a seminar concerning the text of Acts.

5 June, Tuesday, at night, just before penning his letter, he makes good progress on the introduction to Thekla. Otherwise, except for walks after breakfast, lunch, and dinner—the last of these leading to the Radcliffe Camera "to look up some points"—it has been a solid day on Tebtunis. The afternoon brings official word of the capture of Pretoria[79]—flags are immediately up on the High, and Queen's outdoes itself in decoration. The festivities did not suffice to lure him out from the Isis: "No doubt the town is full of bonfires tonight : I have heard gun shots and other tokens of enthusiasm."

6 June, Wednesday. The estimate for plating Thekla, $1.75/page ("rather cheap"), finally arrives in the evening post. "Tebtunis papyri have engrossed me all day."

7 June, Thursday, is an especially noteworthy "day of Tebtunis papyri."

> After tea in the pleasant drawing room [...] I went around to cheer my principals with a few transcriptions. They were amiable and business-like; dropped the Fayûm volume they are making to devote an hour to me.[80] Most of my difficulties were easy for them, of course: but not all. It was great to see them actually doing a papyrus:-

---

we do not report in full above, is uncertain. There are no leases of the requisite length in the relevant portion of the Tebtunis collection in Berkeley. Possibly Goodspeed was referring to the future *P.Tebt.* II 382 ("Division of land") or 397 ("Settlement of claims"). The former of these is a bit short but at least concerns real property, while the latter, which has nothing to do with land, is the right size and appears on the list of papyri assigned to Goodspeed in 1902 (as [T-]703; see App. D). We suspect that Goodspeed was in fact referring to 397, but it is also possible that the piece in question is missing: Two of the T-numbers on the 1902 list (351 and 399) cannot at present be located in Berkeley.

[78] To Father, continuing through 7 June.

[79] "[C]apture of Pretoria": rumored already in the letter of 31 May, but it in fact happened on 5 June.

[80] "Fayûm volume": *P.Fay.*, mentioned already above, 18 May, and published in November 1900. The *Times* of 23 November 1900, p. 5, indicates that it has "just appeared."

The cleverest men at it living, beyond a doubt. H. held the pap., G. the copy: G. suggested readings from the context and his immense knowledge of the literature ; H. verified, or suggested his own.[81] On the whole I came out better than I expected; anyhow I was not discharged .-But it is a serious business keeping up with, or in sight of, such company; and I do not venture to promise myself success at it yet. I am to call tomorrow at 9 at the "book factory" to get some help on my Gizeh study from them. Kenyon has been here, and G. with his usual energy, proposed the Andromeda for the "Hellenic Studies" journal : They are full, however, till this time next year.[82]

This should be soon enough, he thinks, but since he is writing to Father, an assessment of the alternatives seems necessary.

G. and H. offer to shove it into the new German "Papyrus Archiv" of Wilcken's (it prints in English) but I don't wish it buried in Germany. My present feeling is, to give it to "Hellenic Studies" whenever they'll take it. What do you think? Will you talk to George and Charles about it? - I figure that it will help me in future attacks upon Gildersleeve and Wright, to have put something into the Hellenic Journal. ₍(Chas. also thinks so)₎ Then I am now sounding Gildersleeve with a Homeric fragment, and shall soon ask Wright to take a long study ; which seems enough to tax them with just now. Of course Gildersleeve may decline the Iliad bit : it's rather small and slow : if he does I'll send it to Wright. I repeat, the Andromeda seems to me very important : far more sao than the Gizeh "Helen" which so thrills the Germans.[83]

He receives "a beautiful specimen page of Ethiopic Thekla," encouraging him to hasten that project. As Big Tom tolls, he still must finish up his "Gizeh points" in advance of tomorrow's meeting with "the experts."

8 June, Friday:[84]

I have just returned [10 p.m.] from an hour with "The 2 Chiefs of Your boy."[85] They

---

[81]Cf. E. G. Turner 2007, 23: "They were incomparable decipherers; and both had the power of grasping the bearing on old problems of new evidence and of penetrating to the heart of a difficulty even in an unfamiliar field."

[82]"[T]he "Hellenic Studies" journal": The *Journal of Hellenic Studies*. Here and below (see next note) Goodspeed is imprecise in naming the journals.

[83]"[T]he new German "Papyrus Archiv" of Wilcken's": Ulrich Wilcken's *Archiv für Papyrusforschung und verwandte Gebiete*, cf. Keenan 2009, 63–64. Its first fascicle dates to 1900, its first volume (two fascicles) to 1901. It would include Grenfell and Hunt 1901, the famous short description of the excavations at Tebtunis. "George and Charles": Edgar's cousin (George S. Goodspeed, 1860–1905, Yale Ph.D. 1891, professor of comparative religion and ancient history at Chicago) and brother. "Gildersleeve and Wright": see above, n. 67. "[L]ong study": Goodspeed's Gizeh study. "[S]low": reading certain, apparently meaning "[d]ull or tedious in character; boring, tiresome" (*OED*, s.v., I.8.b.). "[T]he Gizeh "Helen"": of course (again!), the epic that got away (Ch. 2).

[84]To Mother, continuing through 10 June.

[85]Perhaps Goodspeed is punning on the title of J. A. Froude's novel about the "Irish problem," *The Two Chiefs of Dunboy*. This was first published in 1889 but reprinted in 1897 in a pocket edition by George Munro's Sons (New York). Froude, whose religious sentiments are notoriously difficult to pigeonhole, was Regius Professor of Modern History at Oxford from 1892 until his death in 1894.

stood around all the time in great shape cleaning up difficulties in my Gizeh study and in 2 little Tebtunis papyri I took over. Then they loaded me up with a whole box (huge tin box) of Tebtunis papyri to consume. We had a good time. They offered to look over Andromeda, which pleased me much.

The morning post included "a card from Nöldeke (noble boy!)"—more help on Thekla, no doubt[86]—and one from his old teacher Gregory, whose sister-in-law, "the adorable Miss Thayer," had passed through Oxford earlier and then revealed Edgar's whereabouts.[87] A last line before signing off for the night, disconnected from what immediately precedes: "I am to call at Queen's oftener, herafter [sic]."

9 June, Saturday. A big day's work on Roman cursive "proves that there are papyri in the immense Tebtunis pile, that I can read, and read as fast as they can be read! I rather feared there wouldn't be." He expects to have worthwhile results, including some complete documents, to show Grenfell and Hunt next Tuesday afternoon.

10 June, Sunday. "I seem to have run through 3 or 4 short papyri today, without really toiling. Of 2 of these I have first class copies made; I think I shall gladden the hearts of my principals Tuesday after tea." Still, he is uncertain about "the upshot of my papyrus labors. Anyway, I shall have learned to read Roman cursive. (You are not to infer that the Oxonians have shown any sign of weakening! They have not)."

11 June, Monday.[88] He visits the Charleses again with pages of questions about Thekla—two weeks to the day from R. H. Charles's offer of help (28 May). As for the rest of the hot day: "a fair lot of Tebtunis pieces," a "few minutes on Thekla at the Bodleian before tea," and plans for an hour's work on Andromeda.

12 June, Tuesday—so hot that Edgar wakes at 6:15—consists of a full day's work on the Tebtunis papyri. Then:

> At 5 I called at Queen's and the men devoted an hour to 9 brand new copies I had to submit. They were a great improvement, certainly, and they quickly put on the finishing touches. I do not flatter any very great hopes about the outcome of this business; but if the joint authorship falls through (I have no objective reason for thinking it will) I am likely to get a small volume of my own out of it.- The thing is, I am getting the best practice and the best instruction in papyrus palaeography that the world affords; indeed the first really systematic and adequate palaeographical instruction I ever enjoyed. Hitherto I have been self-taught, in reading manuscripts, as far as Ive been taught at all.[89]

---

[86] This card is not preserved in the Goodspeed Papers.
[87] "Gregory": See Ch. 1, n. 10. "Miss Thayer": "the daughter of [biblical scholar] Joseph Henry Thayer [1828–1901], and sister of Mrs. Gregory. She is on her way home from 2 years abroad, and is the star of this establishment [the Isis]" (22 May continuation of 21 May to Charles). Gregory's card is not preserved in the Goodspeed Papers.
[88] To Charles, continuing through 14 June.
[89] Despite Krebs's mentoring and Goodspeed's belonging to and enjoying "Schoene's seminar in

While he was at Queen's Grenfell and Hunt "cordially agreed [...] that Andromeda was a much better as well as bigger thing than the Gizeh Epic of unhappy memory."[90] Back at the Isis,

> [w]hen my quarters get too boiling, I descend into the cool and pleasant smoking room, which is usually empty, save perhaps for a funny little Irish dog who slumbers at my feet. I am getting some very good letters out of the TEBTUNIS pile. My instructions are to select the easiest and completest pieces, and neglect the scraps which are innumerable. Hunt has them all fixed up in nice shape between sheets of papers, numbered and straightened out.[91]

On Wednesday, 13 June, after taking "it easy [...] putting some 87 or 8 hours on papyri, and taking frequent walks," Edgar fails to write home, having "turned in early." Next morning he confides, "In case I prove unequal to the collaboration scheme, I trust Andromeda to eclipse the ignominy. But I shall make a big stagger at these papyri before I chuck them." He is going to write Kenyon about placing Andromeda in the *Journal of Hellenic Studies*.

15 June, Friday.[92] He is still working on the Gizeh study and has written to Wright "entreating him to take it" for the *American Journal of Archaeology*. "To day [sic] I visited my principals again. B.P.G. was alone in the book factory, and professed himself at my service, so I submitted 7 or 8 copies to him and he devoted an hour and a half to me. Hunt was out." Edgar has been away from home twenty-one long months, but "[t]he days are flying now; and if I can only average 3 papyri a day all may yet be well! My hour with Grenfell was pleasant and not discouraging."

16 June, Saturday, is largely devoted to Tebtunis papyri with no particular results. The 9:30 p.m. post brings a letter from Kenyon, assuring Edgar "in the most polite sort of way that they will he thinks be glad to take Andromeda" for *JHS* and

---

Greek paleography" in Berlin. See Goodspeed 1953, 107, with more detail in Goodspeed n.d., ch. I, p. 7, where he writes, "I had done already done so much work with actual manuscripts that I found myself at a considerable advantage in this group which was still dealing only with facsimiles." As a graduate student he had done some palaeographical work with Gregory when the latter was in Chicago (Ch. 1). Schoene is Hermann Immanuel Schöne (1871–1941), a specialist in ancient medicine, for whom see Schröder 2012. Of course, everyone was essentially self-taught in reading papyri at this time. There was little institutional instruction, mainly collegial help.

[90] 14 June postscript to 11 June regarding events of the 12th.

[91] "[S]heets of papers": for the most part recycled copies of the *Oxford University Gazette*. Cf. Hunt's 6 October 1920 letter to F. W. Kelsey of Michigan: "I have been transferring the [Maurice] Nahman papyri as I flattened them into sheets of the Oxford University Gazette, which I have always found very convenient for the purpose, being of a suitable size and a substantial unglazed paper which is fairly absorbent. It has the further advantage of costing nothing, as I collect discarded copies from my friends [...] There is plenty of room on the margin of the Gazette for numeration and small notes" (box 84, folder 2, Francis Willey Kelsey subgroup, Kelsey Museum of Archaeology Papers, Bentley Historical Library, University of Michigan). "[N]umbered": Ch. 2, n. 82.

[92] To Father, continuing through 17 June.

print it as desired, with facsimile. "It will thus appear in about a years time – if I can ever get it in shape."

17 June, Sunday, 10:30 p.m.: There is nothing to report about the day's work, but a just-completed dinner at Wadham College has been immensely informative about insiders' views on Oxford. Edgar has learned "much more than I had heard at Queen's ever."

18 June, Monday,[93] a day mostly given over to Tebtunis ("Grenfell's work"), he has received a letter from Gildersleeve

> conveying with unparalleled politeness his readiness (glad, is the word) to use and facsimile my little Iliad thing![94] The Editors are thus all crying for more, as it were [...] and my problem is how to spend all my time on Tebtunis papyri and yet get 5 articles into shape. If I only had somebody to boss me, I know I could do it. To night [sic] I have devoted to Gildersleeve: (He doesn't propose I should pay for the plate!)

A letter from the Bodleian's sublibrarian has also arrived, "enclosing a card from Gregory, indicating what he wishes me to do for him here."[95]

19 June, Tuesday, he cleans up a few Tebtunis pieces and after tea brings them to Queen's for approval. "[Hunt] was very nice about it, as usual. Grenfell was out." A card from R. H. Charles invites him to come over on Friday afternoon to review his (Charles's) points on Thekla. "This recalls a remark of Miss Tunnicliff's at Rome : she ~~she~~ said she thought it simply splendid the way I owned these men! This was not meant as a rebuke."[96] In the evening at the Radcliffe Camera, he works on "Andr- no, - the Bond Homer," which is "progressing fast."

20 June, Wednesday, he

> hammered out one fine papyrus [...] and had it passed with the solution of two or three minor difficulties by G. and H. ₐafter tea.ₐ G. seemed a little anxious, about the Gregory labor: I am myself.[97] [...] I shall cut it to the narrowest limit possible. Grenfell has sent me a ticket to this Agamemnon performance at Bradfield School [...] tomorrow. It promises to be a great affair [...] Strange how well his kindness wears! His last suggestion as to my publishing alone whatever I had left over that did not go into the joint volume struck me as about the best thing yet! This cheers me much: For suppose I do a pap. G. + H. dont care for in the 1902 volume : I'll clap it in one of my own, you see.[98] But I'm saying nothing; these chickens are not yet hatched.

---

[93] To Mother, continuing through 21 June, 9:30 a.m.
[94] Dated 8 June and preserved in box 4, folder 3. It begins, "I shall be glad to have your note [...]"
[95] Presumably Gregory had requested Goodspeed's help in the card that arrived on 8 June, but this is the first mention of the matter in the "Student Travel Letters."
[96] For Miss Tunnicliff, see nn. 20–21 above. "This was not meant as a rebuke": It could only be taken as a rebuke if "own" has the meaning "[t]o acknowledge as having supremacy, authority, or power over oneself; to recognize or profess obedience to (a greater power, a superior, etc.)" (OED, s.v., 4.c.).
[97] Word had reached Grenfell from the Bodleian.
[98] "[C]lap": OED, s.v., IV.10.a: "To apply, place, put, set, or 'stick', with promptness and effect: properly with the implication that the object in question is promptly brought flat and close to the other

He has moved to a new room ("a pearl") at the Isis, with the "same view and price and altitude as before; but 50 % larger, and rather better furnished." Before retiring for the night he works on the Bond Homer.

21 June, Thursday.[99] The day's big event, after a morning's work on Tebtunis, is Goodspeed's attending, with Grenfell's mother Alice and on the ticket Bernard had given him,[100] the performance of *Agamemnon* at Bradfield College, in a village not quite thirty miles south of Oxford—it was in ancient Greek and important enough to be covered by the New York press.[101] Talthybius opened the play "with a trumpet blast."[102] Additional social activities are in prospect, as Miss Tunnicliff, whom Edgar had last seen in Florence back in March, "is coming up on Saturday for 2 days here; her friend Miss MacMahon [*sic*] comes with her."[103] But just yesterday Edgar was protesting that he was "too busy [...] to take in any sightseeing in Oxford."[104]

22 June, Friday. After "arranging some things for the approaching ladies," he

---

surface, but this notion often disappears ... and the word becomes a vivid or picturesque equivalent of 'put', 'place', with the implication of energetic action easily performed."

[99] To Charles, continuing through 24 June, 10:30 a.m.

[100] Grenfell's request to escort his mother to the play was made on 19 May (letter to Mother, in continuation of 17 May). For Alice Grenfell, see Ch. 1, n. 94.

[101] More fully: "I am just back from Bradfield where I saw the Greek play - "Agamemnon". It was great. The theatre is built or excavated in a chalk pit, and is a model Greek theatre, open to the sky (it rained most of the time) and seated just as the ones in Pompeii are. It holds some 2000, and is perfectly embowered in trees and vines. There was a crowd of the finest kind of English; the Greek costumes were ideal. Clytaemnestra and Cassandra admirable, the Chorus (the chief feature of this particular drama)—but adjectives are exhausted. I had an interesting time there, roamed over the college, saw the chapel, a class room, and the rambling quads. The College is 50 years old." For the press coverage, see the *New York Journal*, 27 May 1900, p. 60 (curiously only mentioning performances during the last week in June). The *Journal* article is accompanied by a depiction of the theatre, identical to the one that has been tipped into the second volume of the "Student Travel Letters." See also Macintosh and Kenward 2020, 14, which has a gallery related to the Bradfield productions in 1892 and 1900; the fourth item bears the image of the theatre that appears in the "Student Travel Letters" and reveals that Goodspeed attended the second show of the run. The Bradfield production is Archive of Performances of Greek & Roman Drama (APGRD) ID 782.

[102] Talthybius, of course, is not a character in Aeschylus's tragedy.

[103] "Miss MacMahon": Edgar spells her surname inconsistently. This is Una McMahan (1871–1915), whom Maddison 1917, 210, lists as "Graduate Student in Egyptian, 1908–09. A.B. Smith College, 1894. Graduate Student, University of Chicago, 1894–95, 1896–99, 1911–12; University of Berlin, 1900–01; American School of Classical Studies, Rome, 1902–04; Studied in Oxford, 1906, 1907; Demonstrator in History of Art and Classical Archaeology, Bryn Mawr College, 1907–09, and Reader, 1908–09. Married 1909, Mr. Frank Edgerton Harkness [an attorney]." In 1900 she was working as an instructor in history and mathematics at the Kenwood Institute, alongside "Miss T.": University of Chicago 1899–1900, 139. Though he seems to present her to Charles as an unknown quantity, their paths presumably crossed at Chicago, given their similar academic interests. His remarks about her situation at the Institute, 29 June continuation of 27 June to Mother, which close, "I never knew she was a Phi Beta Kappa until this visit," would appear to confirm this.

[104] 21 June continuation of 18 June to Mother.

works on papyri until lunch and after (3:30 p.m.) and then visits the Charleses again (at 4:15 p.m.) for "an invaluable hour on Thekla" with R. H. Charles, whose

> general criticisms will prove most helpful : his suggestions on corrupt readings are occasionally brilliant, and his answers to my questions I think all I could desire. He advises me to go ahead with my Ethiopic studies, and after we had had tea in the drawing room,- a most pleasant great room - he gave me a reprint of his recent review of Budge's latest, in Hermathena.[105] It is a scorcher, and no mistake.

Charles also conveys the news that Grenfell will be receiving an honorary D.Litt. from Dublin.[106] Goodspeed is amazed that Grenfell has achieved such distinction at such a young age—not much older than Goodspeed himself.[107] He goes to Queen's to offer "felicitations," but Grenfell is at a garden party (which the Charleses are also attending). Hunt, however, is there, providing three emendations for a papyrus in the Gizeh study, the loan of a book (unnamed), and delivery of "one tin box containing say 500 fresh papyri to consume." Goodspeed will get to these tomorrow morning.

23 June, Saturday, "a busy day." Edgar starts early on Tebtunis, finishing one papyrus before breakfast and four more before going over to Queen's to congratulate Grenfell: "a very pleasant call […] both men feeling well." His mentors date the Bond *Iliad* to the Antonines. He does another papyrus after lunch but then must depart for the Great Western station to meet Misses Tunnicliff and McMahan. The balance of the day is spent socializing on the river and attending a performance of scenes from *The Tempest* in the Worcester College Gardens.[108]

24 June, Sunday. He closes his letter to brother Charles with a 10:30 a.m. addition. He had already done two little "paps" (a Grenfellism that Edgar has adopted), but the addition is mainly to explain why the Thekla project, which he had earlier (16 May) deemed finished, was taking so long, which in turn includes a strange admission. The matter must have been brought up in Father's letter of 13 June, mentioned in yesterday's continuation (23 June):

> Pater thinks I have been slow on Thekla: so do I. The reason is, I knew so little Ethiopic; or rather none at all. I'll explain my method on my return. It would have been hazardous to rush into print, in Ethiopic. You see I had to verify every letter of the MS., in Dillmann or through Noldeke [sic] + Charles.[109]

[105] Charles 1899.

[106] Cf. Grenfell's 12 March 1902 letter to Smyly (Hickey 2017, 234–235): "The nice example set by Dublin in giving me a degree was not long in being followed by Germany which has made us [Hunt and himself] Ph Ds of Königsberg. There is no hood, I regret to say. The Dublin one excites much envy among my colleagues."

[107] Grenfell was 30, Goodspeed was 28.

[108] The production was part of the Commemoration Week festivities; see *Jackson's Oxford Journal*, 30 June 1900, p. 5. for additional details.

[109] "Dillmann": theologian Christian Friedrich August Dillmann (1823–1894), author of the leading Ethiopic grammar of the time. This could have been sent by Charles when Edgar was in Cairo: Ch. 2

Later in the day he starts a short letter to Father ("Charles' instructions are to post twice a week, news or no news").[110] He has spent most of Sunday, all Monday, and some of Tuesday sightseeing and socializing. The two misses have been escorted back to the station and have left Oxford, leading to Edgar's assessment of their days there:

> They seemed well, and spoke most appreciatively of my efforts. They are remarkably nice girls, and I am delighted to have been called upon to shew them the glories of Oxford. If only the weather had been any wise decent! There's so much open air work about seeing Oxford colleges that sun is indispensable. A little more time, too, would have made it easier, all round. Miss Mac Mahon [sic] is a Smith- and U of C. girl, but her home was for many years in Quincy, of which place she is a native. Greek is her forte, and she is up in architecture : in spite of all of which erudition she is quite unspoiled and a very jolly girl.[111]

The rest of Tuesday is "devoted to that Gizeh thing of mine, and recuperating!"

Edgar then begins a letter to Mother, undated at the top, but it must belong to 27 June, Wednesday.[112] He brings her up to date regarding his publication program:

> I posted the Gizeh study this afternoon to Wright. It will be a whopper if he prints it ; and I really think he will, as it comes clear from Gizeh. Then I resumed my interrupted labors on Tebtunis papyri, and have made some exhilarating progress [...] It is a great relief to know that Gizeh has gone; and the Gildersleeve Iliad is in its envelope ready to post, as soon as Kenyon answers a small question. So things are moving. Finishing Thekla text is only a matter of time.

28 June, Thursday, 9:00 p.m.:

> I have got pretty satisfactory readings out of three papyri today : one a nice literary bit - a column or two of some Greek historian, whom I haven't yet identified. As he tells a story about Cleomenes and Kephisophon, however, this ought not to be difficult.[113]

He has received "a harvest of letters," including one from Shailer Mathews, not extant, "on the Bond papyrus," as well as

---

with n. 47. "Noldeke": Goodspeed is hit or miss when it comes to the Umlaut or the Noe- spelling, both of which are correct; the No- spelling is not. "Charles": R. H., of course, not brother Charles.

[110] The letter continues through Tuesday, 26 June, 9:30 p.m. (from which section this and the two subseqent quotes come).

[111] "Quincy": Quincy, Illinois, Edgar's birthplace (Ch. 1).

[112] Continuing through 30 June.

[113] Edgar is referring to the future P. Tebt. II 267, not the work of an historian but a fragment of Demosthenes 19. Κηφει | σοφωντα appears in ll. 5–6 of the first column in the editio princeps; "Cleomenes" must be a misreading of l. 1's Μοιροκλεα μεν ε. Despite these early errors the papyrus appears on the list of papyri that Grenfell and Hunt assigned him to edit for the volume; see App. D. For the Oxonians' consent to this assignment, see the Epilogue, citing a letter to Father begun on 1 August, shortly before an excursion to Cambridge.

a gilt edged testimonial from my late fair charges, done in Miss McMahan's best manner. She is a clever girl. They composed it on the babbling Wye,[114] and it was a great document. I think it should go in the letter book, after I've worn it in my hat a while.[115] Tonight I heard from Kenyon: a nice letter, as usual; and in conseqquence my Iliad note is on its way to Baltimore.[116] Tell father to lay that flattering unction to his soul.[117]

By Goodspeed's calculations, the sending of the *Iliad* note plus yesterday's dispatch of the Gizeh study took "2 irons out of the fire" from a total of six: "6 going at once was mildly distracting."[118] He has doubts (eventually unfounded) whether Gildersleeve will accept the *Iliad* fragment "without some murmuring + disputing." If he balks, he will send it to Wright (who, contrary to expectation, seems to have rejected the Gizeh study). In any case, he tells Mother, "You observe the rocket has begun to explode. Now for Thekla text and Andromeda." The Mathews letter was, to his great relief ("Whew! I begin to be afraid of coming home."), full of congratulations on all his "remarkably successful work."

29 June, Friday, is summed up as "an interesting and profitable day."

I got in a fruitful hour before breakfast, cleaning up dark points in 3 [Tebtunis] transcriptions, and promoting them into my "finished" envelope. The number absolutely finished is still small however; but I have kept the standard away up.[119] I did 3 small new ones before lunch, two more before tea, and a 6th before dinner, beside composing a Sonnet![120] To night [*sic*] I shall devote to Thekla text, in the hope of getting it off to Leipzig at once.[121] Translation and comment, though nearly in shape, must wait until I reach America, I am afraid. Just now I must do papyri, all I possibly can.

He expresses delight in his transcribing an "extraordinary magical" text (Fig. 16),[122] the first such he has "ever tackled," but letters are his "chief joy [...] and they are numerous."

---

[114] The river that separates Wales from England.

[115] If it was ever included in the "Student Travel Letters," it is no longer there.

[116] "Baltimore": i.e., to Gildersleeve at Johns Hopkins, where the *American Journal of Philology* was, and still is, based.

[117] Cf. *Hamlet* III.iv.145: "Lay not that mattering unction to your soul."

[118] "6": Thekla, Andromeda, and the Tebtunis papyri were certainly three of the other four "irons." His charge from Gregory may have completed the set; a letter to Charles, written on 2 June in continuation of 31 May, i.e., before the Gregory matter emerged, names only five projects.

[119] "[A]way up": *OED*, s.v. "away," 9.b: "Originally and chiefly *U.S.* Used as an intensifier, chiefly modifying adverbs of distance or time, as *away back*, *away behind*, *away down*, *away up*, emphasizing the extent, remoteness, etc., involved." "Way up" is the modern equivalent.

[120] The sonnet seems not to be preserved but mentioned Andromeda and Thekla; see below.

[121] The text was being sent to Wilhelm Eduard Dragulin, the self-described "Oriental printer" based in Leipzig, for typesetting, not to a journal for publication. Dragulin's "beautiful specimen page" had arrived several weeks earlier; see 7 June above.

[122] The future *P.Tebt.* II 275, which does not bear a T-number (possibly it was written only on its *Gazette*; cf. n. 91 above). Perhaps it is one of the two papyri on Goodspeed's 1902 assignment list from Grenfell (App. D) that is presently unaccounted for.

30 June, Saturday. In the morning, while working at the Bodleian and at the Radcliffe Camera he manages to identify the "tiny Homer scrap" he found yesterday as coming from Book 24 of the *Odyssey*,[123] and to restore "a corrupt passage in Thekla even better than Charles had done : also getting a ray of light on the Magical text."

Having surprisingly failed to write on 1 July, his silence being attributed to a lack of paper, Edgar begins a new letter to Charles on 2 July, Monday. Its contents are complicated because it is misdated to the 3rd, and he backtracks to fill in events of the preceding one and half days before returning to the present one, and then appending a continuation on "Tuesday" (i.e., the actual 3rd). His reports on progress on the Tebtunis side of his work boil down to this:

30 June, Saturday, in the afternoon, presumably after posting his 27–30 June letter to Mother, he did "6 or 7 paps," bringing them into "pretty good shape."

1 July, Sunday. Four more papyri are brought into decent shape.

2 July, Monday. Working in the afternoon and evening, he breaks his record by "closing" 7 or 8 papyri, "mostly fine ones. Some I confess were very short: but the beauty of the thing is the excellence of the results, rather than their numbers." Among them is a fifth Homer fragment. He is encouraged.

3 July, Tuesday. Progress slows, but he has done four or five papyri, adding one of these to his "finished list." He has "identified another big Homer fragment, this time of Iliad 13."[124] He also reports that on Monday he "read the letter of the Emperor Gordian [...] a small and easy papyrus, which the Oxonians consider one of the great finds of the year, though we are of course very far from sure that it's an original. Still it may be : anyway it's a fine little letter."[125] (Fig. 17) The day was not all work, however: In the morning he went out to "Sunnyside" on Banbury Road to visit the "Scriptorium in Dr. Murray's back yard," in reference to James Murray and his *Oxford English Dictionary*.[126] Murray "spoke admiringly of Grenfell, as everyone does." This seems to have been a pleasant and instructive diversion for Edgar, but the mail that he received during these days included a letter entailing a different sort of distraction. The "missive" in question came from Gregory,[127] who

---

[123] *P.Tebt.* II 432 *descr.* (T-468); not in the 1902 list (App. D). Edition: Keenan 1971, 201–202.

[124] *P.Tebt.* II 429 *descr.* (T-666); not in the 1902 list (App. D).

[125] "[L]etter of the Emperor Gordian": the future *P.Tebt.* II 285 (T-421; not on the 1902 list). It is more precisely a rescript. Goodspeed's comment about its being an original is puzzling, given that the first word (θεός) indicates that Gordian was dead when it was copied.

[126] The exact address: 78 Banbury Road. The scriptorium, a garden shed with a 50' x 15' room, stood just behind Murray's house on land owned by St. John's College. See Murray 1979, 241–243, with fig. 14 on 241 (exterior view); also figs. 1 (frontispiece) and 15 on 260 (interior views, Murray at work).

[127] Gregory's letter (box 4, folder 8), in a tiny calligraphic hand, was written from his home address in Leipzig on 29 June. Its requests are as Goodspeed describes them—and a bit more. Gregory was updating the manuscript descriptions in his *Prolegomena zu Tischendorfs* Novum Testamentum Graece (1884, 1890, 1894) while preparing his *Textkritik des Neuen Testaments* (1900, 1902, 1909). Goodspeed never did examine the Earl of Crawford's manuscripts.

Figure 16: Goodspeed's "extraordinary magical" papyrus,
the future *P.Tebt.* II 275.
Courtesy of the Center for the Tebtunis Papyri, University of California, Berkeley.

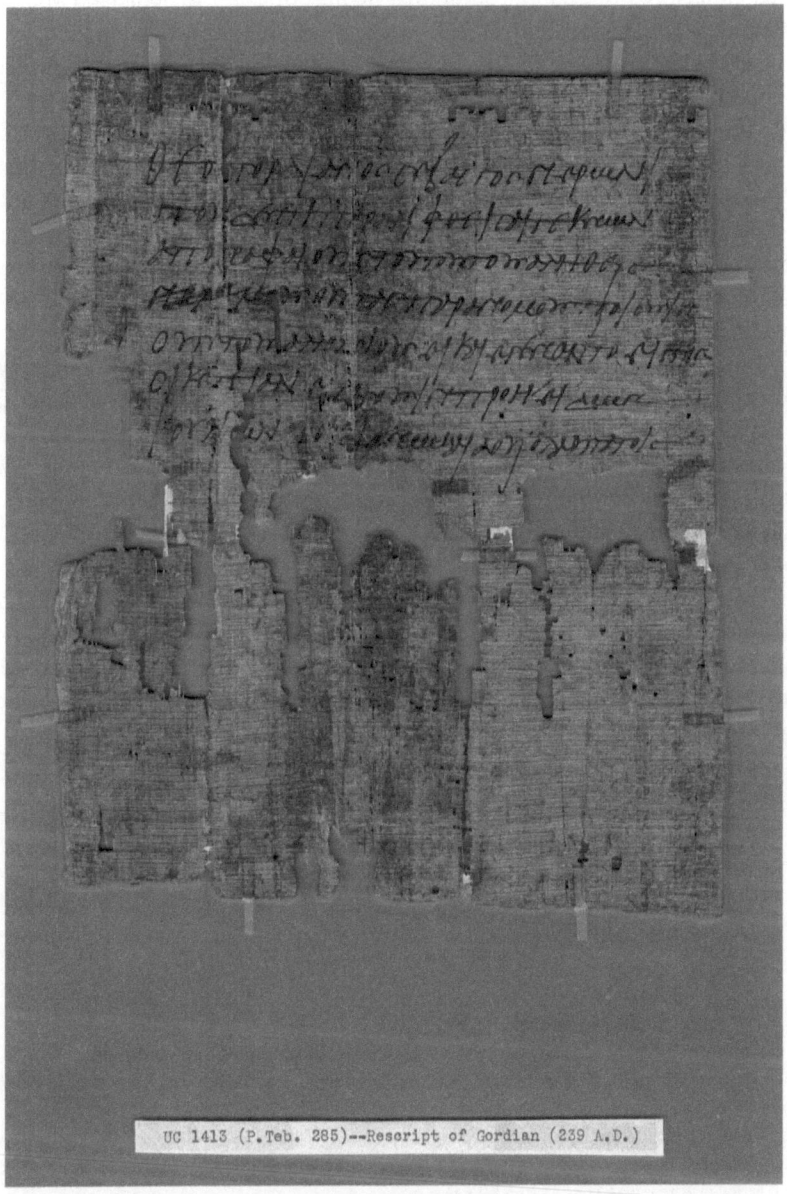

Figure 17: The "letter of the Emperor Gordian,"
the future *P.Tebt.* II 285.
Courtesy of the Center for the Tebtunis Papyri, University of California, Berkeley.

wants Goodspeed to examine additional manuscripts at the Bodleian (which he visits that Monday morning), as well as items in Cambridge, London, and, worst of all, at Haigh Castle, the Cheshire residence of the Earl of Crawford. This will eat up a week's time, which Goodspeed cannot sacrifice. "I have other fish to fry. Still Ill do the British [Museum] for him and Bodleys; and we'll see about Crawford."

4 July, "the Glorious Fourth," Wednesday.[128] The day was "properly celebrated," largely devoted to social activities: boating with some compatriots staying at the Isis, visiting Kirsopp and Isabel Lake. "A note from Miss McMahan enlivened the morning [...] My Tebtunis labors have amounted only to deciphering one long complete papyrus and revising another: but as both go into the "finished" list, I am content."

5 July, Thursday. Progress is slow. He has "revised and passed" two papyri, and then done two more, "one pretty thoroughly. This," however, "is is not fast enough." Five more letters arrive, including another from Miss McMahan and one from Wright, written in response to Edgar's own sent in advance of the Gizeh study. Wright is cordial but not promising when it comes to swift publication: "Still I have hopes; and with in [sic] a year will do.- What a slow world! Grenfell alone can publish fast."

6 July, Friday. He has gone, by way of Winchester, for the sights there, to London to do some work at the Museum and to attend the English track and field championships.[129] He is staying again at 10 Bedford Place, meeting up with some American friends.[130] He cannot believe reports from China, mid-Boxer Rebellion, that foreigners have been massacred.[131]

7 July, Saturday.[132]

> I arose with the lark at Bedford Place: (i.e., 8.40 am) and put in a whacking morning: 4 hours at the Museum; I looked up Homer points in the big reading room, did points on the Ethiopic manuscripts in the Oriental room, worked up 2 or 3 manuscripts for Gregory in the Manuscript room, and called on Kenyon. My interview with him was satisfactory. He will have a nice piece of Andromeda facsimiled in the Hellenic Journal.

[128] To Father, continuing through 6 July.

[129] American athletes on their way to the Paris Olympiad, including some from the University of Chicago, were also participating, hence Goodspeed's interest. See further, e.g., "New World Athletes Opened the Eyes of the English People," *Philadelphia Inquirer*, 22 July 1900, p. 13.

[130] The R. C. H. Catteralls, who are accompanied by the William Lyon Phelpses. The Catteralls will visit Goodspeed back in Oxford, arriving 31 July 1900; see the Epilogue for details. Catterall's wife, we recall (above, n. 20), was Miss Tunnicliff's sister.

[131] Cf. "All Foreigners in Peking Dead?" *New York Times*, dateline: London, 2 July 1900. Edgar's disbelief was justified: This was "fake news" *avant la lettre*.

[132] As related to Mother in a letter subsequently (it is unknown when) dated to 8 July, i.e., Sunday; this letter has a continuation dated (by Goodspeed at the time of writing) to "Monday 10 am July 10 [sic]." The next letter in the sequence was written to Charles on Monday evening and dated (after the fact) to "July 9" (corr. from "10").

After seeing Catterall in the Manuscript Room,

> [i]n the Oriental I met Crum the Coptist, who treated me very well.[133] All I wanted was to borrow his centimetre measure, but he learned my name, and greeted me cordially : said Grenfell had been dining with him and told him I was working with them. He had also seen me doing Ethiopic in the Oriental room : he even remarked that I had contributed to the Berlin Urkunden, hadn't ?I?- Anyway, I got the centimetre measure, and ₐweₐ promised to meet again in Oxford.[134]

After lunch he goes to the Gower Street Station of the Metropolitan Railway, popping in at University College on the way to inquire after Petrie and Mace. They are out, but he makes a quick stop at Petrie's annual exhibit:[135] "It reminded me of my call there with Coffin last July, - fateful incident!" From Gower Street he proceeds by underground—the car is crowded and full of smokers, "the air choking : but worse outside than in"—to Waltham Green Station and from there to the athletic grounds near Stamford Bridge. He twice visits the dressing room to meet with Amos Alonzo Stagg and the Chicago athletes before taking in some events. "From the Univ. standpoint, I think we need not be ashamed: for we got two men into the finals."[136] Before departing for Oxford via Paddington, he visits the locker room a third time to say goodbye: "[T]hey seemed glad to see me." Edgar is back in Oxford about 9:10 p.m., but feeling run down. In two days' time he will report a sore throat, a malady for which he will hold London "responsible."

8 July, Sunday.[137] In the morning

> I called on B.P.G. who had just returned Saturday from London. Hunt was still at Romford Hall: he returns to day [sic]. Grenfell was feeling well, reported a good time,[138] and asked me to dine with him Tuesday [the 10th]. I reluctantly consented. It now seems doubtful about my being able to take papyri home to work upon:[139] which somewhat relieves me, I must admit.

9 July, Monday. In the morning, "I did a few papyri, rather lamely." Nevertheless, as later in the day he writes to Charles,[140]

---

[133] Walter Ewing Crum (1865–1944); Bierbrier 2012, 136–137: "Crum shares with Steindorff the premier place among Coptic scholars of modern times." See Cromwell 2014 for a full appreciation of his contributions to Coptic studies.

[134] This seems not to have happened.

[135] Exhibit catalogue: Petrie 1900.

[136] "The Chicago team won second in the half-mile run, third in the 100-yard dash, third in the quarter mile run and second in the hurdle": *Dixon Evening Telegraph*, 1 August 1900, p. 2.

[137] As reported in a continuation from Monday morning (see n. 132).

[138] Which included, as we have seen, dining with Crum.

[139] "[H]ome": Since Goodspeed seems to have done most of his transcribing at the Isis, and certainly not at Queen's, the reference must be to Chicago. Cf. Gregory's 18 July 1900 letter to Edgar (box 4, folder 8): "Could you not take them to America with you?"

[140] Continuing through 12 July.

> The afternoon has been reasonably productive of papyrus results: it better be, for to morrow [sic] night I am to make a general showing to the Oxonians after dining with them at Queen's.- Unless I chuck the dinner, on account of this surprising cold of mine, as I am tempted to do.

Edgar hoped "to have some 80 rough copies to submit" after Tuesday's dinner, "but it will take a big day's work in copying and revising to do it, I fear. Various medicaments I am trying are improving my throat," however, and he was not too ill to visit Mrs. Betteridge, a departing American friend and fellow Baptist, for tea.[141]

10 July, Tuesday. When the moment of truth arrives, Goodspeed begs off. He writes at night (10 p.m.), explaining to Charles:

> My London cold has passed naturally from my throat to my lungs, and head: it will now wear slowly and miserably off. Meantime I feel like anything but work, and all paps look alike impossible. Still I have made some progress in several ways [...] I did not dine with Grenfell tonight: My cold was really too bad, so I wrote him a note this morning [...] Tonight I am preparing Thekla text (break this gently to Father) for the printer. It really must go.

11 July, Wednesday. The day, like the preceding one, has been very hot. Edgar "hammered out 6 or 8 small papyri, "passing" five of them finally. I fear B.P.G. will think my results small." Nevertheless, he felt able to accept an invitation from Mr. Thomas, "a great expert," to watch his swimming demonstration on the Isis.[142] That evening: "Rejoice with me! Thekla text is really ready to post to Leipzig, to the printer's! This is a vast relief. It's in its envelope, and tomorrow I shall post it."

12 July, Thursday, again very hot.[143] He reads "6 or 8 small papyri," his toil being cheered by the mail, including a note from Miss T. "I have Posted! Thekla-text to Leipzig."

13 July, Friday.[144] Rain brings some relief. Edgar is again fully engaged with Tebtunis: "I set out to do ten, great and small : and did nine, three of them very nice ones indeed." He identifies a fragment of *Iliad* 16.[145] "There must be 20 literary pieces great and small among these 750 papyri." He also wants "awfully to get to Cambridge for a day to see Schechter's great collection of parchments and to meet

---

[141] Mary Caroline Allen Betteridge (1856–1941), wife of Walter Robert (1863–1916). Mr. Betteridge was professor of Hebrew language and literature at the Rochester Theological Seminary; his obituary: *The Standard*, 25 March 1916, pp. 951–952.

[142] Ralph Thomas, "swimming's first historian," and a member of the International Swimming Hall of Fame: https://ishof.org/ralph-thomas-(gbr).html (accessed 16 July 2020).

[143] Despite Goodspeed's remarks during this period, its weather (with one exception; see n. 157 below) was not extraordinary enough to merit mention in Burt and Burt 2019.

[144] Writing to Father, continuing through 15 July.

[145] The future *P.Tebt.* II 430 *descr.* (T-261, eventually edited in Carp 1972, 10–12; on the 1902 list [App. D]).

the Lewis and Gibson twins."[146]

14 July, Saturday: Another day for Tebtunis work, "pleasant and gratifying." He reads

> five or 6 papyri, 3 of them pretty satisfactorily. This means, as it usually does, that the others were very fragmentary. I am equal to most any complete one. One I read between lunch and tea was a fine one: I think I made out every word of its 30 odd lines correctly: an encouraging result.- My first labor was a huge column of Iliad XI, the longest papyrus column known I think: 58 lines. This is twice the usual length.[147]

15 July, Sunday. He reads five "fairly successfully" and revises a sixth.

> They are almost all documents of respectable length [... N]ow if I can only keep at work steadily till the 19th! To night [sic] I am writing Gregory. I fear my lame response to his appeal will sour him: but I really cant help it: I must seize the present hour for myself: this I feel to be the chance of a lifetime.

16 July, Monday,[148] "hot, sultry and oppressive," is a discouraging day. He receives "a postal from Gregory" adding assignments to the manuscript project. "Quite impossible! I haven't even time for Andromeda and Thekla, my "charges fair" (as my late admirable sonnet says!)." He read

> but two papyri, one pretty satisfactorily: the other a long fragmentary thing, I find tonight I had already done, a mon͜th͜, before. Alas! But when one has read 150 papyri, a mistake occasionally will occur.[149] I have now made a schedule of papyri read which will save further vain repetitions.

17 July, Tuesday ("very hot"). In the morning he worked on another big *Iliad*, "parts or wholes of five columns in an immense uncial hand."[150] After lunch he "sorted papyri, and after getting one box in order, went at another papyrus which

---

[146]Cf. Hoffman and Cole 2011. Solomon Schechter (1847–1915) was simultaneously reader in Talmudics at Cambridge and professor of Hebrew at University College London when Goodspeed visited and of course the great collector of those manuscripts from the Cairo Genizah housed in Cambridge. "[T]wins": Agnes Smith Lewis (1843–1926) and Margaret Dunlop Gibson (1843–1920), "the Westminster Sisters," enthusiastic backers of the Genizah project and significant scholars of Semitics in their own right.

[147]Goodspeed is referring to the future *P.Tebt.* II 266 (T-417; on the 1902 list [App. D]). For data on the number of lines per column in literary rolls, see Johnson 2004, 217–230. *P.Tebt.* 266 (Trismegistos 60437) is the penultimate entry in Johnson 2004, 230; it is surpassed only by *P.Oxy.* LXIV 3155 (*Iliad* 15; 63–64 lines/column). As a metric, Johnson places greater emphasis on column height measurement (Johnson 2004, 58).

[148]To Mother, continuing through 18 July. The undated first portion of the letter was later assigned (cf. n. 132) to 17 July, a Tuesday, but it is clear that it was begun on Monday the 16th.

[149]"150 papyri": A mere week before he was struggling to complete "80 rough copies."

[150]Goodspeed is again referring to the future *P.Tebt.* II 265 (T-547; on the 1902 list [App. D]); as we have seen, he was "piecing together" this papyrus at the end of May, 26 May to be exact. The remains of six columns are in fact preserved.

I have since finished." He then stops work and sets out to visit Professor Charles. En route he overtakes Grenfell on Queen's Lane and

> walked on with him up New College Street to Holywell.[151] He was very cordial: asked me in to tea, but I declined as I was on my way to Charles'. Then he said I must come to dinner Friday or Saturday. I told him how many papyri I had done, and he seemed quite satisfied : Mrs. Grenfell came up at this point, and I proceeded to 17 Bradmore Road.

Upon arrival at the Bradmore Road residence,

> [t]he maid conducted me into Charles' great study, where the professor was at work sitting at a huge flat desk, completely covered with papers. He was in his shirtsleeves, and immediately rose to receive me. Mrs. C. was "going out" to tea : so Charles and I had it alone in the garden. In a corner of the garden at a table three or four young nieces of the professor's were having their tea, and the dog, a "[sic] rough English terrier of the wire haired variety divided his time between us. Well, we had a fine talk, the dog, Charles, and myself. He was mighty nice (this applies to both Charles + the dog,): told me all about his new book on the "[sic] ascension of Isaiah, which he thinks the oldest of noncanonical writings, putting it back some parts of it to 88 AD.[152] He shewed me the proofs: and explained a lot about it. We talked a little about Thekla: and after tea he urged me to stay for some tennis, ₐwith him + the girlsₐ even starting upstairs for some tennis shoes for me: but I begged off, and left. Well he's a delightful man as B.P.G. says: and I'm mighty glad to have gotten in with him a little.

18 July, Wednesday, "hotter than ever." He revises two papyri and reads four new ones, "none entirely satisfactorily. To night [sic] I am writing R. F. [Harper] about Thekla,[153] and sending Blass the rough copy of Andromeda."[154] He closes his letter by expressing relief "about the Tebtunis volume: the back of my job seems to be broken." He will later calculate, "Our joint volume now promises to contain about 100 papyri, with a big catalogue of the rest of the 700."[155]

19 July, Thursday.[156] A slow day in papyri; it is "too too hot to work."[157] Nev-

[151] New College Lane would have preceded New College Street on this walk.
[152] Charles 1900.
[153] Robert Francis Harper (1864–1914), the younger brother of President Harper. He was professor of the Semitic languages and literatures and managing editor of the *American Journal of Semitic Languages and Literatures*, where Thekla would first appear (Goodspeed 1901a). Because Harper was in London, Edgar would receive a positive response just days later, on the evening of 23 July. (Goodspeed there refers to the journal as *Hebraica*, its title from 1884–1895.)
[154] For Blass, see Ch. 1, n. 119. As we have seen (25 May), this was Grenfell's recommendation.
[155] 23 July in continuation of 22 July to Father. For the final composition of *P. Tebt.* II, see Ch. 2, n. 82. Goodspeed greatly underestimates the number of fully edited papyri, while overestimating the size of the "catalogue."
[156] To Charles, continuing through 21 July.
[157] Regarding this day's weather, Edgar reports (20 July continuation) that it was "99° in the shade: hottest ever known here"—an exaggeration. Burt and Burt 2019, 136, record the high as 32.0° C (89.6° F); this day is more significant for its range (low-high), only one of three recorded in July exceeding

ertheless, work he does: one papyrus before lunch, two and a half before tea, another half before dinner, and two between dinner and 8:30 p.m. coffee: "Total six, all rather well done." It "has been a great day for mail": Five items from family, plus one from Miss T., now in Cumberland, and Gildersleeve has also written. He has received Edgar's edition of the *Iliad* fragment and incorporated a correction subsequently sent. It will appear in the journal's autumn number. ""Proof will be sent from the printers probably in the course of next month." Quick work, I say! I wrote the thing like lightning; the papyrus is only about 1 inch x 3 or 4, and I was afraid he'd think the whole thing too thin.- I am much pleased."

20 July, Friday. "Today's record": a glance at Andromeda before breakfast, three Tebtunis papyri before lunch, one before tea, two before dinner, two before coffee; since coffee, one: total, nine, "but some copies are rough enough!" Edgar finds the news from the Paris games "cheerless"—did Coach Stagg keep the Chicago athletes out of the competition because it was Sunday? "If so, he was right, but should have kept them home."[158] The morning mail brought "a nice letter from Gregory [...] handsomely acknowledging my notes, and freely absolving me from any more toil for him: a most characteristic letter."[159] Gregory's letter, written on 18 July, also advises Goodspeed, "[B]e careful about your health while you are busy with those 800 papyri. I do not see how you can stop working on them by August. Could you not take them to America with you? Could you not stretch your stay?"[160] At night word comes from Dragulin that the Thekla text had arrived in Leipzig. "To morrow [sic] I shall devote to cleaning up papyri and getting my copies in shape to shew the Oxonians after dinner." (He had apparently chosen Saturday over Friday in response to Grenfell's invitation during their recent walk together, 17 July.)

21 July, Saturday. In the morning he receives a thank-you gift from Gregory, "a copy of Harnack's latest work, a small volume of lectures on the "Essence of Christianity," delivered to large student audiences in Berlin.[161] It seems a splendid series of appeals to them to accept the Gospel. I am glad to have it." Edgar spends the day, as promised, getting his transcriptions "into shape for this evening." Late

---

20° C. In Goodspeed's day, the July record high was 33.9° C (93.0° F), set, coincidentally, 19 July 1825 (Burt and Burt, p. 133).

[158]"Before the boys went over there was an understanding that there were to be no Sunday races. Quite an argument ensued when they found that plans had been made for Sunday races without regard for the promises and agreements to the contrary. We were so disgusted [reported the Chicago team's trainer] that we would not take part and left": *Dixon Evening Telegraph*, 1 August 1900, p. 2.

[159]Box 4, folder 8.

[160]"800 papyri": the 100 papyrus editions *plus* the 700 of the catalogue presumably; cf. above under 18 July with n. 155. In transmitting his notes to Gregory, Goodspeed must have mentioned these figures to suggest the extra pressure caused by the former's unexpected assignment, thereby perhaps excusing the omission of the Earl of Crawford's mss. Gregory perhaps misread this to mean that Goodspeed was singly responsible for all 800 papyri.

[161]Harnack 1900.

at night, 11:00 p.m., "just back from Grenfell's," he describes the evening's dinner and aftermath. Dinner is served to only a "small table of men" in the Senior Common Room.

> [A] jolly and frivolous mood prevailed. All the older dons being away, Grenfell pronounced the brief grace-before-meat, "Benedictus benedicat" and -after-meat, "Benedicto benedicatur".[162] A general assault was made, B.P.G. leading, upon David (known as "King") who seems to be junior bursar of Queens. A series of complaints were addressed to him, because the magazines didn't come, the lawns were in bad condition, the Room's afternoon paper was a noon 𝑛edition instead of an evening, as in the other colleges: there was no ice and no proper ice chest, and the beer was bad. David [...] finally fled from the scene, to fulminate postals against the magazines, news agents etc.[163] We sat a long time in the dusk, then in Grenfell's room he and Hunt looked over my copies for an hour and a half. They seemed pleased at the number of them, and marked a lot of them as material for the book, also making numerous emendations which will be helpful. G. let me out a private gate into Queen's Lane at 10.30[.]

22 July, Sunday, to Father.[164] "The day has been swallowed up in a reaction from my excessive labors of the past week. I <u>did</u> transcribe a big column of a fourth century contract (lease of a pottery, I think) then went to church."[165] The afternoon, after revision of a papyrus "with very encouraging results," was given over to social activities and leisure.

23 July, Monday, is "paralyzingly hot." To make things worse, "The morning's mail" had brought "a postal from B.P.G. telling me to call to day [sic], as they had forgotten one or two things. I may say I feared the worst[.]" Goodspeed works on revisions, under great pressure and "with poor success." At 5:30 p.m. he called at Queen's

> with several rough copies, prepared to be sacked chucked or whatever the phrase

---

[162] "May the Blessed One give a blessing … Let praise be given to the Blessed One" (or: "Let a blessing be given by the Blessed One"). For these two-word, alliterative, before- and after-meal graces see Dixon 1903, 165, R. H. Adams 2013, xiii–xiv ("this short formula became very popular, particularly in Oxford"), xvi, 82. See above where Goodspeed refers in parentheses to the "responsive Latin grace" recited in the Great Hall at Queen's after dinner on 25 May. "[M]eat": Oxbridge (Old English) term for food, as also that of the *KJV*; *cibum* or *esca* in Latin.

[163] "David": the Rev. Albert Augustus David, Junior Bursar since 1899, and eventual headmaster of Clifton College in Bristol, at which Grenfell had been educated, and where Grenfell's late father had been assistant master (1870–1889). See *Who's Who* 62 (1910) 484.

[164] Continuing through 24 July, but with nothing newsworthy on that third day beyond an attempt to finish the Thekla introduction ("still rough").

[165] The future *P.Tebt.* II 342 (T-372; not on the 1902 list [App. D]). Not after all a lease, but a report of confiscated property in the Hermopolite nome featuring in its best preserved column a pottery and appurtenances that were under lease. The dating to the fourth century—the late second is correct—was presumably based upon a palaeographical estimate made before the chronological limits of the papyri from the Roman town were fully known.

is. However, they only wished to suggest that henceforth I should devote myself to those particular pieces which I should later annotate and edit for the volume, while they quietly intimated that as no one would know who did which, I perhaps better take the easier ones : Homers, leases, letters, etc. leaving the more imperfect and exacting documents to them. Of course this is not flattering; but it is frank, practical, timely, and generous. Don't you think so? I am much relieved, and have new courage, for this, the last lap of my great labor.[166] It begins to look as though I had succeeded- not gloriously, perhaps; but I did not expect to shine in comparison with these twain."[167]

---

[166] Goodspeed's metaphor may be Pauline. Cf. 2 Tim. 4:7: "I have fought a good fight, I have finished *my* course, I have kept the faith"; 1 Cor. 9:24: "Know ye not that they which run in a race run all, but one receiveth the prize? So run, that ye may obtain."

[167] "[G]loriously": Cf. perhaps Exod. 15:1, "for he hath triumphed gloriously." "[T]hese twain": undoubtedly influenced by the *KJV* (cf. Ch. 1, n. 89). *OED* notes, "In Middle English *twain* ceased to be confined to the masculine, and became merely a secondary form of *two*, used especially when the numeral followed the noun. Its use in the Bible of 1611 and in the Marriage Service, and its value as a rhyme-word, have contributed to its retention as an archaic and poetic synonym of *two*." According to Samuel Johnson, *Dictionary*, s.v., "An old word, not now used but ludicrously" (McAdam and Milne 1963, 429).

Epilogue

As I sailed home after two solid years abroad, what had they given me?[1]

From this point on, that is, following the evening conference with Grenfell and Hunt on 23 July, Goodspeed becomes less informative and less specific about his papyrological work. His letters over the weeks before departure, in a script that is less consistent than earlier in the summer and often strikingly large, talk a lot about showing visitors around Oxford, time spent on the water (frequently in a "Canadian canoe"),[2] an interlude at Cambridge, and socializing in general. Letters to Mother, 25–28 July, and Charles, 29–31 July, bring little new concrete information. On Friday, 27 July, it is cool enough for Edgar to work in his room again. He revises some transcriptions and does some copying. On Saturday, 28 July, he makes two more transcriptions and does further revising. "A fine note from Miss T." arrives in the evening. On Sunday, 29 July, he revises a papyrus, goes to church; then: "After tea I read a fresh papyrus, and revised a nice horoscope."[3] On Monday, 30 July, he revises four or five papyri. On Tuesday morning, 31 July, he anticipates the arrival of friends from Chicago, the R. C. H. Catteralls, with their son, Ralph, along with their friends, the William Lyon Phelpses.[4] They

---

[1] Goodspeed 1953, 115.

[2] "T. [=Thomas] Tims on Christ Church meadow" (25 July to Mother) furnished the canoe. Tims, who died 2 April 1908 at age 63, was a well-known boat builder and had served as waterman to the Oxford University Boat Club since 1863 (*Oxfordshire Weekly News*, 1 July 1908, p. 2).

[3] The exact papyrus Goodspeed means is unclear. The content of *P.Tebt.* II 276, an astrological extract concerning the effects of the positions of the planets (*apotelesmata*), might have suggested a horoscope to him, while *P.Tebt.* II 274 is a planetary almanac in which the signs of the zodiac would have stood out to a reader. Neither text appears on the 1902 list (App. D), and Smyly is credited "for the[ir] elucidation" in the preface of *P.Tebt.* II, p. vi.

[4] "Catteralls": For Ralph Henry Charles Catterall (29 March 1866–2 August 1914), see the obituaries in *The Phi Gamma Delta* 37.1 (October 1914), 71–72; the *Cornell Daily Sun*, 4 August 1914, pp. 1–2; and the *New York Times*, 4 August 1914, p. 11. Catterall 1903, an expansion of his 1902 University of Chicago doctoral thesis and his only book, is regarded as a classic treatment of the subject. He died "at the [summer] home of William Lyon Phelps, with whom the family had a long and close

will reach the Isis Boarding Establishment after dinner,[5] just as he and Andrew Wyant, another Chicago friend Edgar happened to bump into on the High that afternoon,[6] are about to leave for their "second pull" on the river. The evening post brings a letter from Miss T., now in "Auld Reekie."[7] Edgar closes his own letter to Charles that Tuesday evening with the admission: "This is not work by a long ways, though, is it? I must hit it up,[8] somehow: I am loosing my grip."[9]

A letter begun to Father on 1 August describes a visit to Queen's with Catterall, then instructor in modern history at Chicago.[10] Edgar had

> offered to take Catterall to Grenfell to get a voucher for the Bodleian privileges, but Phelps said his letter from the Librarian of the British Museum would surely do for both, so I withdrew, telling C. to call on me if he needed me. He did so after lunch: we went at once to Queen's: Hunt had some coffee made for us, and we got the voucher filled out.-[11] They shewed us a pile of photographs Grenfell - no Hunt - had taken at Tebtunis;[12] and Catterall was induced to have a cigarette.

Goodspeed takes Catterall's smoking not as an action for reproval, but as a sign of Grenfell's hospitality.[13] He continues:

---

friendship" (https://www.lib.uchicago.edu/e/scrc/findingaids/view.php?eadid=ICU.SPCL.CATTER-ALL, accessed 13 July 2021). His wife, Helen Honor Tunnicliff Catterall (1870–1933), has already been introduced (Ch. 3, n. 20). Their son and only child, Ralph, was born in 1897. The family's papers are archived at the SCRC (cf. next note). "Phelpses": William Lyon Phelps (1865–1943), Ph.D. Yale 1891, already an extremely popular teacher, would achieve legendary status as Lampson Professor of English (appointed 1901) at Yale; he was also a famous preacher and public intellectual; his wife (m. 1892): Annabel Hubbard Phelps (1869–1939).

[5]The Catteralls' receipt for their stay at the Isis has been inserted at the front of Helen's diary for the period: Helen Tunnicliff Catterall and Ralph C. H. Catterall Family Papers, box 3, folder 5.

[6]Andy Wyant (1867–1964), nicknamed "Polyphemus" (he was 6'3" at a time when the average height of an American male seems to have been between 5'7" and 5'8"), received his B.D. degree from the Divinity School of the University of Chicago (1895) and was a football star under Stagg (Ch. 3, n. 60). Having played at Bucknell before coming to Chicago in 1892, he eventually (1962) would be inducted into the National Football Foundation Hall of Fame. He had been ministering in Goodspeed's former home of Morgan Park (Ch. 1) since 1895. Obituary: *New York Times*, 18 June 1964, p. 35.

[7]"Old Smokey" in Scots dialect, i.e., Edinburgh.

[8]*OED*, s.v. "hit," "to hit up 1. To force up; to speed up. With *it*: to put on pressure; to make efforts in a certain direction."

[9]"Loosing": not an error for "losing." See *OED*, s.v. "loose," 6.a, "To make loose or slack; to loosen, slacken, relax, make less tight."

[10]The letter continues through 3 August.

[11]Cf. Helen's diary, 1 August 1900 (Catterall Family Papers, box 3, folder 5): "Mr. Goodspeed introduced Ralph to Dr. Grenfell who secured him admission to the Bodleian Library to work there."

[12]Hunt was almost invariably the photographer; cf. Coles 2007, 7, and Rathbone 2007, 220–221. This seems to be another example of Goodspeed's inclination to credit almost everything to Grenfell, little to Hunt—here, however, corrected.

[13]Even less reason for reproval is that Edgar's father was a smoker: C. T. B. Goodspeed 1932, 67 (a friendly joke about how Thomas will spend his retirement: "He will play billiards and smoke"), 70 (he lights a cigar when about to read his morning newspaper). Of course, we have seen a couple of

> I am pleased to state that I have done some work to day [sic].- I had a swell note this morning from Mrs. Lewis the Cambridge Scholar, inviting me to a luncheon at her beautiful home Castle-brae. Grenfell says it's one of the finest in Cambridge - "which" he says "is rather a mean place"!

Mrs. Lewis's note, which remains loosely inserted in the "Student Travel Letters" right before Edgar's missive describing it, also mentions that Rendel Harris, whom Goodspeed had met the previous summer,[14] was back from America. He had attended the Congregation at the University of Chicago and there met Edgar's father and mother. This was during a tour of the United States in whose last month, July 1900, Harris had given a series of lectures in Chicago.[15]

A second note also arrived this day.

> Schechter the Genizah MSS. man writes that he will shew me the collection anytime I come: So imagine me Cambridge bound. I have perhaps forgotten to intimate that Miss Tunnicliff is to reach Cambridge Monday or Tuesday, and has expressed her approval of my suggestion to meet her there.[16]

He concludes his news of the day: "The Oxonians consent to my doing the Demosthenes as well as the Homers."[17] The next day, Thursday, 2 August, is largely consumed by sightseeing with Wyant, who is to leave early on Friday, and Mrs. Catterall, "never more delightful" when the three share tea. A cold that emerges in the evening puts the Lewis luncheon at risk, but this disappears the next day, during which Edgar is more devoted to scholarly interests, including time spent "revising the big papyrus."[18]

Preparations having been made, including the loan of Mrs. Catterall's trunk,[19] Edgar travels to Cambridge on 4 August, staying at 2 Pembroke Street ("opposite Pembroke College, and close to the fine building of the Pitt Press"), remaining there until 8 August. The evening before leaving Oxford he believes the visit to Cambridge a mistake, confessing to Mother the next day, "I fell asleep last night in deep disgust with my self for ever proposing this Cambridge visit."[20] But events of

---

incidents where Edgar had found smoking, and alcohol, offensive and intolerable.

[14] See Ch. 1 with nn. 104, 105.

[15] Harris sat next to Thomas Goodspeed at the Congregation Dinner, 3 July: letter to Mother, 16 July 1900, with (for the date of the Dinner and Harris's lecture titles) University of Chicago 1900a, 141, and 1900b, 146. More on the lecture tour: Falcetta 2018, 137–138.

[16] Miss McMahan (Ch. 3, n. 103), Miss T.'s traveling companion, would also be coming.

[17] "Demosthenes": *P.Tebt.* II 267. As we have seen (Ch. 3, n. 113), Edgar initially misidentified this text. He had been set straight or had independently discovered his error in the interim.

[18] "[T]he big papyrus": Based on "the Homers" just mentioned, this is probably the "immense Tebtunis Iliad" that Goodspeed had begun "piecing together" on 26 May, the future *P.Tebt.* II 265 (see Ch. 3). His own Andromeda likely would have been mentioned by name.

[19] The loan is mentioned in Helen's diary, 3 August 1900 (Catterall Family Papers, box 3, folder 5).

[20] He had mentioned the idea to Father, 13 July (see Ch. 3). This letter to Mother continues through 7 August.

the 4th, specifically the elegant luncheon at Castlebrae with Rendel Harris among the guests, lead to a change of view: "I feel now that I have not been foolish in it." On Monday the 6th he accomplishes the main (scholarly) goal of his trip, writing that evening at 6:30 p.m.:

> This morning I called on Schechter. A big ˄squat˄ grey haired and bearded German Jew.[21] He smoked and talked awhile : I seemed to know more Semitic Scholars personally than he. We walked out to the tram, took it a ways, then he stopped to buy some cigars, and we finally reached the library. He took me to the collection, and his assistant shewed me a lot of MSS. The size of the collection is truly portentous: 3000 documents alone, besides thousands of literary (biblical, liturgical etc) pieces and numerous parts of printed books. Hebrew and Arabic predominate : there is some Syriac and Coptic, very, very little Greek.- Well, I wouldnt have missed it for any thing. Schechter talked very freely; he's an interesting old boy. After the Genizah stuff, I got an attendant to shew me some leaves of "D" (Codex Bezae), which is a beautiful Manuscript.[22] It is the great treasure here, as Alexandrinus is at London, and Vaticanus at Rome.

That afternoon Goodspeed called on Rendel Harris and showed him Andromeda; Harris reciprocated by showing some of his Syriac "treasures."[23] "He [also] spoke of his talk with you and the president," Edgar mentions to Mother, "and seems to think W. R. [i.e., President Harper] approves my present ventures."

Preceding Goodspeed's reports of his visits with Schechter and Harris, however—in fact, the opening of the 6 August portion of his letter—is a short sentence that perhaps reveals his true priority for Cambridge: "I have found the girls." Edgar would, in any case, spend the balance of this excursion with Misses Tunnicliff and McMahan. A day packed with sightseeing left him "too weary" to write to Charles on the 7th, so he saved his account of that day for the next morning.[24] The highlight was some post-dinner canoeing on the Cam,

> up and down its surface for an hour or more in twilight and moonlight. The moon rising full through the great trees, and reflected in the great river, with many a college bridge and tower, made the experience a remarkable one; and we agreed surpassed even Venice.

But this pleasure had a price: Next day, 8 August, after failing to see Miss T. off

---

[21]Though partly trained in Vienna and Berlin, Schechter (Ch. 3, n. 146) was born in the equivalent of today's Romania. For other descriptions of Schechter, including notice of his fondness for cigars, see Hoffman and Cole 2011, 6–10.

[22]"D" was the siglum for the Greek uncial portion of this bilingual (Latin-Greek) manuscript of the New Testament that *inter alia* contains most of the four Gospels.

[23]Edgar had also seen "a lot of his [Harris's] Syriac and Greek manuscripts" during his 1899 visit (19 September 1899 to Mother, Ch. 1, n. 106). Both visits may thus be considered the fulfillment of an invitation extended by Harris in a letter of 22 September 1897 (box 4, folder 17), written from 5 Park Terrace, Cambridge.

[24]This letter continues through 9 August.

to London "by extraordinary clumsiness," Edgar himself would depart for Oxford, having developed "a beastly bad back" from all the paddling, and another cold—"It is almost incapacitating." Cheering him, however, was the company of Miss McMahan, who had "finally weakened, and decided to come here." Back at the Isis, Mrs. Catterall has Edgar transferred to the Catterall-Phelps table, with Una as his neighbor: "This makes dining attractive[.]"[25] Still, thoughts of his work commitments weigh heavy. That morning, he had described the coming ten days, the rump of his time in Oxford, as "a delirium of toil," and in the evening he was not feeling his best "just now when I need every ounce" of energy. "Well, we'll see.-I have some remedies." Another reminder of tasks remaining was a "nice letter" from Blass, supporting the Hellenistic date of Andromeda: "[P]oor girl! she's only Alexandrian."[26]

The remedies, or one of them, would do the trick: On 9 August, he declares his back better thanks to a "hot water bag. They are good for everything." Reinvigorated, he devotes the rainy day to "constant and productive toil," mainly on unspecified revisions. He talks with the "charming Miss MacMahan from dinner till coffee" and then shows some photographs of his travels. "You must meet her," he tells Charles, "when she returns from Greece next May."

On 10 August he begins writing to Father,[27] describing the business of one of his last face-to-face meetings with Grenfell and Hunt:

> This afternoon I called at Queen's; I found Hunt, and had a good time. Grenfell came in soon with Gradenwitz of Königsberg,[28] who is visiting them at Queen's. Both my principals looked through my big 47 column "accounts",[29] and they recommended its publication. G̶r̶Hunt made several notes off it, for use in their present volume,[30] and gave me some suggestions. They also looked over some 30 copies I took in to them, and decided I might prepare them for publication. I hope to have ten more before I sail. Meantime I am copying. I asked Hunt to let me bring in Andromeda, for help in piecing her together; and he very willingly consented.[31]

[25] The quoted sentence ends "though Phelps seems hardly civil." Here and elsewhere Goodspeed seems to dislike Phelps or to react to Phelps's dislike for him. In any case, Phelps is one of the very few (Western, Anglophone) individuals he does not find congenial; perhaps his sentiment took root during the year they overlapped at Yale.

[26] The quoted words after the colon are in parentheses. Edgar says, further, he will bring Blass's letter home and show it to Mother ("I'll shew it to you"), but no letters from Blass are listed among the Goodspeed Papers. They would have been filed in box 1, folder 19.

[27] Continuing through 13 August.

[28] For Otto Gradenwitz (1860–1935), who was first and foremost a legal historian, see Kaser 1964. Gradenwitz's university would later confer honorary degrees on Grenfell and Hunt; cf. Ch. 3, n. 106.

[29] Goodspeed is referring to the future *P.Cair.Goodsp.* 30, a papyrus in his personal collection, by far the larger of the two unrolled in his mother's kitchen in October 1897 (Ch. 1, with n. 51).

[30] "G̶r̶": As earlier (above with n. 12), he begins by crediting Grenfell, then corrects himself. "[P]resent volume": presumably *P.Fay.*, which would appear in November (Ch. 3, n. 80).

[31] Between Grenfell and Hunt the latter was the designated conservator. This was the case when they were in the field (App. B) and also back in Oxford (see Ch. 3, 12 June, with n. 91). Hunt would

After dinner and before coffee he escorts "Miss McMahan to the Mesopotamia walk [...] We had a pleasant time."³²

Next day, a Saturday, in the afternoon, Edgar gets "a blue ribbon for good behavior" by taking young Ralph Catterall punting on the Cherwell; after dinner Una helps him take the punt back. The balance of the day is occupied, once again, with unspecified "labors [...] to considerable purpose." On Sunday, he does "a big copying job" and other work after tea. Most of the rest of the day is spent with Una: first, services at the cathedral, walking back to their lodgings "through Christ Church Meadows, returning under the great trees of the Broad walk," and then a second and longer stroll after dinner, out southeast to Littlemore by way of Cowley. In Cowley, they "had a glorious view of Oxford's dreaming spires [... A]ltogether the walk was a pronounced success."

Monday, 13 August, Goodspeed worked on Andromeda before breakfast. At 9:45 a.m. he called on Grenfell and Hunt,

> and we tried to piece Andromeda to gether [*sic*], in vain[.] Four parts of columns are in order; but four more are not. They were very kind, especially Hunt. Grenfell accepted four or five more pieces I had elected, and they ran over a Gizeh copy of a Ptolemaic letter I had made. They revised it most helpfully, and recommended that I give them copies of my Ptolemaic Gizeh things, which they would revise at Gizeh in December.³³ This is kind, rather than flattering. I revised till tea.

Afterwards he canoes with Una: "The Char and she were alike delightful." Meanwhile, Father, in a letter Edgar has just received, has expressed himself "abundantly satisfied" with Edgar's accomplishments while abroad. "Certainly in travel little more could have been asked," Edgar modestly agrees, "but I do not," he promptly confesses, "seem to look back upon two years of solid work."

It is to his mother that he describes the activities of his final days in Oxford, 14–17 August. On the 14th, Tuesday, he revises some papyri and now has his "forty pretty well in sight." After tea it is back on the river with Una, canoeing "way up the "Char" to Marston Ferry, and photographing her and the canoe to my heart's content [... W]e were both happy."³⁴ Then dinner at the Isis, now made more pleasant—it "suits me down to the ground"—by the absence of the Phelpses (in Cambridge) and the earlier hours preferred by the Catteralls ("for the sake of the little lad"). Next day he starts before dawn (the canoe has to be retrieved from Parson's Pleasure), filling the morning with errands and last-minute photographs before turning to work after lunch:

---

reconserve Goodspeed's Andromeda in 1914; see Meliadò 2008, 11–12.

³²A footpath running from the University Park to King's Mill Lane, with a bridge (now made of concrete) crossing the Cherwell.

³³*P.Cair.Goodsp.* 3–9 are Ptolemaic, 3–4 are letters. On p. 3 Goodspeed thanks Grenfell and Hunt for their "help on many difficulties in" all the Gizeh papyri (*P.Cair.Goodsp.* 1–15).

³⁴None of these photographs are present in the Goodspeed Papers.

I fussed over a tough letter to a potter's wife, at Bodley's:[35] then had tea, and got down to the pleasant and rapid task of cleaning up my forty "selects". I did great execution till dinner; which Miss MacM. attended in a most enchanting heliotrope gown.

After dinner he grumbles about the arrival of a "mob" of Americans—"they will sit at our table and mar our – i.e. my – happiness"—before returning to his "first "volume" of copies for Grenfell and Hunt."

On the 16th, Thursday, the Thekla proofs arrive, "[a]nd they are fine. It's the swellest thing I ever did." But these are duplicates because three weeks ago Dragulin had "stupidly sent" the proofs and copy from Leipzig to Goodspeed's London address, 10 Bedford Place. There is a final dinner in the Queen's Common Room in the company of Grenfell and Hunt, Sayce and Magrath, "the gray bearded provost of Queen's,"[36] after which Edgar offers a concluding assessment of his summer's work with Grenfell and Hunt:

Well, the thing is over, and at least I have not failed.- I can not tell myself I have succeeded; but at Queen's after dinner tonight, Grenfell and Hunt assigned me some 50 of my copies to do for the volume, whereas I had expected less than 40. They also expressed themselves as obliged to me, and seemed to think I had done enough to please them. It was an anxious hour for me: and I am glad it is over, and over so pleasantly.

The 17th is filled with errands, copying, and his final packing. After tea, there is time for one last punting expedition.[37] He has coffee in the evening with Una, who "said a handsome thing about my Oxford services, and we parted. She has been the jolliest kind of company, and I have greatly enjoyed her presence here." He continues: "So ends my Oxford chronicle, and the world opens once more before me; with first London and then the Ocean,-"wide as its waters be[.]""[38]

So yes, he heads for London, where, on 18 August, he settles in again at 10 Bedford Place, two blocks from where Miss Tunnicliff is staying.[39] From about

---

[35] *P. Tebt.* II 414, not on the 1902 list (App. D).

[36] John Richard Magrath (1839–1930), provost since 1878. A prolific writer, he published in 1921 a two-volume history of the college. Sayce: Ch. 1, n. 44; here Edgar reports that the "entertaining" Sayce "says one of his great ₄or great great₄ grandmothers traced her descent back to the days of Julius Caesar, + had it in writing. This was before the time of Fernando Jones [1820–1911; one of the earliest settlers of Chicago, arriving ca. 1835]." Sayce's other topics that evening included teetotalers and the Rev. Sabine Baring-Gould (1834–1924), whose anonymously published novel *Mehalah* (1880) he praised.

[37] Edgar, presumably due to haste, is not clear regarding who was present: certainly Mrs. Catterall and little Ralph.

[38] Cf. Job 30:14 (*KJV*): "They came *upon me* as a wide breaking in *of waters*." A less likely direct inspiration: the old Scottish folksong, "The Water is Wide."

[39] A short letter to Charles runs from the 18th through 3:00 p.m. on the 19th. Miss Tunnicliff is at 35 Upper Bedford Place, Russell Square, according to a "certificate of posting of a registered postal packet" dated 17 August 1900; this is mounted in a travel scrapbook, box 18, Helen Tunnicliff and

noon to 7:00 p.m. he collates his Thekla proofs with one of the British Museum manuscripts, "doing practically all of it." After a visit with "R. F." [Harper], also staying nearby,[40] he drops in on Miss Tunnicliff at 8:30: "I'm 'fraid it was a long one. She was finer than ever." On Sunday, 19 August, a train delay allows him to spend much of the day sightseeing with Miss Tunnicliff, whom he had tracked down and "caught […] at the door of S[t]. Margaret's" in Westminster. Eventually departing from Waterloo Station at 3:30 p.m., he reaches Southampton and then boards the S.S. *Grosser Kurfürst*, the vessel that will take him home to America.[41] During the voyage, his letter writing continues (Charles had suggested he write to the very end of his travels),[42] but the letters reveal little about his continuing scholarly activities on shipboard, though he does mention correcting his Thekla proofs, revising its translation based on R. H. Charles's suggestions, and beginning an introduction to Andromeda. On his first full day at sea, 20 August, he receives his "steamer letters" from family and friends, including missives from both Miss McMahan (enclosing Oxford photographs) and Miss Tunnicliff. He expresses displeasure with the Germans and German Americans ("not a desirable lot") in his part of the ship; much worse, the "Polack anarchist" ("looking sour + plainly meditating mischief") who is one of his five cabin mates.[43] On 25 August, two days before landfall, he finds himself "poring over Farrar and Lightfoot" and significantly anticipating, "It certainly is going to be delightful to spend one's days with these men: it beats papyri."[44]

Ralph C. H. Catterall Family Papers. Upper Bedford Place is now known as Bedford Way, i.e., Russell Square lay between the lodgings of Edgar and Miss T.

[40] See Ch. 3, n. 153. Harper is staying a "[h]alf a block east" from Edgar.

[41] A new liner of the Norddeutscher Lloyd shipping firm, built in 1899 and launched in Danzig. The vessel's crew was interned in New York in 1914, and after the United States declared war, it became the troop transport U.S.S. *Aeolus*. See Kludas 1991, 62–63.

[42] The journey is covered by a single long letter to Father, 19 August through 5:00 p.m., 29 August.

[43] "Polack": "*Polack*, for a Pole, is old in English, and the *OED* traces it to 1599 [now 1561]. Horatio uses it in 'Hamlet,' Act II, Scene I" (Mencken 1977, 375). *OED*, s.v., now classifies it as "derogatory and offensive." The others in the cabin: "grocery keeper, hotel waiter […] ‚Hebrew,‚ and countryman."

[44] "Farrar": Frederic William Farrar (1831–1903), dean of Canterbury Cathedral, 1895–1903; "Lightfoot": Joseph Barber Lightfoot (1828–1889), bishop of Durham Cathedral beginning in 1879. Both were biblical scholars, prolific writers on a wide variety of religious and intellectual topics; they were what these days would be called public intellectuals. Goodspeed seems particularly taken with Farrar, "delightful but dangerous," able to "make the dry bones live!" (cf. Ezekiel 37:1–14). It is not possible to be sure what works of theirs Goodspeed is referring to, but the books seem to have been new (their pages required cutting), and the purchase of the Lightfoot at least was recent (mentioned in the 15 August continuation of 14 August to Mother). Perhaps it was Lightfoot 1889–1890, a set of volumes with sources in their original languages, whose absorption certainly would require considerable "poring over." The Farrar may be Farrar 1889. No matter the works, the approving reference to their authors reinforces the sense that Goodspeed craved a respite from papyri, for the time being if not for the long term.

✤ ✤ ✤ ✤

It will take over fifty years for Goodspeed to put the finishing touches on the story his "Student Travel Letters" narrated in such minute and intimate detail. They will be found, of course, in *As I Remember*, which presents his mature reflections on his accomplishments abroad.[45] These include a "closer acquaintance" with Greek papyrus documents and a "working alliance" with Grenfell and Hunt. Of these, the latter appears accurate, at least for a period of years.[46] More revealing is the use of the word "acquaintance" in reference to papyri, for indeed, Goodspeed's prominence as an *editor* of such texts all but ended in 1907 when *P.Tebt.* II finally appeared.[47] There Grenfell and Hunt credit him not as co-author; instead, the title page, albeit in type sizes equal to their own, acknowledges the "assistance of Edgar J. Goodspeed, Ph.D., Assistant Professor of New Testament and Patristic Greek in the University of Chicago," without specification as to his exact editorial contribution.[48] The preface, besides crediting him with compilation of "the bulk of

---

[45] Goodspeed 1953, 115. "Abroad in the Nineties" (Goodspeed, n.d.), ch. VII, pp. 13–14, gives a different assessment, moving swiftly from papyrology (cf. the extract quoted near the beginning of Ch. 3) to Goodspeed's success in Ethiopic studies (i.e., Thekla). A final sentence, scrawled in a hand that seems to speak its age, acknowledges four scholars whom he met in his time abroad for their "friendly interest and understanding" over the years: "Krüger, Grenfell, Charles and Harris," but not Hunt.

"Krüger" was (Hermann) Gustav Krüger (1862–1940), professor of church history at Giessen and a guest lecturer in Chicago (Goodspeed 1953, 125). Goodspeed had apparently met him during his tour of German universities (cf. Ch. 1). Goodspeed 1953, 109, is unclear on this ("… to Giessen, where Gustav Krueger has always been my friend"); there is no mention in Goodspeed n.d. We have failed to uncover evidence in the Goodspeed Papers for Krüger's importance to Goodspeed; in other words, there are no incoming letters where one would expect to find them, in box 5, folder 13. The explanation must lie in the lost "Student Travel Letters vol. 1."

[46] Up to *P.Tebt.* II (1907). Two later articles—Goodspeed 1908 and 1910—and *P.Chic.* (1908) note their assistance, but this is something different.

[47] For Goodspeed's later editions, see the previous note. *P.Chic.* is largely a republication of earlier work.

[48] "[N]ot as co-author": Contrast Grenfell's letter of 3 January 1900 (quoted in full in Ch. 2). Goodspeed inscribed a copy of *P.Tebt.* II, now part of his collection at Denison University, to his father: "Thomas W. Goodspeed, | In gratitude and affection | From Edgar J. Goodspeed | Nov. 16, 1907." This suggests some pride in his contribution, but many years later (Goodspeed n.d., ch. III, p. 8), he would seem to play it down, expressing delight in the mere appearance of his name on the same title page with Grenfell and Hunt's: "[W]hen in 1907 they published their second huge Tebtunis volume [*P.Tebt.* II], they most generously put my name with theirs on the title page!" In any case, the title page seems to be at odds with the preface of *P.Tebt.* I, dated May 1902: "The Roman documents have already, to a considerable extent, been deciphered by Dr. E. J. Goodspeed, of Chicago University, who will collaborate with us in their publication" (p. x). It may be recalled that the Roman material was originally envisioned for the first volume of the Tebtunis series. A letter from Grenfell to Smyly (IE TCD MS 4323, item 83) indicates, however, that a decision had been made as early as 9 July 1900, when Goodspeed was still in Oxford, to privilege the crocodile papyri. The extent, if at all, to which Goodspeed's performance as a collaborator impacted this decision is unclear. In print, Grenfell and Hunt noted (*P.Tebt.* I, pp. viii–ix), "The Tebtunis papyri reached England in May, 1900, but during the rest of that

the indices," does state that "in the summer of 1900, while we were occupied with other work, these papyri were studied by Dr. E. J. Goodspeed, who deciphered part of those here edited and is associated with us in their publication"—but what part did Goodspeed decipher, and what exactly was the nature of the association from Grenfell and Hunt's perspectives (which need not have been identical)? A clue perhaps resides in a 5 November 1902 letter from Grenfell assigning Goodspeed forty papyri to edit in full for the volume, but it is impossible to verify whether these forty were the "part of those here edited" to which Grenfell and Hunt's preface refers.[49] Nor is it possible to determine the extent to which Goodspeed was responsible for the final printed versions of the papyri assigned to him. It is conceivable that soon-to-be chronic and lifelong problems with his eyesight hindered further work on papyri, but this ailment did not keep him from a life's productive work on other kinds of manuscripts, though perhaps clearer to read.[50]

That aside, we cannot fail to surmise that in his meeting with Grenfell and Hunt on 23 July 1900 he saw in their politely phrased ("… perhaps better …") nudge to "take the easier" papyri the plain truth of their assessment of his papyrological abilities—not "flattering" but (indirectly) "frank."[51] This may have confirmed the apprehension, indeed fear, that lay behind his misgivings when the summer before he had been invited under pressure to work on Grenfell and Hunt's as yet undiscovered papyri.[52] It also may have prompted recollection of the duo's frolicsome jape at Jules Nicole's expense in 1898 and their candid opinions about "Krebs, Wilcken, Wessely, Revillout, Mahaffy, and other palaeographers" as expressed during his first visit to Queen's on 31 July 1899.[53] During the summer

---

year the editing of *Fayûm Towns and their Papyri* and the *Amherst Papyri* left us no time for other work. We were anxious however not to postpone indefinitely the commencement of the publication of so valuable a collection, and the claims of the papyri from the crocodile-mummies seemed the most urgent." This last assertion finds support in Grenfell's letters to Smyly in the summer of 1901 (e.g., IE TCD MS 4323, items 43 and 44), which reveal that he and Hunt were pleased with the crocodile texts, in particular the προστάγματα (royal decrees, such as the future *P.Tebt.* I 5).

[49]Were these identical to the "forty selects" mentioned above (cf. 15 August)? For the full, annotated text of Grenfell's letter, which gives the maximum extent of Goodspeed's editorial contribution to *P.Tebt.* II, see App. D.

[50]"[E]yesight": As reported in Goodspeed 1953, 123–124, Goodspeed was in danger of losing his sight; this occurred soon after his marriage in December 1901. When staying at New College in the summer of 1899 (see Ch. 1) he complained of visual grogginess caused by reading and writing by candle light. He was helped when his scout provided a lamp: "Those candles were near being the death of me" (letters to his mother, 6 August 1899 in continuation of 3 August, and to Charles, 9 August in continuation of 8 August). Note also Grenfell's postcard of 29 May 1902 (Goodspeed box 4, folder 9), which closes, "I hope your eyes are better," and Goodspeed 1953, 162 (long before Goodspeed had begun his translation of the New Testament his oculist had forbidden him "to do any close work at night").

[51]Ch. 3; cf. the explicit instructions on 12 June.

[52]Ch. 1.

[53]Ch. 1. We suspect that Grenfell was the instigator of the former and the more outspoken on the latter. Note in support of this suspicion the quip about his then newfound friend, papyrologist and

of 1900 he must have calculated where he himself ranked in their estimation and adjusted his sights accordingly. Moreover, it had been, as Nick Gonis reminds us, "a very hard apprenticeship," offering little in the way of guidance (given Grenfell and Hunt's other priorities that summer) and no open access to the papyrological resources, much less residence, as proposed the previous summer, at Queen's College. Goodspeed did the bulk of his Tebtunis and other work alone at the Isis; his "contact hours" with Grenfell and Hunt were relatively few. It is perhaps significant, or perhaps not, that he was not invited to contribute to any publications beyond the second Tebtunis volume. That there would have been nothing personal about this is shown by a friendly letter from Grenfell, 12 February [1908], full of scholarly advice, returning the proofs for Goodspeed's "Karanis Accounts," musing about a lecture tour through various American cities, and asking for his help in making arrangements in Chicago should the tour materialize.[54]

Yet another clue may reside in the absence of a course in papyrology at Chicago until the Autumn 1920 term, and in Goodspeed's failure to repeat this course in the years following.[55] And while it is true that he did collaborate on a Greek papyrus reader in 1935, the stated aim of this volume is to illustrate the language of the New Testament.[56] Here, and for that matter in his entire post-1910 oeuvre, papyrology is exclusively a *Hilfsmittel* for Religious Studies.[57] Once again, *As I Remember* is illuminating. There it is clear that Goodspeed regarded his return from abroad as a life boundary, and he closes the door on the period with the suggestive rhetorical question, "What was I being fitted for, anyway?"[58] Papyrology, in its narrow sense at least, was not his answer. The enthusiasm ignited in Chicago by

---

archaeologist Pierre Jouguet, in a letter of 18 March 1901 to J. Gilbart Smyly: "But nature did not design a Frenchman of the Midi for either a scholar or an excavator" (Hickey 2017, 227).

[54] It, of course, did not. Grenfell's letter: box 4, folder 9. "Karanis Accounts": Goodspeed 1908.

[55] The course description reads as follows:

45. Greek Papyri.—Their discovery, character, and significance, especially for New Testament studies. The principal collections. Paleographical study of facsimiles and originals.
Mj. [= a "major" course for degree requirements] Autumn, 1920, Professor Goodspeed.

There appears to have been no training in papyrus editing. See University of Chicago 1920, 57.

[56] Goodspeed and Colwell 1935, viii. It is Colwell who teaches the papyrology course when it reappears in Autumn 1931. His course description is consistent with the aims of the *Reader*; cf. University of Chicago 1930, 43.

A bill of appraisement for posthumous donations by Goodspeed to Denison University's William Howard Doane Library indicates he continued to acquire or be sent papyrological books for his personal library into the 1930s, including *P.Tebt.* III, Part 1 (1933; noting editorial assistance from the then-deceased Grenfell), but not Part 2 (1938; a posthumous publication for Hunt). His *P.Oxy.* set ended with vol. XVII (1927), Hunt's last volume in the series (a solo one). The latest papyrological item in the list is *P.Ryl.* III of 1938 (the year after his retirement from Chicago), but this is a volume of *Theological and Literary Texts*. Although earlier volumes in the list include important editions of documentary papyri, volumes from the 1930s lean almost exclusively to those of religious interest.

[57] Cf. Goodspeed 1953, 161, 171, 192.

[58] Goodspeed 1953, 115.

first sight of the Ayer papyrus, we make bold to suggest, was fatally dampened by his second summer in Oxford, and perhaps by the realization that Grenfell, and Hunt, too, presented models of genius in papyrology that he could never hope to match. There was no shame in that. At the time only Ulrich Wilcken could have been seen to equal them as all-round documentarians.[59] Whatever the reasons,[60] Goodspeed's effective withdrawal from the field meant that the seeds of papyrology sown in Chicago and nourished in Berlin and Gizeh and Oxford had fallen on the stony ground; the good soil in America lay elsewhere, but it would not begin yielding fruit for another decade or so.[61]

---

[59] Cf. Goodspeed 1953, 101: Krebs and Wilcken, "then considered the best Greek paleographers in Germany." Goodspeed did not meet Wilcken during his tour of German universities, begun on 15 February 1899 (see Ch. 1), possibly because Wilcken was excavating at Herakleopolis (3 January–21 March: Bierbrier 2012, 577) during the first five weeks of Goodspeed's German travels, and Breslau, Wilcken's university at the time, should have fallen early in Goodspeed's itinerary. In any case, it is not on Goodspeed's list.

[60] Which may also have included a lack of interest in the related field of Egyptology, implicit in a letter to Father begun on 16 October 1899: "I'm not an Egyptologist[.]" Nevertheless, he would serve as the local honorary secretary in Chicago for the EEF/EES from 1910/1911 until at least 1931 (thus the annual reports of the Fund/Society). Goodspeed became a subscriber to the Graeco-Roman Branch in 1899/1900 (for which the volume was *P.Fay.*, not the copy of *P.Oxy.* II that he received in Cairo in mid-November 1899; Ch. 2), but he let his subscription lapse until 1904/1905, possibly a sign of his post-Oxford interest in the discipline.

[61] "[E]lsewhere": specifically in Ann Arbor, at the University of Michigan. The vision and drive of Francis Willey Kelsey (1858–1927; biography: Pedley 2012), professor of Latin, would be the engine for the field's American renaissance, but once again Bernard P. Grenfell would play a critical role, just before declining health would take him away from papyrology (1920) and then from life itself (1926). General survey of the Michigan collection: Verhoogt 2017. An ample account of the field's rebirth, including the contribution made by Wisconsin's William Linn Westermann (1873–1954), appears as the introduction to the forthcoming volume marking the centenary of the Michigan papyrus collection (*P.Mich.Cent.*).

For a more positive assessment of Goodspeed's papyrological contributions, though in conclusion not fundamentally in conflict with ours (because it stresses Goodspeed's championing the value of papyri for New Testament studies), see Danker 1988, 125–128. In the early forties, when he was at U.C.L.A., Goodspeed expressed a renewed interest in the Tebtunis papyri, but this was neither lasting nor resultful; see App. G.

Appendix A

The Ayer Papyrus and Goodspeed's "Last Graduate Year"

In *As I Remember* (Goodspeed 1953, 98), Goodspeed writes, "But it was not until my last graduate year at Chicago that I saw my first Greek papyrus." This is the sentence as it appears revised in version 2 of *As I Remember*'s typescript, p. 92, in replacement of a sentence scribbled over on p. 91: "It must have been in my last graduate year that I saw my first Greek papyrus."[1] The shift from the subjunctive mood on typescript to indicative in the book has served to cover the author's initial doubt and made definite what, as will be shown, would better have been left uncertain. The issue may seem minor, but the dating of Goodspeed's first sighting of the Ayer papyrus may be seen as marking the exact beginning of papyrology in America, if only such an exact date could be recovered.

A "prequel" to this is the problem of precisely dating the acquisition of the Ayer papyrus itself and its arrival in Chicago, where a similar lapse of memory, this time on the part of Edward Ayer himself, seems to have occurred. As the story is told in what must be considered Ayer's official (and only) biography (Lockwood 1929, at 191–196, much here in Ayer's own words),[2] while on a Mediterranean–Black Sea cruise on the S.S. *Fürst Bismarck* that set sail in autumn 1894, with passengers including Mrs. Ayer and various "royal couples" of Chicago, Ayer left his traveling companions and jumped ship during a stopover in Cairo—an exciting first time for him in that bustling city. Inspired by antiquities on display in shops near Shepheard's Hotel and a desire as first president and cofounder to stock the newly opened (2 June 1894) Field Columbian Museum,[3] he judged the five days

---

[1] The sentence on the relevant page in version 1 (p. [99]) has been covered by a pasted-on replacement strip. The underlying text cannot be read.

[2] Possibly taken from one of Ayer's travel memoirs. While those for his travels in the American West and Mexico are among his papers at the Newberry Library (visited by us, 9 January 2020), we have not located any for his Egyptian adventures.

[3] Ayer does not state the name of his hotel, only that antiquities shops were nearby; for the

allotted by the cruise's itinerary to be insufficient. "I stood on the porch for a few minutes and then went back to our [hotel] room and said to Mrs. Ayer, 'Emma, I'm not going on this steamer. I'm going to stay here for a month or six weeks and make a collection for the Field Museum.'" On this, the first of his shopping sprees in Egypt, aided by "Mr. Emil Brugsch-Bey, an Austrian [sic]," director of the Gizeh Museum, he spent $20,000 on Egyptian antiquities.[4]

The same story in essence, but with notable differences as to expenditure and timing, is told in a 12 May 1894 article in the *Chicago Tribune* (p. 13), celebrating Ayer's return after three months abroad, mostly "spent in the land of the Nile hunting valuable relics." In this enterprise, he had "the assistance of Bachs [sic] Bey, Curator of the famous Gehirez [sic] Museum," and it was with contributions from fellow cruise members that he spent $6,000 on antiquities for the museum in Chicago.[5] In other words: much less than $20,000, not all of it his own, and not an autumn cruise after the Museum's opening but a winter-spring cruise beforehand. As for the papyrus, our principal concern here, a letter to Goodspeed from Ayer, written from the Old Colony Building on 29 October 1897, states, "I found this three years ago in a small shop in Cairo."[6] Ayer's letter goes on to say he left the papyrus for a year at the Gizeh Museum for an expert opinion, which never materialized, apart from generic identification of the text as mathematical; he returned next year only to reject an offer of £50(!) and reclaim the papyrus.[7] So when Ayer in 1897 says he bought the papyrus three years ago, i.e., in 1894, and Goodspeed 1903b states that Ayer "brought the papyrus from Egypt to the Field Museum" in 1895, the years are surely accurate. Within the latter it is possible to be even more precise since Field Museum records show that Ayer's second expedition to Egypt started from Chicago on 5 January 1895; he was back in town before 3 June; the papyrus was received at the museum on 20 August.[8] It is there

---

identification here, which is suggested, at any rate, by his description, cf. the Chicago *Daily Inter Ocean*'s comic account of the cruise, "Wanderers at Home," 18 May 1894, p. 3. Shepheard's is where he stayed during his second trip to Egypt: letter of 19 March 1895 written by Ayer on hotel stationery, Field Museum Library, Ayer EE 1895–1901 (corrected from "1894–95"), Directors Correspondence.

[4] Brugsch Bey was German (born in Berlin), not Austrian (Bierbrier 2012, 83). For the early assembly of Egyptian antiquities collections for Chicago institutions through private benefaction like Ayer's, partly inspired by the World Columbian Exposition and ambient "Egyptomania": Teeter 2010. Ayer's expenditure of $20,000, if reported accurately (see below), was roughly equivalent in 2019 to $613,000 according to the Consumer Price Index (Williamson 2021).

[5] The *Inter Ocean* article (n. 3 above) corroborates the *Tribune*'s dating. It also states that Ayer, along with banker Lyman G. Gage, did not meet up with the cruise until Cairo (on 23 February specifically), having travelled instead via London and Paris. According to the *Inter Ocean*, the *Bismarck*'s first Mediterranean stop was Gibraltar, followed by Algiers, Genoa, Ajaccio, and then Alexandria.

[6] Box 1, folder 13. "Old Colony Building": an early Chicago skyscraper at 407 South Dearborn, still standing. Ayer's letter was in reply to Goodspeed's lost inquiry of 23 October.

[7] He does not specify whether the pounds were Egyptian or British.

[8] 5 January start: letter of 3 December 1894 to Mr. Sabatino De Angelis, Naples, Italy, Field Museum Library, Ayer EE 1893–94, Directors Correspondence. Return before 3 June: letter written from the

registered as the gift of D(avid) G(ilbert) Hamilton (not Ayer), he and Ayer being named as "Collector/Source."[9] Presumably Ayer purchased the object with Hamilton's money; the *Tribune* account of Ayer's "relic hunt" cited above lists Hamilton among those who "donated $1,000 to be expended for whatever suited [Ayer's] fancy."[10] (Fig. 18)

How long after 20 August 1895 Goodspeed got his first glimpse of the papyrus is a related but more important question for the reason stated above. As there mentioned, he first wrote "it must have been" on typescript, then changed this to "it was not until" his "last graduate year at Chicago" that he saw the Ayer papyrus. If strictly calculated, this would have been the year leading up to the 1 April 1898 conferral of his Ph.D.,[11] that is, the period from 2 April 1897 to 1 April 1898. He had heard about the manuscript at a meeting of the New Testament Club whose records (one box) in the SCRC at the University of Chicago contain printed programs (in folder 1), but none for the academic years 1896–1897 and 1897–1898; these might have narrowed the range of possible dates, even perhaps have supplied an exact one. Failing that, on 27 January 1897 we find Goodspeed writing to W. W. Beman (1871–1922), mathematician at the University of Michigan, about the Ayer papyrus.[12] From the letter it is apparent that De Witt Burton had told Beman about it; Beman had expressed interest to Goodspeed; Goodspeed was writing back. Goodspeed, in his "early hand," smaller and neater than that of the "Student Travel Letters," describes the piece at first (more extensive description follows) as "the little papyrus fragment Dr. Breasted lately found in the Field Museum." Just how "lately," he does not say. Finally, as Goodspeed later recalled the sequence of events (Goodspeed 1953, 100), it was engagement with the Ayer papyrus that spurred his desire to purchase his own papyri. The first in the series of letters about that enterprise, gathered in Chapter 1, is dated 5 February 1897 and surely presumes prior correspondence to and from Egypt stretching back into 1896. Thus the year-by-year sequence of events with regard to the Ayer papyrus may be reconstructed as follows:

Old Colony Building to Museum Director F. J. V. Skiff, Field Museum Library, Ayer EE 1895–1901 (corrected from "1893–94"), Directors Correspondence. 20 August accession: Field Museum Library, Accession File A230.

[9] See https://collections-anthropology.fieldmuseum.org/catalogue/1225921 (consulted 11 October 2018).

[10] Hamilton (1842–1915), son of one of Chicago's founding fathers, Polemus Draper Hamilton (1813–1891), was, according to his obituary (*Chicago Tribune*, 17 February 1915, p. 11), a prominent Baptist lawyer and "streetcar magnate," among many other activities. He also served on the board of trustees of the University of Chicago.

[11] Unless Goodspeed's recollection of a March 1898 convocation is accurate (Goodspeed 1953, 95). See Ch. 1 with n. 11.

[12] Wooster Woodruff Beman Papers, Bentley Historical Library, University of Michigan, box 1, folder 3 (correspondence 1892–1897).

Figure 18: The Ayer papyrus.

© The Field Museum, image no. 31327, cat. no. 31327, photographer Lauren Fitts.

1894: Ayer buys the papyrus in Cairo.

1895: He brings it to Chicago from Egypt.

1896: Breasted "finds" it (a curiosity, no doubt) and brings it from the Field Museum to his office at the University of Chicago; Goodspeed hears about it at a New Testament Club meeting and sees it next day in Breasted's office.

1897: He confers by letter with palaeographical and mathematical experts and prepares an edition of the text (cf. Ch. 1).

1898: He publishes his edition in the *American Journal of Philology* (Goodspeed 1898a).[13]

Goodspeed, in sum, misremembered the date of first sighting, or, in retrospect, conceived of his "last graduate year" in very broad terms.

---

[13]The journal's editor, Basil L. Gildersleeve, acknowledged receipt of Goodspeed's "paper on the Ayer papyrus" in a letter dated 6 December 1897 (box 4, folder 3). When our manuscript was in press, Mills McArthur alterted us to the *Chicago Chronicle* of 29 January 1897, p. 7, which claims that Goodspeed, with the assistance of Professor E[liakim] H[astings] Moore [of Chicago's Mathematics Department], had "completed the task of deciphering" the Ayer Papyrus.

Appendix B

Edgar's Letter to His Mother about His Visit to Tebtunis[1]

Sat. Feb. 17. 10.15 a.m.

My dear Mother

This is Wasta,[2] or el-Wastah, 57 miles from Cairo, and I have just gotten into the train for Medinet-el-Fayoum. My huge basket of vegetables and I have a compartment, 2d class,[3] to ourselves. It is large, and comfortable, but pretty dirty. - The day is cool and fine. The man forgot to wake me at the SIMA,[4] till 7.30 : so I skipped breakfast, + hurried to the train in a cab, taking what was to have been my lunch as a breakfast on the train. The ride from Cairo was interesting : for we passed all the great groups of Pyramids with the morning light on them : Gizeh, Abousir,[5] Dahshur, Lisht, Mêdum.[6] On the whole I am not sorry to have had a long night's sleep, for I turned in last night at 12 after a fussy lot of packing. - My vegetables make an interesting pile : filling a native basket holding about a bushel and a half. The fields through which we have passed are beautifully green, with occasional

---

[1] For additional notes on this letter, see our rendering of it above in Ch. 2. Goodspeed's hyphenations (sometimes marked by a proper hyphen, sometimes by a mere interpunct) at the ends of lines are represented by "|". We do not indicate the red underlining that was later added to the letter; cf. Ch.1 with its n. 22 as well as n. 28 below.

[2] Edgar may have enclosed a (now lost) photograph of Wasta.

[3] Note Baedeker 1898, 177: "The natives almost invariably travel second class, and those who wish to make a nearer acquaintance with the country and the people should, perhaps, select a second-class compartment, in spite of its offering less resistance to the incursion of the yellow desert sand."

[4] A pension on "Shāri'a el-Maghrābi" (now Shāri'a 'Adlī), near the Turf Club and the "Azbekeya" (Ezbekīyah) Gardens; cf. Baedeker 1898, 23, and *Egypt and How to See It* 1907, 158. Source of the vegetables: "The mistress of our pension had very kindly bought them for me!" (Goodspeed n.d., ch. VII, p. 6).

[5] "Abousir" overwrites another word, not deciphered. None of the options listed in Baedeker 1898, 177, seem to suit the traces.

[6] "Mêdum": "d" corrected from "i"?

spaces of yellow blossoms like mustard. We came up from Cairo in two hours. I shall not reach Grenfell's however until toward six,[7] having a long wait in prospect at Medinet. I think I shall spend it seeing the ruins there.

12.15. Medinet el Fayoum- I am enjoying coffee and pastry at the Hotel Karoun Cafe in Medinet. The place is interesting, especially its creaking water wheels, for irrigating : self-working, right in the city. I leave here at 4.15. The proprietors and waiters here are of course Italian - and yet hardly of course, for they are often Greeks.-[8] I have the name of an antiquities dealer here, whom I must see. The Rainer papyri I saw in Vienna come from Crocodilopolis, where I now am.[9]

2.15 I am indeed! I'm seated on the dirt on top of Kûm FARIS, the highest rubbish mound of Arsinoe. All about the mound are mud brick ruins - a whole city of them. Beyond them are the green fields and palm groves of the "First Oasis" - rimmed round by far Libyan hills.[10] The minarets of Medinet shew above a thin line of trees to the southward. It's an unusual place, with the swift current of [the] Bahr Yusuf running right through the town.[11] One mud brick bridge is a veritable rialto with shops along each side of it![12] - Awfully funny. A teacher in the Gov't school is walking about with me.[13] I called on Mahmoud Refsbai, a papyrus dealer; he had nothing.[14] My mentor assures me Hunt went to Gizeh today : but he calls

---

[7] In fact, he would not arrive at the camp until about 7:30; see below.

[8] In the 1907 census, the Fayyūm's population was 441,583; of these individuals, 195 are recorded as Greeks and 20 as Italians. See Ministère des finances 1910, 32–33.

[9] "Crocodilopolis": one of the ancient names of Madīnet. The "w" in "where" is a correction.

[10] "First Oasis": This can hardly be a reference to Strabo, who refers to the Great Oasis (i.e., Dakhla and Kharga) as ἡ πρώτη (27.42); Goodspeed must mean the Fayyūm itself, which is not actually an oasis. The "r" in "rimmed" is a correction.

[11] After the initial letter of "Yusuf" (possibly written as "J"), Goodspeed refreshed his ink. When he put pen to paper once again, he began the word anew, overwriting his first attempt.

[12] The "e" of "each" is a correction. In Goodspeed n.d., ch. VII, p. 6, "Rialto" (capitalized) is canceled and replaced above with "Ponte Vecchio."

[13] The "G" in "Gov't" is apparently a correction.

[14] The reading "Refsbai" is difficult. Whatever Goodspeed intended, Westerners have struggled with the name, creating seemingly irresolvable orthographical uncertainty. In records on Otto Rubensohn's activities (November 1901–1903) in behalf of the Preussisches Papyrusunternehmen and then Deutsches Papyruskartell, the dealer appears as Rifai or Riffai (information from Holger Essler, email, 23 June 2012). Francis W. Kelsey's diary refers to him as Mahommed Rifaa (entry on 26 February 1920) and Mohammed Rafaa (27 February 1920); see box 4, Francis W. Kelsey Papers, Bentley Historical Library, University of Michigan. Elsewhere in Kelsey's papers, Grenfell renders the name as Mahmoud Rifaa (see box 15, folder 3, Francis Willey Kelsey subgroup, Kelsey Museum of Archaeology papers, Bentley Historical Library, University of Michigan). Pedley 2012, 271, somehow ends up with Mohammad Rafar, an apparently false spelling (a typographical error?) that is picked up by Hagen and Ryholt 2016, 247, s.v. "Mohammed Rafar" (fl. 1920), cf. p. 101; they have a separate entry on p. 237 for Mahmud Rifai (fl. 1900–1905), cf. p. 101, a dealer based in Madīnet al-Fayyūm. The two are surely identical. Meanwhile, Magdy Aly, email, 23 June 2012, suggests that Refā'ī (رفاعى) is the correct rendering of the name. "[H]e had nothing": confirming H. O. Lange's experience in failing to find antiquities

him "Hunt kin" + may mean another man.[15] Away to the E. I see the pyramid of Hawara near which the Ayer papyrus was found.[16]
[p. 2]

4.15 pm- Still Medinet - Seated in the 3rd class carriage of the narrow gauge line running south. We are waiting for the little train to start. As I hastened to the station, after a long ramble in the ruins of Arsinoe, a man accosted me- a tall native, a fellah:[17] ˏbarefooted,ˏ dressed in a long blue garment,[18] + wearing a white turban. He handed me a twisted scrap of paper. I read "Dear Goodspeed :[19] The bearer of this, Mohammed Mansour,[20] has come in to Medinet to buy planks + will return to Damian in the same train as you. There will be a camel waiting which will take your luggage. Come on yourself in advance with one or two of the other men. Yours B.P.Grenfell." Thoughtful thing of Grenfell, sending the note. The afternoon has been fine, + I have taken some photographs.

Umm el Baragat, Feb. 18. 6 pm. I am seated on a big packing case in front of Grenfell's tent. The sunset which has been very beautiful is just ending. My day has been divided between following Grenfell over his excavations in the Ptolemaic Ceme|tery this morning, and looking over 6700 Roman papyri with Hunt in G's tent this afternoon, I.e., until tea, when Grenfell joined us, and later we three went out together to the excavations.

I arrived here last night after a rapid walk of an hour from the train, escorted by 3 of Grenfell's most trusted men.[21] They carried me over canals on their shoulders, led me by the hand when it was very rough, and closed in a solid group about me when the dogs of each village or hamlet rushed upon us! I was glad when we neared the tents at about 7.30 ; the starlight had made the plain reasonably light however.[22] Grenfell came out to meet us, and then Hunt with a lamp in his hand. They made me welcome, + I washed up in Gre⌊f⌋nfell's tent. After which we had

---

worth purchasing in Madīnet al-Fayyūm, also in 1900 (Hagen and Ryholt 2016, 99–101); he was hoping to buy papyri for Danish collections.

[15] The reading "mentor" is difficult. Presumably Goodspeed is referring to "Refsbai," but the reference could be to the "teacher in the Gov't school." "Hunt kin": This is a huge stretch, but it is just possible the speaker, perhaps with heavy accent, is referring to Hunt by his nickname "Huggins," a datum Goodspeed picked up the preceding summer during one of the dinners at Queen's College (Goodspeed n.d., ch. III, p. 9). Of course, if Hunt had gone to Gizeh, he had already returned since he was on hand to welcome Goodspeed at 7:30 p.m. (see below).

[16] "Ayer papyrus": Ch. 1 and App. A.

[17] "[F]ellah": "tiller of the soil," an Egyptian peasant.

[18] "[L]ong […] garment": i.e., *jalābīyah*.

[19] The "e" in "Dear" is a correction.

[20] The "o" of "Mohammed" is a correction.

[21] Goodspeed seems to have refreshed his ink before beginning this sentence.

[22] The "l" in "light" appears to be a correction from "b." Possibly Goodspeed intended to write "bright."

a mighty good dinner, and a fine talk till bedtime. [p. 3] Grenfell lives well, and means to. He doesn't believe in what he calls the Petrie methods in this particular.[23] We had cold turkey, toma|to sauce, potatoes, boiled rice; a blanc-monge with prunes; coffee; and everything was nice. After a talk, we adjourned to a nice little tent allotted me, and concocted a bed.[24] There was the usual frame standing perhaps 18 inches above the sand: on this we assembled George's blan|ket,[25] one from Grenfell's establishment, one from Hunt's: an air cushion from H; a Norfolk Jacket of Grenfells, my mackintosh, and later my clothes. My mattress was the usual "lihaf" or thick comforter,[26] doubled. Altogether I did well, and slept rather better than at Petrie's. Hunt retired early; I talked till 10 30 with BPG[.]

Monday 1-15 p.m.[27] ˌFeb. 18/00ˌ[28] I am jolting along on the narrow gauge to Medinet. The day is a little hazy with sand, the open cars are very comfortable however: I have this compartment to myself: (at least I had when I began that sentence)) [sic] I must resume where I left off. I was awakened Sun|day morning by hearing the swift steps of passing Arabs on the hard sand outside.[29] They were Grenfell's men gathering from the adjacent villages. Mahmoud brought me some water and I joined G. + H. in Grenfell's tent for a fine breakfast at 7.20.[30] We had oatmeal, eggs and bacon, bread, jam and tea : all first class. I must explain that B.P. and his men lay off on Saturday and work Sunday. I suppose Sat. is the local market day.- That is at least Petrie's method : I mean, to make the local market day his rest day.[31] - Anyway I walked out with Hunt after breakfast to the town mounds, where he shewed me the ruins of their Coptic church, with its pictures of S[t]. George and the dragon, etc, and its 2 pretty columns. [p. 4] Then I walked on alone to the barren level desert which Grenfells men have pitted with thousands of little holes:- The Ptolemaic cemetery. I may tell you in confidence, what hardly anyone in Gizeh knows, that the fellows have had in a way a greater year than at Oxyrhynchus : they have found more Ptole|maic papyri than anyone ever found before! They are keeping this fact rather dark.- You see in this ceme|tery, they found a lot of crocodile mummies, wrapped in cloths stiffened with big pieces of

---

[23]"[T]he Petrie methods in this particular": Petrie's camps were famously spartan, their meals heavily reliant on tinned goods; cf. Drower 1995, 229, 243, 269, 276, 319, 393, 414.

[24]Goodspeed refreshes his ink before writing "concocted."

[25]George: George S. Goodspeed, Edgar's cousin, mentioned above in Chs. 1 (n. 82), 2 (n. 36), and 3 (n. 83).

[26]"Lihaf": Arabic for "coverlet, blanket." From this word to the end of the page the ink is darker.

[27]The first "1" of "1-15 p.m." is a correction.

[28]This superlinear addition, in red ink, is later than the main text; it was probably included in conjunction with the red underlining (cf. n. 1 above). In any case, it is incorrect: Monday was the 19th.

[29]Goodspeed seems to have written "hear" first and then corrected this to "hearing." The ink of the correction is darker, suggesting that it was not made immediately (cf. next note).

[30]Goodspeed refreshed his ink for the latter part of the word "Mahmoud," from "h" onward.

[31]For the Saturday respite, cf. Ch. 2 (Grenfell's letter of 5 December 1899).

papyrus : also a good many human mummies finished in the same way. They are now figuring on three volumes from this years digging. They thus wish me more than ever to come to Oxford to work on the first one, which will be devoted to a selection from the 700 Roman papyri I saw yesterday.- While it might be more flattering to be taken on for the Ptolemaic ones, I am on the whole well pleased with the Roman field, as it covers my period, and I've had experience in Roman papyri. Moreover papyri from the time of Augustus, as some of these are,[32] are hardly less rare than Ptolemaic pieces.-[33] Well: if Cal. is favorable, I am to go to Oxford about May 1 and remain till Sept 1.- The dates are Grenfell's: for he says I'll want a holiday! - I spent the morning, following Gren|fell from pit to pit among his men: he is rather short : and walks briskly about, his surveyor's staff in his hand, a broad white felt hat pulled over his eyes, and the invariable cigarette in his teeth.-[34] I photographed him, I hope successfully. The afternoon I spent with Hunt till tea: when as I wrote last night, we all three went out to the excavations,[35] 10 minutes walk from the tents.- Grenfell is working 140 men, these days[.][36]

After dinner, we sat about the little table in Grenfell's tent and talked till nearly 10. The tent is full, with G's bed and the dining table, chairs and a few boxes, besides piles of clay lamps, Ptolemaic vases and little bronzes, etc. The moon was up when I sought my tent: also a wind which shook [p. 5] the tents all night.- At sunrise I got up, and again we were together for breakfast in Grenfell's tent.[37] I walked with him to the work: he is a fast walker : and the wind cool and dust laden was against us. I spent an hour and a half with G. among the men: then said goodbye, and joined Hunt in the tents where he was separating papyri from the wrapping of those Ptolemaic crocodiles! They found about 1000 crocodile mummies, of course only a few of them "papyrifer."[38] Ah! We are entering Medinet: 3 p.m.

Medinet 3.45. In 15 minutes I go on to Cairo, having only a stop of indefinite

---

[32] "[P]apyri from the time of Augustus": Cf. Hanson 2001, 604, n. 43, and App. C below. But we also note that Grenfell and Hunt thought for a time that some of the crocodile papyri, specifically those from crocodiles 1 and 19, were of Augustan date; cf., e.g., IE TCD MS 4323, item 46, letter from Grenfell to Smyly, 5 May 1901, and Grenfell and Hunt 1901, 378.

[33] The "r" of "hardly" is difficult.

[34] The final "e" in "cigarette" is a correction.

[35] The "e" of "went" is a correction, possibly from "a."

[36] For the staffing of the excavation, see also App. C.

[37] The second "a" of "again" seems to be a correction.

[38] Cf. *P.Tebt.* I, p. vi. "Papyrifer" strikes us as a Grenfellism.

length at Wastah, which I shall reach at 5.30.- I was telling you about Hunt and the crocodiles. Around the tents are piled pots and mummies of men and crocodiles; a few nice little crocodile mummies were in a box and on the ground under my bed![39] I watched Hunt damping out Ptolemaic pieces, + laying them away in sheets of paper for a while: talked over my Gizeh transcriptions with him,[40] and at 11.05 left those hospitable tents behind, and struck off on foot with Mahmoud Mansoor, for the railroad. We reached it in 1 hr. 40 min. good walking,- along a rapid little canal first, then across the desert and past a town or two. We crossed little cultivation, it seemed to me. When we reached the railway, there was no station; I really dont see how Mahmoud knew it would stop there : - he spread out his wrap on the dust for me to sit on;- and I proceeded to demolish a substantial lunch of chicken, duck and native bread,[41] which G. had sent with me in a sand proof box.-[42] This, with a bottle of mineral water and my bag, Mahmoud had carried in that same big outer garment, slung from his neck, all the way from the tents. When we reached the railway, and he took it off, he uttered an explosive "alhamdu lillah."-"Praise God"- for which I couldn't blame him.[43] He waited till my train came at 1.15 + saw me on board_[p. 6] -At this point I transfer my activities to a 2^d class carriage, the Wastah train having pulled in.-

So ends my visit to Grenfell's camp. I could have seen little more by remaining longer. I feel that it was emphatically the thing to do, coming out here, 2 hard days of travel, for two nights and a day at Grenfell's camp. I shall have no more memorable day of Egypt to look back upon. I wish you could have seen the little cluster of tents there in the blowing desert! The "cultivation" is only a hundred ˬor 2ˬ yards away to the north, and this brings mosquitoes; but on the other sides is desert, and the tents look lonely enough there on the bare sand. There are three tents with 6 ft walls "Egyptian officers' tents" the type is called : they are 12-sided, and lined :[44] Mine was smaller, but very comfortable for one. My wash stand was unique :[45] an ancient pot, nearly four feet high, into the top of which the bowl just fitted! The walk from the train to the camp Saturday with those three men was a great experience. They could talk no English, but made me understand

---

[39] Cf., e.g., P(hoebe) A(pperson) H(earst) M(useum of) A(nthropology) inv. 6-21633, which appears (bottom right) in an archival photo of Hunt's; see Rathbone 2007, 205. The photo in question likewise includes what appear to be two cat mummies, and perhaps these were also among the "little crocodile mummies" under Goodspeed's bed.

[40] "[S]heets of paper": See Ch. 3, n. 91.

[41] The first "and" in this clause overwrites a string of three or four letters that seems to begin with "M" ("Mahm"?).

[42] The "s" of "sand" is a correction.

[43] "[H]im" seems to be corrected from "his."

[44] For these tents, see Ch. 2 at end, Goodspeed's photos (Figs. 10 and 11), and the photo in Rathbone 2007, 199.

[45] Goodspeed seems to have refreshed his ink before writing "unique."

some things in Arabic. They wanted to know whether I knew Petrie, and were happy as children to learn that I did,: [*sic*] and also Mace and ˄Quibell and˄ McKee|ver. -⁴⁶ Then the boy who led, and who set a killing pace, inti|mating to me that at this rate "Misser Grenfell" walked it in one hour,-⁴⁷ asked if I knew Ali? - Ali you remember, is Pe|tries famous "head man".⁴⁸ When I said I did, and gave as glow|ing a description of Ali as my Arabic would permit, they became ecstatic, and informed me altogether that the afore|mentioned leader was Ali's brother.⁴⁹ My tent at the Camp was an old one of Grenfell's: a 12 sided tent, with 3 ft. walls: and about ten feet in diameter. From mine to the cook's was about 50 yards, outside dimensions. In the shelter of sand + dura stalks South of the cook's tent, some 40 or 50 of Grenfell's non local men live.- Sunday morning at 7, there were quite a hundred extra locals squatting with baskets + mattocks behind the cook; they, eager to be hired. After breakfast, B.P. selected 8, and the rest were sent away.

Edgar

Feb. 19. Monday. 4. p.m. en route.

[Perpendicular to the main text in the right margin, in an increasingly minuscule hand:]

Both men offered to look over any difficulties in my Gizeh transcriptions for me: and in every way were most kind. - Tues. 8 am.⁵⁰ Ar. 10.30 p.m. 2 hrs late⁵¹ + walked Cairo till 11.15 hunt -⁵² ing a place to sleep. Sima, Villa Victoria + Bristol

---

⁴⁶"Mace and Quibell and McKeever": For Arthur C. Mace, who would soon (1901) begin to excavate with Reisner, see Bierbrier 2012, 346–347, and Ch. 2, n. 8; for Quibell, see Ch. 2, n. 22. "McKeever" is a mistake for (David Randall) MacIver (1873–1945), on whom see Bierbrier 2012, 347–348. Presumably Goodspeed's transcription of the name is a rendering of its pronunciation.

⁴⁷"Misser Grenfell": perhaps an exact aural transcription (see preceding note), however offensive to modern ears.

⁴⁸"Ali": ʿAli Muhammad es Suefi, from the Fayyūm village of al-Lāhūn; see Quirke 2010, 301–302, and refs. He was "the idol of the [Abydos] encampment" according to Goodspeed's 4 December 1899 letter to his mother. Petrie's admiration and affection for ʿAli: Drower 1995, 226, characterizing their friendship as "deep and lasting."

⁴⁹Quirke 2010, 301, identifies two brothers for ʿAli, both younger: Mahmoud and Yusuf (the youngest).

⁵⁰An indication of when Goodspeed picks up the letter again (the morning following his return to Cairo).

⁵¹"Ar.": "Ar(rived)." Cf. Grenfell's letter of 5 December (transcribed above, Ch. 2), which indicates an 8:20 arrival time in Cairo.

⁵²The two syllables of "hunting" are separated by an apparent fold, and the continuation of the text on the other side of the fold is misaligned. Goodspeed's hyphen leads the eye across the fold to the continuation.

full : Angleterre too dear; + finally stopped here at the Eden, also too dear.[53] Met Wollaeger in the hall![54] had tea at 11.30, + went to bed. I fear I cant finish today.[55]

---

[53]For the Sima, see above, n. 4; the Villa Victoria, Baedeker 1898, 24 ("a quiet house pleasantly situated near the Place de la Opéra"), cf. Ch. 2, n. 12; the Bristol, Ch. 2, n. 10; the Angleterre, Baedeker 1898, 24 ("in the new quarter of Isma'iliya, with 100 rooms, terrace, garden, Anglo-American bar, etc., pens. in Jan.–March 70–80 [piastres]"), and *Egypt and How to See It* 1907, 24 ("greatly appreciated by those who desire a quieter life than is possible in the larger establishments; it is, however, first class, and quite as well managed as any of the big hotels"), 156; the Eden: Ch. 2, n. 133. Baedeker 1902, 24, records "pens. from ca. 50 pias.," the same as the Bristol and less than the Villa Victoria.

[54]The reference is to "Dr. Wollaeger, our Milwaukee friend and Heidelberg Ph.D.," mentioned in a letter to Mother from Haifa, in a 6 p.m. continuation on 2 January 1900. He had joined Goodspeed's party in visiting sites in Galilee: Goodspeed n.d., ch. V, pp. 5–9.

[55]The events subsequent to Goodspeed's arrival in Cairo are also mentioned in a letter to Charles begun later on 20 February.

Appendix C

Grenfell and Hunt's Account of the Tebtunis Excavations

(*New York Journal*, 10 June 1900,
"American Magazine" supplement, p. 23)[1]

Ancient Egyptian Treasures Hidden in Mummies and Crocodiles
By Bernard P. Grenfell and Arthur S. Hunt,
Directors of the Phoebe A. Hearst Exploring Expedition.

Our excavations at Behnesa, the ancient Oxyrhynchus, in 1897 yielded an unrivaled collection of papyri of the Roman and Byzantine periods. Since then it has naturally been our ambition to make a find of similar importance for the Ptolemaic period.[2] For such a discovery, the district which offers the best chances of success is the Fayum, not only on account of the great number of Graeco-Roman sites in it, but by reason of the practice which prevailed there in the third and second centuries B. C. of **using up old papyri instead of cloth as the background for painted plaster in making up the cartonnage of mummies**. A cemetery of early Ptolemaic mummies in which the cartonnage consisted of strips of Greek and demotic papyri, stuck together by glue or merely by water, was discovered ten years ago in the Fayum by Professor Flinders Petrie, and the papyri from them, edited by Professor Mahaffy, form the principal collection of Ptolemaic documents extant.[3] In

---

[1] In the interest of facilitating comparison between Grenfell and Hunt's two popular accounts of the excavations, we have set in **bold** language strings that also appear (verbatim, though ignoring punctuation, orthography, and typesetting) in the *Athenæum* account (Grenfell and Hunt 1900). Unsurprisingly, Grenfell and Hunt assume a more knowledgeable reader in the more literary English publication, though space constraints may also account for some of their brevity there. For the excavators' engagement with the press and the public, see Montserrat 2007.

[2] Cf. the more concise beginning of the *Athenæum* article (hereafter *A*.): "One of the chief objects of our excavations in the Fayûm has been to discover another cemetery of Ptolemaic mummies with papyrus cartonnage like those found by Prof. Flinders Petrie at Gurob."

[3] For Mahaffy, see Ch. 1, n. 89; Stanford and McDowell 1971, 183–187, address his work on the Petrie

1898-9 we, too, found in the Fayum a similar cemetery of papyrus mummies; but unfortunately **damp had ruined the papyri**, which dropped to powder at the touch.[4] This year, however, our luck changed in a manner which surpassed all our hopes, and our new collection of papyri promises to be of even greater importance for the earlier **period than the Oxyrhynchus find was for the** later.[5]

Last Winter our excavations **were conducted on behalf of the University of California, with funds provided by Mrs. Hearst.** The site which we had selected is called Umm el Baragat, and is situated on the edge of the desert in the south of the Fayum. **The mounds, which form an oval half a mile in length**, indicate that it was once a town of some importance, and **it is surprising that the** place had remained quite unknown to archaeologists.[6] **The explanation is partly that** Umm el Baragat **is in a poor and until recently not very accessible district, but still more the fact that the major portion of the** site is **later than the Arab invasion**,[7] and the few native diggers who had tried to find antiquities there had met with no success.[8] **Only the southern** parts **of the** town **facing the desert were Roman, the line of demarcation clearly indicated on the mounds by the change in the pottery** upon the surface.[9] At the extreme south end some Ptolemaic fragments **were mingled with the Roman** potsherds, **and we began work along** this side on December 3, 1899.[10]

Starting with forty men and boys **whom we had brought with us, chiefly old hands at papyrus digging, we soon increased the** number **up to 100 and later to 140** by taking on local applicants.[11] To obtain workmen was never easier, though the daily wage we pay is 15 cents for a man, 10 cents for a boy, i. e., practically the market rate of unskilled labor in the Fayum. We follow Professor Petrie's system of paying each pair of workmen a "bakshish" for everything they find, and with luck a workman may increase his earnings by 25 to 50 per cent, possibly by much more.[12] Every Sunday morning (Saturday being the market day at the nearest village was our "day off") our camp was besieged by a crowd of would-be work-

---

papyri. His edition is *P.Petr.* I–III (the third volume appeared only in 1905 and was co-edited with Smyly, for whom see Ch. 1, n. 96). The papyri were recovered from mummies excavated at Kawm Madīnet Ghurāb (Gurob; cf. previous note).

[4] This was at Baṭn Ihrīt (ancient Theadelpheia); cf. *P.Fay.*, p. 55.

[5] A. has "Ptolemaic" instead of "earlier" and "Roman and Byzantine" for "later."

[6] In A., this clause concludes: "site had hitherto escaped the notice of not only archæologists, but native diggers."

[7] "[L]ater than the Arab invasion": Cf. Keenan 2003, 129–137.

[8] A. has "it" for "Umm el Baragat"; "rather inaccessible" for "not very accessible"; and "mounds, including those near the cultivation, are, as at Behnesa," for "site is." It has "and *sebakh*-diggers had, therefore, found nothing of importance" as this sentence's concluding main clause.

[9] A. has "part" for "parts," "site" for "town," and "is" for "were."

[10] A. has "potsherds" for "fragments" and lacks "potsherds" after "Roman"; "that" also takes the place of "this."

[11] A. has "workmen" for "men and boys" and "number" for "numbers." For the composition of the labor force, cf. Quirke 2010, 41–43.

[12] Cf. Quirke 2010, 98–100. Grenfell had cut his teeth in Egypt working with Petrie at Coptos in 1894.

ers.¹³ Though the half Bedawi [Bedouin] settlers on the outskirts of the Fayum make less satisfactory diggers than the fellahin of Upper Egypt, we were able, having so large a power of selection, to get together a very fairly intelligent lot.¹⁴

The first day's excavations yielded a number of demotic and Greek papyrus-fragments of the Roman period, mixed with some hieroglyphic, a discovery which indicated the proximity of a temple.¹⁵ And, in fact, it was not long before the plan of a large enclosure disclosed itself, 110 metres long by 60 wide, with walls 3 metres thick.¹⁶ The northeast corner was occupied by a small temple, dedicated to Seknebtunis, one of the numerous forms under which the crocodile-god, Sebek, was worshipped in the Fayum, his special province; while round the sides of the enclosure were built the houses of the priests in a series of rooms two to four deep.¹⁷ The temple itself, which was built chiefly of brick, with some stone, had been ruined down to its foundations and produced no antiquities, but the houses yielded many Greek papyri of the first three centuries A. D., with a few Ptolemaic and some fine domestic [sic] rolls.¹⁸ Most of the papyri found in the temple enclosure appear to be concerned with the priests, and promise, therefore, to be of special interest.¹⁹ Other finds in these houses included two small boards [sic] (each numbering about 150) of Ptolemaic silver and copper coins, and several native [sic?] statuettes.²⁰

We next proceeded to examine other houses in the Roman town. In several

---

¹³"[D]ay off": See App. B with n. 31; cf. Drower 1995, 271.

¹⁴For the distinction between the Bedouin and *fellāḥīn*, cf. Quirke 2010, 91–92. "[P]ower of selection": On Sunday, 18 February 1900, Grenfell selected only eight locals out of "quite a hundred" (see App. B).

¹⁵A. has "pointed to" for "indicated."

¹⁶A. puts "disclosed itself" at the end of the sentence and has "110 by 60 mètres" as the enclosure's dimensions.

¹⁷A. replaces "dedicated to" with "of" and "the Fayum, his special province" with "his nome." It also supplies "brick" between "small" and "temple." In the *Journal* piece, information concerning the construction materials of the temple is delayed until the next sentence ("which was built chiefly of brick, with some stone").

¹⁸A. has "a good number of" for "many" and "demotic" for "domestic," which is presumably a typesetter's error.

¹⁹A. has "these" for "the papyri found in the temple enclosure."

²⁰A. has "the temple enclosure" for "these houses" and "hoards" for "small boards" (presumably another typesetter's error). It also has "some votive" for "several native." It is not clear whether Grenfell intended "native." For the hoards, actually 140 and 108 pieces, see Milne 1935, 210–212. A letter of Reisner to Mrs. Hearst, 17 April 1900, included "a list of objects found by Grenfell and Hunt in the Fayum" (George and Phoebe Apperson Hearst Papers, BANC MSS 72/204c, The Bancroft Library, University of California, Berkeley). The original letter and list are lost, and the copy of the list at the Hearst Museum is imperfect; it does, however, mention "1 headless statuette," "2 inscribed marble statuettes" (= PAHMA inv. 6-20313–4), "1 statuette Sobek(?) [the transcription of this word is garbled] on pylon" (= PAHMA inv. 6-20315), and "1 statuette figure standing on crocodiles" (= PAHMA inv. 6-20317). Cf. also Ch. 2 with nn. 83–84 and Ch. 3 (the "battered little blue glaze lion" that Goodspeed "picked up at Grenfell's last February").

of these papyri were fairly plentiful, noticeably a group of cellars containing documents of Augustus's time, and some rooms on the floor of which we found bundles of from ten to fifteen rolls.[21] Altogether the Roman town produced about 200 well preserved Greek documents, literary fragments being few and unimportant.[22] Beside papyri, we found, as in other Fayum sites, numerous coins, terra cottas and tools, ornaments and domestic objects of various kinds, made of stone, wood, bronze, iron, glass, pottery, etc., among which we may signal a little box containing one gold, two silver and one bronze ring,[23] and two little bags bound together, one of which held a pair of silver earrings, the other 120 first century tetradrachmas.[24]

The excavations had so far lasted four weeks, and a week was then devoted to clearing an early Coptic church, which had upon the walls interesting paintings, with inscriptions,[25] depicting besides St. George and other Saints, scenes of the torments of hell.[26] The church, of which the floor was four metres from the surface, was built of small clay bricks, and had been filled up with sand, while the walls were bent and cracked with the pressure of the surrounding rubbish mounds. The process of excavation was attended with some danger to those concerned, since few of the walls would remain standing for a longer time than was just sufficient for photographing them and copying the inscriptions. Fortunately, however, although we had one or two narrow escapes, there were no accidents.[27] But it was with a feeling of relief that on January 5, 1900, we started work upon the cemetery.

This lay immediately to the south of the town, and proving varied and extensive, occupied our energies for more than two months.[28] Four groups of ancient Egyptian tombs were discovered; two of these belonged to the Middle Empire, one being XII. dynasty, the other somewhat later, and two to the New Empire, probably XXII.-XXVI. dynasty.[29] In all of these classes of tombs we found

---

[21] *A*. has "two or three" for "some" and omits "from" later in the sentence. For the Augustan papyri, see App. B with n. 32. For "bundles," cf. Verhoogt 1998a.

[22] *A*. has "houses" for "Roman town" and inserts "of various kinds" after "documents." "[U]nimportant": an indication that the significance of one large fragment, Dictys Cretensis's "diary" of the Trojan War (the future *P.Tebt.* II 268 = Trismegistos 59665) had not yet been discerned.

[23] The list of finds (n. 20) includes "1 gold serpent shaped ring," "3 silver rings," and "1 bronze ring."

[24] The list of finds (n. 20) mentions "3 silver earrings." For the tetradrachms, actually 119 of them, see Milne 1935, 212.

[25] *A*. has "was spent in" for "then devoted to" and "on" for "upon."

[26] Cf. Ch. 2 with n. 86 and the references there given.

[27] For the church and its archaeological zone, see further Keenan 2003, 132–136. Note also O'Connell 2007, 812–813.

[28] *A*. has "was" for "lay," "proved" for "proving," and "occupying us" for "occupied our energies."

[29] *A*. puts a colon after "discovered" and omits "these belonged to." It also adds "of the" before "twelfth" (it uses words instead of Roman numerals). Finally, it has "of the New Empire" instead of "to the New Empire." For these cemeteries and their designations in the Hearst Museum inventory, see O'Connell 2007, 813.

scarabs, beads, amulets, alabaster vases, pottery and various small objects.[30] No tomb was strikingly rich, nor indeed was a very rich burial to be expected, for in Pharaonic times Tebtunis (such we found to be the ancient name of Umm el Baragat) was probably merely a fishing village on the shore of Lake Moeris; but the existence of ancient Egyptian burials at Umm el Baragat is a matter of some importance.[31] Hitherto the only remains in the Fayum which date from the Pharaonic period have been found on the highest plateau at the entrance to the province or at the back of the Birket el Kurun, the modern representative of the great Lake Moeris, which still filled most of the Fayum in the time of Herodotus[.] The level of the oldest tombs at Umm el Baragat will provide a new terminus ad quem for determining the height and extent of Lake Moeris in the time of the XII. dynasty.[32]

Of greater interest, to ourselves at any rate, was the Ptolemaic cemetery, which seems to have been a centre of burial for other villages besides Tebtunis. One group of tombs contained painted coffins and mummies with uniformly cloth cartonnage, and appears to belong to the first half of the third century B. C., before the practice of using papyrus cartonnage existed in the Fayum.[33] In the burials of the next hundred years, however, when the coffins, if any, were of plain wood or pottery, mummies with papyrus cartonnage were common.[34] Most of the large tombs had, as usual, been plundered anciently, and in many of the others damp and salt had wrought much damage.[35] Nevertheless, we obtained about fifty papyrus mummies in sound condition, with fragments of as many more.[36] When to these are added those which we found later on at another site (see below), the papyri, partly Greek, partly demotic, from these mummies, will, we expect, be about as numerous as the Flinders Petrie papyri.[37] Until they have been separated from each other, cleaned and flattened out—a lengthy and difficult process—it is impossible to ascertain their contents and

[30] A. has this sentence in the passive ("were found") and extracts the pottery from the main list of the finds ("besides much pottery").

[31] A. has "None of the Pharaonic burials" for "No tomb." After "rich," it skips right to the adversative clause, which displays some shared verbiage with the longer *Journal* text: "but the fact of their existence at Umm el Baragât is a matter of some importance for determining the height and extent of Lake Mœris in pre-Ptolemaic times."

[32] For Hunt's correspondence with the archaeologist Gertrude Caton-Thompson (cf. Bierbrier 2012, 108) concerning the pharaonic remains at Tebtunis and the level of Lake Moeris, see App. F.

[33] A. has "containing" for "contained" and lacks the "and" before "appears." In addition, it has "was common" for "existed" and appends "if, indeed, it yet existed" to the end of the sentence.

[34] A. substitutes "where pottery or plain wooden coffins were used, or else there was no coffin at all" for "when the coffins, if any, were of plain wood or pottery."

[35] A. lacks "as usual" and substitutes "other cases" for "of the others" and "havoc" for "damage." It also employs "or" between "damp" and "salt."

[36] A. has "parts" for "fragments."

[37] A. has "afterwards" for "later on," "v. inf." for "see below," and "approximately" for "about." It also omits "Flinders."

to state whether the proportion of fragments of lost classical authors is large or small.[38]

The Ptolemaic cemetery also contained a very large number of **mummied crocodiles,** that animal being held sacred in the Fayum.[39] **Some thousands of these creatures were found, ranging in size from** full-grown specimens of **13 feet long to baby crocodiles just out of the egg.**[40] Apparently the priests of Tebtunis could not have too many crocodile mummies, for we found **numerous sham** crocodiles, **which, when opened, proved to contain** nothing more than **a bit of bone or** some eggs.[41] **The importance of this cemetery is due to the fact that in some cases the crocodiles were wrapped up inside one or more layers of** the ancient equivalent of old newspapers—i. e., sheets of papyri, **while vacant spaces, especially in the head, were stuffed with papyrus rolls.**[42] These papyri were nearly all Greek, **but occasionally a large demotic roll was found buried beside a crocodile.**[43] As may be imagined, to pack up **a good-sized crocodile in several folds of papyrus, many correspondingly large documents were necessary, and though, as was inevitable, decay from within or damp from without had irreparably injured many of the papyri, the balance which remains in a good or fair state of preservation is very considerable, and includes many large and important official documents, with some literary fragments.**[44] The crocodile papyri **cover the last century and a half B. C.,** while the papyrus mummies belong to the earlier Ptolemaic period, so that our collection of Ptolemaic papyri from Tebtunis is very complete, and the result of our find **is approximately to double the extant amount of Ptolemaic papyri.**[45]

[38] *A.* joins this sentence to the preceding one with the adversative conjunction "but." It is also more concise than the *Journal* article, omitting "from each other, cleaned" and the appositive "a lengthy and difficult process," and reducing "and to state whether the proportion of fragments of lost classical authors is large or small" to "or to estimate the number of classical pieces."

[39] *A.* transitions to the crocodiles in this manner: "Adjoining the cemetery of papyrus mummies was a large cemetery of mummied crocodiles." It omits the explanation of the crocodile's religious significance.

[40] *A.* has "the fully grown animals" for "full-grown specimens of."

[41] Again *A.* is more concise, appending "besides numerous sham crocodile mummies which when opened proved to contain merely a bit of bone or a few eggs" to the preceding sentence.

[42] *A.* lacks the explanatory text "the ancient equivalent of old newspapers—i. e.," and renders "sheets of papyri" as "papyri sheets."

[43] *A.* begins, "All these, with a few exceptions, were Greek." This is overstated—there are a significant number of demotic crocodile papyri in Berkeley—but perhaps inadvertently, given the early date of the articles. Grenfell and Hunt (1901, 378) note, "Nearly all of these papyri are Greek, though occasionally a demotic roll was found buried beside a crocodile." These rolls were left in Gizeh; cf. Verhoogt 1998b, 14.

[44] *A.* has "in order to enclose" for "to pack up."

[45] *A.* concludes the paragraph, "The papyri from the crocodiles cover the last century and a half B.C., and the effect of the Tebtunis find, as a whole, is approximately to double the extant amount of Ptolemaic papyri written in Greek." The absence of the famous story of the discovery of the papyri wrapped around and stuffed into the crocodiles (see *P.Tebt.* I, p. vi) from the *Journal* and *Athenæum* articles is puzzling—its popular appeal is obvious. It is absent from Goodspeed's 1902 *Chicago Tribune*

The Roman Cemetery yielded several portrait heads on wood similar to those which have been found at Hawara and Rubayyat, one, a portrait of a youth, being particularly well executed.[46] Two other **specimens are of unusual interest—the one containing on the back a sketch of the portrait on the front, while on the back of the other are memoranda for the painter, giving a brief description of the salient features of the deceased.**[47] When we had finished **Umm el Baragat a week was devoted to** exploring **another Ptolemaic cemetery** about **six miles to the west.**[48] **A few more mummies with papyrus cartonnage were** found in the earlier tombs, and in two of the later Ptolmaic [sic] burials we found a large wooden box elaborately fitted up inside with the various requisites for a lady's toilet, e. g., combs, pins, powder boxes, alabaster scent flasks, etc.[49] We concluded our excavations on March 25.

The antiquities other than papyri will, with the exception of **a representative selection** retained by the Gizeh Museum, be sent direct to the museum of the University of California. **The most important of the demotic papyri,** including those found in the town or buried beside the crocodiles and eight large rolls tied up together in cloth which were discovered in the Ptolemaic Cemetery, remain at Gizeh. **The rest of the papyri,** i. e., including all the Greek, have been sent **to Oxford for publication.** This will be a somewhat **long and difficult undertaking,** in which

---

article, but included in his 1904 *Independent* article. We wonder if it is not a product of some later "elaboration" of the excavation narrative, though Goodspeed many years later recalled having heard the story from Grenfell (and Hunt?) during the first evening of his visit to the Tebtunis excavation site, 17 February 1900 (see further Ch. 2, n. 120). In any case, Grenfell and Hunt's account itself would receive embellishment; cf. the rendering in Deuel 1965, 151–152. Montserrat 2007, 28 n. 2, mentions "media references" to the discovery, but his citation, Deuel, does not provide any. The influence on a popular song that Montserrat posits for the find is, moreover, chronologically impossible, and the part of the song that he quotes makes no specific mention of a crocodile mummy.

[46] A. lacks the text in the plain font. The portrait in question is probably PAHMA inv. 6-21377, which Hunt photographed in the field (EES Hunt photograph 55), but 6-21378b cannot be ruled out.

[47] A. omits "other" and adds "—instructions which show that these 'portraits' were to a large extent imaginary" to the end of the sentence. The portraits to which Grenfell and Hunt refer are PAHMA inv. 6-21378a and CG 34253 (in Cairo), respectively (though PAHMA inv. 6-21377 also has traces of such instructions on its back). For inv. 6-21378a, see *P.Horak* 18; for CG 34253, cf. Edgar 1905, p. xvi ("[A] badly injured panel from Gharaq has a few memoranda on the back about the features of the deceased, an indication that the picture was not painted straight from nature.") and n. 1 ("[f]rom the excavations of Grenfell and Hunt, 1900"). Grenfell and Hunt's account above would seem to suggest that Tebtunis was the actual origin of this portrait, as may EES Hunt photographs 70 and 71, which depict it and another panel; but perhaps Edgar was speaking loosely (cf. Ch. 3, n. 32).

[48] A. has "After finishing" for "When we had finished" and omits "exploring" and "about." For this site, Kawm al-Khamsīnī (Khamsin), see Ch. 3, n. 32.

[49] A. is considerably more concise: "Here a few more mummies with papyrus cartonnage were discovered." "[L]arge wooden box," etc.: The box is PAHMA inv. 6-21596 A, B; its card record indicates that it contained 6-21604 ("iron, pointed object") and 6-21597 ("wooden box fragments").

we hope to have the assistance of one or two other scholars, English and American.[50] Subsequently a selection of the papyri will be returned to the Gizeh Museum, while the major portion will go to the University of California.[51]

        BERNARD P. GRENFELL.
        ARTHUR S. HUNT.

---

[50] The "i" of "in" (in "in which") is broken. "English" presumably refers to the Anglo-Irishman Smyly, who had just been asked to collaborate on the Ptolemaic texts: Ch. 1, n. 96.

[51] A.'s penultimate paragraph reads, "The Gizeh Museum has kept a representative selection of the miscellaneous antiquities and the most important of the demotic papyri. The rest of the papyri are on their way to Oxford for publication. Subsequently they will be divided between the museums of Gizeh and the University of California, to which the other objects will be sent direct." A.'s closing paragraph echoes the *Journal* article in indicating that the editing of the papyri "will be a long and difficult undertaking," but it also provides the reasons for this (the preparatory work that must be done on the cartonnage and the crocodile papyri, Grenfell and Hunt's other commitments).

Appendix D

Grenfell's Letter to Goodspeed about His Contribution to *P. Tebt*. II

(Goodspeed box 4, folder 9)

Queen's College
Oxford
Nov. 5th [1902]

My dear Goodspeed,
                      Tebtunis I has been out over a week now. I hope that a copy has reached you by the time you get this. With regard to your papyrus 30 of the accounts Im afraid we cant suggest much,[1] but here are a few remarks (on nos xvi-xxix you already have our criticisms, I think)[2]
introd. πιττακιον occurs as 'receipt' in the Coptos tariff of Domitian's reign.[3] vide Wilcken Ost. I on ἀποστόλιον[4]
Col. 3.25 συνβολη also occurs in Tebt. I; it hasn't anything to do with συμβολικά
Col 4.7 margin ?οὐχ εὑ(ρίσκεται)
Col 6.22,[5] note 'raphan<u>us</u>', not '-nous'
Col 13.15 ἀνθ' οὗ

---

[1] "30" is a later addition in another hand, presumably Goodspeed's. The papyrus in question is the future *P.Cair.Goodsp*. 30.
[2] "[N]os xvi-xxix": another reference to *P.Cair.Goodsp*. texts.
[3] "Coptos tariff": *SB* V 8904 (= *OGIS* 674 = *IGR* I 1183 = *I.Portes* 67). See, e.g., Burkhalter 2002 for discussion of this inscription and the specific Greek terms mentioned here.
[4] Wilcken Ost. I = *WO* I or *O.Wilck*. I.
[5] "Col. 6" is a correction.

~~14.22~~⁶ κοῦφα cf. P. Fay. Towns 133.6.
21. 18, note Wilcken's theory of the land tax is all
wrong; vide our discussion in ~~Fay.~~ Tebt. I p. 39
~~22.25~~⁷ (ακανθων cannot be right   ? ἀνθ' ὧν - For
the construction ὑπὸ σῖτον "carrying corn" cf. Fay. Towns p324
23.9 & 15. Βακχ(ιάδος) is more likely than Βακχιωτων
~~24.16~~⁸ ἐλέας of course = ἐλαίας. i.e. olives
25.18. ?ὥσ(τε) τελώνῃ
[p. 2]
35.20 κνιδίου means a ~~jar of~~ Cnidian ~~wine~~ measure ˏof wineˏ
see Wilcken Ost I. 765
Now as to the future. We are well on with Oxyrh.
III and shall have finished writing it by Dec. 6
when we leave for Egypt,⁹ whence we shall return
in April. We expect to have the volume off our
hands by the end of June, and wish to devote July
and August of ~~next~~ 1903 to revising the Tebtunis
Roman papyri. Then we hope to write the major
part of the volume (or rather of our share) in
the autumn and have it printed during the
winter of 1903–4, so that it can appear in
1904, as foreshadowed in the preface to Tebt. I.
We have looked through your copies again
and selected the following to be done by you;¹⁰
14, 460,¹¹ 545, 561, 679, 427, 727, 411, 721, 450, 7,
226, 239, 267, 1, 524, 538, 101, 61, 351, 725, 96,
334, 350, 415, 286, 488, 249, 703, 326, 426, 698,¹² 549,
425, 261, 417, 547, 399, 233, 376.¹³ This list is slightly
different ˏfromˏ and I think larger than, what was arranged
previously; if there are any in it which you dont
understand, you can leave them to us. <u>Can you
let us have your copies of these</u> (ready for publication)

---

⁶The cross-out, in blue, is a later addition, no doubt Goodspeed's.
⁷The cross-out, in blue, is a later addition, no doubt Goodspeed's.
⁸The cross-out, in blue, is a later addition, no doubt Goodspeed's.
⁹Grenfell's "III" may be a correction from "II."
¹⁰The word "looked" may be a correction from "worked."
¹¹This numeral was overwritten, making it appear darker.
¹²The "9" of "698" may be a correction from "0."
¹³The numbers are "T-numbers," for which see Ch. 2, n. 82. A list of their corresponding publication numbers appears in App. E.

[p. 3]
<u>by July 1st 1903?</u> Please do them in the
style of our Fayum Towns ˏand Amherst papyriˏ etc,[14] with short introductions
and <u>translations</u>, but dont bother about notes, when
you have any thing [sic] particular to say.[15] You might
keep as far as possible in translaˏtˏing
technical terms etc to the equivalents used by
us, and avoid 'Americanisms'.[16] Cross-references
from one papyrus to another should be put in in
pencil, as we cant say yet what the numbers will
be. We have now abandoned Roman numerals
altogether except for numbering columns (vide
Tebt. I).[17]
I hope we are giving you enough notice,
and that you have time enough for doing these
40 documents. It isnt worthwhile your spending
time over 'cruxes', for we shall have to go into
these ourselves carefully anyhow. With regard to
the literary texts you might give a collation of
the Homers with Ludwich's recent edition of Il i-xii
and of the Demosthenes with Blass ˏin the Teubnerˏ (supplemented
by Bekker if necessary).[18]
[p. 4]
If you could send me by return the references to
your publication of the Gizeh papyri, I should be
very grateful, for we shall be sending our catalogue
to the Press by the 5th Dec.[19]
Prof Burton called the other day, but unfortunately
on the eve of his departure, so I was

---

[14] Grenfell first wrote a comma after "Towns," then inserted "and Amherst papyri" above the line, and then squeezed in "etc" before the comma.

[15] The "u" of "you" is a correction; Grenfell may have started to write "you've." Either Grenfell has omitted "dont" before "have," or "any thing" is a mistake for "nothing."

[16] There is a deletion after "possible" ("to" may be the word that was crossed out). The second "t" of "translating" seems to have been squeezed in after the word was written.

[17] Grenfell and Hunt used Roman numerals for publication numbers in, e.g., *P.Fay.* and *P.Oxy.* I, II. *P.Tebt.* I, the first of their volumes to employ Arabic numerals, had appeared a few months before in August 1902.

[18] Ludwich 1902; Dindorf and Blass 1885; Bekker 1854.

[19] "[O]ur catalogue": *P.Cair.Cat.* Grenfell wants to know the Cairo papyri that Goodspeed has edited (cf. *P.Cair.Goodsp.*).

unable to entertain him, as I was desirous of doing.[20]

I hope you and Mrs Goodspeed are both flourishing.[21]

      With best remembrances from Hunt,
          Yours ever
               Bernard P. Grenfell

P.S. After Dec. 6 our address is Cairo till April 1. We shall begin digging at Hibeh again about Jan. 1.[22]

---

[20] For Burton: Ch. 1, n. 9.

[21] The "-ris-" of "flourishing" is a correction. "Mrs Goodspeed": Goodspeed had married the former Elfleda Bond (1880–1949), daughter of his benefactor, Joseph Bond (Ch. 1 with n. 66), on 3 December 1901 (Goodspeed 1953, 118).

[22] Cf. Grenfell and Hunt 1902–1903, 1–3.

Appendix E

Concordance

T-numbers Assigned to Goodspeed[1] and Their *P.Tebt.* II Publication Numbers (*italicized*)

14	*300*	725	*267*
460	***640***	96	*388*
545	*418*	334	*420*
561	*330*	350	*353*
679	*371*	415	*415*
427	*378*[2]	286	*289*
727	277	488	***442***
411	*394*	249	*369*
721	*405*	703	*397*
450	*377*	326	*421*
7	*387*	426	*406*
226	*403+419*	698	***593***
239	*408*	549	*375*
267	*411*	425	*335+404+424*
1	*333*	261	***430***
524	*380/**622***[3]	417	266
538	*381*	547	265
101	*304*	399	n/a
61	***596***	233	*396*
351	n/a	376	*283*

- *n/a* indicates that the papyrus with this T-number has not been located in Berkeley.
- A publication number in bold indicates a piece that appeared among the volume's "descriptions" (i.e., not in a full edition). *P.Tebt.* II 371 received a partial edition in the main part of the volume.
- Documentary texts have their publication numbers underlined.

[1] See App. D. As mentioned near the end of the Epilogue, it is impossible to determine whether Goodspeed brought these assignments to completion in their final forms.

[2] The reading of the T-number on *P.Tebt.* II 378 is uncertain.

[3] T-524 seems to have been applied to two different papyri. We presume that Goodspeed was assigned 380 instead of 622, a single poll-tax receipt in the group 617–637.

Appendix F

Hunt's Letters to Gertrude Caton-Thompson

Concerning the Pharaonic Remains at Tebtunis and the Level of Lake Moeris

(Caton-Thompson papers, Griffith Institute, Ashmolean Museum, University of Oxford)[1]

Letter I

6 Chadlington Road
Oxford

11 July 1926

Dear Miss Caton-Thompson

I am afraid that my information will not help you very much, but it is at your service such as it is. The Umm el-Baragât excavations were 26 years ago, and my recollections are somewhat dim. It was intended to publish some account of the cemeteries, and of the antiquities in Vol. III of the Tebtunis Papyri, but owing to my late colleague Dr Grenfell's ill health there has been one postponement

---

[1] We reproduce these letters principally for the information that they furnish regarding the pharaonic remains at Tebtunis; a thorough investigation of the site during this period remains a desideratum. Tebtunis's pharaonic remains were signaled as relevant for the historical height of Lake Moeris already in the very first press account of the excavations that appeared: "In the tombs adjacent to the town the discovery of a very large cemetery, the earliest monuments dating from the 12th dynasty, is of especial importance for determining the position and height of Lake Mœris. It proves that the estimate of Captain Lyons [Bierbrier 2012, 344] which places the level of Lake Mœris at 23 mètres above the sea is the highest which can be entertained, these remains, which are the first to be discovered on the second of the three plateaus into which the Fayum is divided, being also at about that level. The exaggerated nature of Herodotus' statement as to the size of the lake is thus finally proved" ("Archaeological Discoveries in Egypt, 1899–1900," *Times*, 24 April 1900, p. 12). This issue is well beyond the scope of the present monograph; for Caton-Thompson's treatment of it, see, e.g., Caton-Thompson and Gardner 1934.

after another,² and the only printed records so far are brief summaries in the Athenaeum 1900, pp. 600–1 and the Archiv für Papyrusforschung I pp. 376–8.³

The oldest cemetery was a group of Middle empire graves on a ~~small~~ rise at a short distance from the town ruins in a SE direction, beyond the Roman cemetery and at the E. end of the main Ptolemaic cemetery. A New Empire cemetery lay farther to the S. ~~of~~ over a ridge, ˬwith a smaller group on the NE side of it.ˬ⁴ The geography was something like this:

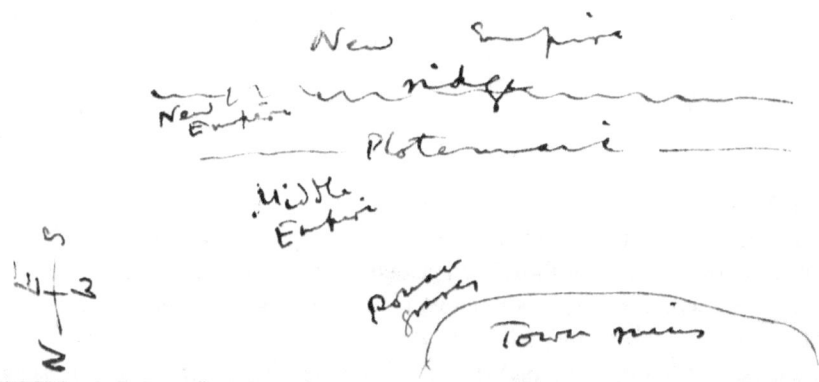

[p. 2]
The Middle Empire tombs were ˬ(a)ˬ of small size, the coffins being plain stone or (rectangular) wood, when there were any. Some had been plundered. The objects found consisted of pottery and small objects –beads, scarabs, amulets, kohl pots etc. (b) slightly farther east, a row of large tombs, without coffins (the bodies were much decayed, & possibly wooden coffins had perished); pottery and small objects ˬmuchˬ as in (a). The bulk of the O.E. [Old Empire] pottery and a selection of the small antiquities accompanying it went to the Cairo Museum (including a small alabaster kohl pot with lid, limestone ditto, scarabs, beads, glassware,⁵ small bronze objects) – the rest to California University, on whose behalf the excavations were undertaken.⁶ Whether these would furnish evidence of the kind you want I cannot say; we were not especially looking for it.

We too worked for a short time at Qasr es-Sagha and found one unplundered

---

²Grenfell had just died, 18 May 1926.
³For a third "printed record," see now App. C.
⁴The inserted text is squeezed into the space following the colon in the next sentence.
⁵The reading is a difficult one; only the "gl-" is certain.
⁶"O.E." would seem to be a mistake for "M.E." The list of finds (App. C, n. 20) does not include any "Old Empire" objects in its enumeration of the material "retained by Gizeh Museum"; it does mention "46 Middle Empire pots" and "a number of beads, scarabs, ushebti-figures, etc., from the new and the middle empires." Among the Tebtunis objects in Berkeley, PAHMA inv. 6-20817, 6-20876, and 6-20877 are alabaster kohl pots dated to the Middle Kingdom.

tomb with a large inscribed ˏwoodenˏ sarcophagus – now at Cairo.[7]

Please let me know if there is anything that I can usefully add to the above.

Yrs. faithfully[8]

A.S. Hunt

Letter II

15 July 1926 [letterhead: Queen's College, Oxford.]

Dear Miss Caton-Thompson

I should say that our evidence was distinctly against the theory of submergence, at any rate so far as the earliest cemeter~~y~~ies wa~~s~~ere concerned. The smaller tombs were ~~somewhat~~ only about 1 – 1½ m. deep, so that if they had been covered with water for any lengthy period, wooden coffins could not have survived at all, I imagine, much less have retained their rectangular shape. In the N.E. tombs too there were remains of wooden coffins, some certainly much decayed owing to
[p. 2]
damp, but still recognisable reeds on which the body was sometimes placed had also survived. I don't think that bones had rotted appreciably, though I cannot speak definitely as to that; pottery was in pretty good condition, I feel sure, but that you can easily verify at Cairo.
Yes, we made one or two allusions to the M.E. tombs at Umm el-B. in Fayum Towns,[9] and it certainly never occurred to us that the water level had subsequently been higher. Whose theory is this, by the way? It seems to need a considerable backing.

Yours faithfully,[10]

A. S. Hunt

---

[7] "[L]arge" is a correction (the overwritten word seems to have ended in "t"). For the find in question, see Grenfell and Hunt 1900–1901, 5–6.

[8] "Faithfully" is written quite rapidly: "f-th-f-ly."

[9] Cf. *P.Fay.*, p. 6.

[10] "[F]aith-" in "faithfully" is a correction. Perhaps Hunt had started to write "sincerely."

Appendix G

Goodspeed's Proposal to Transfer Some Tebtunis Papyri from Berkeley to U.C.L.A.

In 1937 Edgar J. Goodspeed retired from his professorship at the University of Chicago. Next year, he and his wife Elfleda moved to the Bel Air section of Los Angeles close to U.C.L.A., where from 1940 to 1942 as a part-time lecturer he taught classes in the "History of the Founding of Christianity."[1] In that time he came to believe that he owed his and Elfleda's cordial reception at the university in part to a connection established by his past work on the Tebtunis papyri: "After all," he later wrote (Goodspeed 1953, 287), "I had worked on California's papyri and helped publish them some forty years before!"

In the wake of Goodspeed's lengthy reticence about his contribution to the Tebtunis enterprise, this statement jars.[2] Perhaps it is simply the product of an accomplished man's ego; the great success that he later found as a New Testament scholar, indeed a public intellectual, had given him a substantial one. But it may also reflect a curious reconnection, mental if not physical, that he had with the Tebtunis papyri about a decade before *As I Remember* was published. In late 1942—four years after the first shipment of papyri had come from Oxford to Berkeley (1938), four years after his own settling in Los Angeles, and just after his full retirement from teaching—Goodspeed recommended transfer of part of the papyrus collection from Berkeley to U.C.L.A. His own motives for this recommendation remain

[1] He was affiliated with the Department of History, and his title was "Lecturer in the History of Religions." According to the UCLA *General Catalogue*, digital copies of which are accessible from https://www.registrar.ucla.edu/Archives/General-Catalog-Archive/UCLA-General-Catalog (consulted 29 July 2020), he taught the indicated two-credit course for three years, always in the spring semester (1940, 1941, 1942). In points of detail this contradicts the account in *As I Remember*, which refers to teaching in winter sessions and termination at age seventy (Goodspeed 1953, 287, 300).

[2] As we have seen, his assessment of his contribution in "Abroad in the Nineties" is more modest: Epilogue, n. 48.

vague (see below). Inasmuch as he was no longer teaching, the papyri would serve him no pedagogical purpose. He had long ago abandoned the practice of papyrology in its narrow sense (cf. the Epilogue), so he would probably not have contemplated fresh editorial work on them, and the papyri themselves were devoid of Christian content, thus not in accord with his primary interests of so many years. Nevertheless, his proposal generated correspondence, samples of which are to be found in the records of the University's Office of the President archived at Berkeley's Bancroft Library.[3] These items amount to a partial dossier of seven items that tell the middle part of the story—anything pertinent to the initial recommendation or its final disposition must be extrapolated, in the first instance, from the surviving correspondence, in the second, from the fact of the recommendation's eventual and mysterious failure. Parties to the correspondence, aside from Goodspeed himself, are Robert Gordon Sproul (1891–1975), president of the University of California at Berkeley (1930–1952);[4] George Albert Pettitt (1901–1976), Sproul's assistant since 1939 and middleman for the Goodspeed proposal; Professor Alfred L. Kroeber (1876–1960), anthropologist and longtime director of Berkeley's Museum of Anthropology;[5] and Professor William Hardy Alexander (1878–1962), chair of the Department of Classics (1942–1948).[6]

The earliest item, 26 October 1942, is a memorandum from Pettitt to Sproul summarizing Kroeber's initial reaction to the Goodspeed proposal. Kroeber thinks that (1) the collection, having already been fully studied and published, would provide little stimulation to further scholarship; (2) the papyri are "too valuable to be used or even handled by students, graduate or undergraduate"; (3) the contents of the papyri are already known at U.C.L.A. (presumably through the library's possession of the published volumes). Since "the originals now have chiefly an historical and prestige value," the principal concern is their best possible preservation. Goodspeed's exact intentions are (to Kroeber) obscure, except for the idea of displaying some samples in the U.C.L.A. library.

Goodspeed's "objectives," as subsequently understood by Pettitt and expressed in a letter to Kroeber, 7 January 1943, were to secure "a few of the more spectacular examples [...] for display purposes" and a "respectable" number of

---

[3] Office of the President records, CU-5, Series 2, 1942:231 (1 item), 1943:447 (6 items, not counting duplicates). We are grateful to Emily Cole for bringing this material to our attention.

[4] Sproul, perhaps most associated today with the anti-communist "Loyalty Oath" controversy (1949–1951), oversaw a period of tremendous growth for the University. An extensive collection of oral histories concerning him: Regional Oral History Office 1986; press obituary: *New York Times*, 12 September 1975, p. 36.

[5] For Kroeber, a pivotal figure in American anthropology (and father of author Ursula K[roeber] Le Guin), see, e.g., Parsons 1961; a typical press obituary: *Oakland Tribune*, 5 October 1960 (p. 19, front page of section). Unsurprisingly neither takes issue with his actions toward the Native American man known as Ishi specifically or indigenous peoples more generally, behavior now subject to critical reappraisal.

[6] Hardy: https://dbcs.rutgers.edu/all-scholars/8502-alexander-william-hardy (consulted 30 July 2020).

others to explore possibilities for their further (unspecified) study. Goodspeed, according to Pettitt, "said that it would be quite all right to have all of the material sent down [to Los Angeles from Berkeley] put between glass and bound before shipping"—unaware that some 1700 of the papyri, including "the more spectacular examples," had already been sealed in Vinylite in 1940 by Edmund H. Kase, Jr. (cf. *Transactions of the American Philological Association* 71 [1940] xliv–xlv). Kroeber soon (letter of 11 January) brought Alexander into the loop, inquiring of him whether the Department of Classics might have an interest in the papyri, especially since, Kroeber has obviously now learned, "some of them remain unpublished." He credits Goodspeed as "an eminently suitable person to do anything further" on the papyri, given that he "was one of the three authors of Volume 2 of the three published volumes of the Papyri." He asks for Alexander's reaction, pending consultation with his department. Meantime (still on 11 January), Kroeber recommends to Pettitt doing "everything possible to facilitate further study of the Papyri by Professor Goodspeed." He proceeds to educate Pettitt on the history of the papyri, "technically the property of the Museum of Anthropology" while they were in England for editing, but turned over to the University Library upon their arrival in Berkeley. "They were secured," he tells Pettitt, "with funds supplied by Mrs. Hearst in connection with her financing of the Reisner Egyptian Expedition." He now backs anything that will further the collection's study, including (it seems) splitting its housing between Berkeley and Los Angeles and cooperative study involving the Classics Departments of both campuses. Pettitt's handwritten remarks, signed "GAP" in the upper right of a copy of this letter, inform President Sproul that

> [t]his [letter] will indicate further progress in Dr. Goodspeed's request for placement of some of the Tebtunis Papyri at Los Angeles. I saw Dr. Goodspeed during my last southern trip and am quite charmed by him. He was deeply pleased by the fact that you had remembered his suggestion. I think we may work something out.

Alexander's reaction came soon ("January 19, 1943," with "1943" corrected by hand from "1942") in a densely packed, one-page letter sent to President Sproul, composed later on the same day of the Department's meeting in which the topic was considered. In short, the Department was opposed to shipping papyri from Berkeley as "not in accordance with the best university practice in these matters of ancient documents [...] The general principle is that the Scholar interested should visit the place where the documents are deposited, not that the documents should be shipped to the Scholar." In other words, if Goodspeed wanted to study them, he should come to Berkeley, this insistence intending no disrespect to Goodspeed's reputation as one "whose competence in the field is a matter of general knowledge in university circles."

A month later, in a second memorandum to Sproul, 17 February 1943, Pettitt reported that Alexander, now better informed about the background of the proposal, had removed his objections—on two conditions: (1) that the papyri to be shipped be bound in glass or plastic to protect "against further fragmentation in transit"; (2) that there be no permanent division of the collection, the transfer being classified "as a temporary loan." Pettitt reports Kroeber's assent, adding Kroeber's recommendation that Goodspeed should "at his convenience come to Berkeley to make a personal selection of the specimens that interest him."

Finally, 26 February 1943, Sproul writes to Goodspeed confirming the results of his conversation with him, apparently by phone (but this is unstated), and of Pettitt's recent personal visit with Goodspeed in Los Angeles. (It is uncertain whether this refers to a second visit or to the visit already mentioned in Pettitt's handwritten addendum to Kroeber's letter of 11 January.) "[T]here are," Sproul tells Goodspeed, "no objections at Berkeley to the temporary loan of selected specimens [...] for further study on the Los Angeles campus." Kroeber will gladly assist Goodspeed if he should come to Berkeley to make his selection. From a handwritten notation at the lower right of Sproul's file copy of the letter, apparently in Pettitt's hand, it can be concluded that Goodspeed did plan to come up to Berkeley—but in Kroeber's absence. Addressed to a "Mr. Stevens,"[7] the notation indicates, "Goodspeed is coming north next month. Whom should he see in Kroeber's absence?" Below this, in thicker writing, is an arrow pointing down to the name "Gifford."[8]

There the dossier comes to its end—a loose one that does not confirm Goodspeed's coming to Berkeley and making his selection. We only know that no papyri were ever shipped to Los Angeles from Berkeley and presume that, despite unanimous approval of the parties concerned—Sproul, Pettitt, Kroeber, Alexander—for reasons that await discovery, the Goodspeed recommendation never came to fruition.

---

[7] Frank Clifford Stevens (1885–1965), executive secretary, Office of the President. His oral memoir of his forty years of service: Regional Cultural History Project 1959.

[8] Edward Winslow Gifford (1887–1959), then associate professor of anthropology and curator at the Museum.

Figure 19: Goodspeed in the year in which *As I Remember* appeared.
Unknown photographer, 14 March 1953. *Los Angeles Herald Examiner*
Photo Collection/Los Angeles Public Library.

WORKS CITED

Abdel Azim, M., and N. Ayyad. 1948. "A Preliminary Report on the Value of Palm-Leaf Traps in the Survey and Treatment of Streams Infested with Snails." *Transactions of the Royal Society of Tropical Medicine and Hygiene* 42:231–246.

Abt, J. 2011. *American Egyptologist: The Life of James Henry Breasted and the Creation of His Oriental Institute*. Chicago: University of Chicago Press.

Adams, H. 1918. *The Education of Henry Adams: An Autobiography*. Boston: Houghton Mifflin.

Adams, R. H. 2013. *The College Graces of Oxford and Cambridge*. Oxford: Bodleian Library.

Allison, R. W. 1975. "Guide to the Edgar J. Goodspeed Papyri." *Zeitschrift für Papyrologie und Epigraphik* 16:27–32.

American Library Annual. 1916–1917. New York: Office of the *Publishers' Weekly*.

Andrews, E. n.d. "A Journal on the Bedawin, 1889–1912." 2 vols. Unpublished typescript in the library of the American Philosophical Society.

Annual Report. 1907. *Annual Report of the Board of Foreign Missions of the United Presbyterian Church of North America*. Philadelphia: Patteson Printing House.

Annual Report. 1916. *Annual Report of the Board of Foreign Missions of the United Presbyterian Church of North America*. Philadelphia: publisher omitted.

Archive of Performances of Greek & Roman Drama. Directed by F. Macintosh. http://www.apgrd.ox.ac.uk

Army Map Service. 1947. *El Gharaq Elsultani*. 1:100,000. Washington, DC: United States Army.

Bademan, R. B. 2006. "'Monkeying with the Bible': Edgar J. Goodspeed's American Translation." *Religion and American Culture: A Journal of Interpretation* 16:55–93.

Baedeker, K., ed. 1898. *Egypt: Handbook for Travellers*. 4th ed. Leipzig: Karl Baedeker.

———. 1902. *Egypt: Handbook for Travellers*. 5th ed. Leipzig: Karl Baedeker.

Bagnoud, M. 2016. "P.Gen. inv. 187: Un texte apocalyptique apocryphe inédit." *Museum Helveticum* 73:129–153.

Bekker, I., ed. 1854. *Demosthenis orationes*. Vol. 1. Leipzig: Bernhard Tauchnitz.

Bell, H. I. 1952. "Sir Frederic George Kenyon, 1863–1952." *Proceedings of the British Academy* 38:268–294.

———, and R. S. Simpson. 2004. "Hunt, Arthur Surridge (1871–1934)." *Oxford Dictionary of National Biography*, 23 September 2004. https://doi.org/10.1093/ref:odnb/34055

Bernard, C., ed. 1922. *Jules Nicole, 1842–1921*. Geneva: Édition *Revue mensuelle*.

Bierbrier, M. L., ed. 2012. *Who Was Who in Egyptology*. 4th ed. London: Egypt Exploration Society.
Bissing, F. W. von. 1901. *Metallgefässe: Catalogue général des antiquités égyptiennes du Musée du Caire, nos. 3426–3587*. Vienna: A. Holzhausen.
———. 1902. *Fayencegefässe: Catalogue général des antiquités égyptiennes du Musée du Caire, nos. 3618–4000, 18001–18037, 18600, 18503*. Vienna: A. Holzhausen.
———. 1904–1907. *Steingefässe: Catalogue général des antiquités égyptiennes du Musée du Caire, nos. 18065–18793*. 2 vols. Vienna: A. Holzhausen.
Blass, F. 1897. Review of J. Nicole, *Le laboureur de Ménandre*. *Literarisches Centralblatt für Deutschland* 48:1648–1650.
Blight, D. 2018. *Frederick Douglass, Prophet of Freedom*. New York: Simon & Schuster.
Borchardt, L. 1899. "Der zweite Papyrusfund von Kahun und die zeitliche Festlegung des mittleren Reiches der ägyptischen Geschichte." *Zeitschrift für Ägyptisches Sprache* 37:89–103.
Boutros, R. W. 2005. "The Christian Monuments of Tebtunis." In *Christianity and Monasticism in the Fayoum Oasis*, edited by G. Gabra, 119–131. Cairo: American University in Cairo Press.
Boyer, J. W. 2015. *The University of Chicago: A History*. Chicago: University of Chicago Press.
Breccia, E. 1935. "In Egitto con Girolamo Vitelli." *Aegyptus* 15:255–262.
Budge, E. A. W. 1898. *The Nile: Notes for Travellers in Egypt*. 6th ed. London and Cairo: Thomas Cook & Son.
———. 1920. *By Nile and Tigris: A Narrative of Journeys in Egypt and Mesopotamia on behalf of the British Museum between the Years 1886 and 1913*. 2 vols. London: John Murray.
Burkhalter, F. 2002. "Le 'tarif de Coptos': La douane de Coptos, les fermiers de l'*apostolion* et le préfet du désert de Bérénice." In *Autour de Coptos: Actes du colloque organisé au Musée des Beaux-Arts de Lyon (17–18 mars 2000)*, edited by M.-F. Boussac et al., 199–233. Lyon: Maison de l'Orient méditerranéen-Jean Pouilloux.
Burt, S., and T. Burt. 2019. *Oxford Weather and Climate since 1767*. Oxford: Oxford University Press.
Cannadine, D. 2001. *Ornamentalism: How the British Saw Their Empire*. London: Penguin Books.
Carp, T. C. 1972. "Some Documentary and Literary Papyri of the Roman Period." Ph.D. dissertation, University of California, Berkeley.
Caton-Thompson, G., and E. W. Gardner. 1934. *The Desert Fayum*. London: Royal Anthropological Institute of Great Britain and Ireland.
Catterall, R. C. H. 1903. *The Second Bank of the United States*. Chicago: University of Chicago Press.
Charles, R. H. 1899. "Mr. E. A. W. Budge's Edition of the Lives of Mabâ' Ṣĕyôn and Gabra Krĕstôs." *Hermathena* 10, no. 25:397–406.
———. 1900. *The Ascension of Isaiah: Translated from the Ethiopic Version, Which, together with the New Greek Fragment, the Latin Versions and the Latin Translation of the Slavonic, Is Here Published in Full*. London: A. & C. Black.

———. 1916. *The Chronicle of John, Bishop of Nikiu, Translated from Zotenberg's Ethiopic Text*. London: Williams and Norgate.
Clark, W. 2006. *Academic Charisma and the Origins of the Research University*. Chicago: University of Chicago Press.
Cobb, J. H., and L. B. Jennings. 1948. *A Biography & Bibliography of Edgar Johnson Goodspeed*. Chicago: University of Chicago Press.
Coles, R. 2007. "Oxyrhynchus: A City and Its Texts." In *Oxyrhynchus: A City and Its Texts*, edited by A. K. Bowman et al., 3–16. Graeco-Roman Memoirs 93. London: Egypt Exploration Society.
Cook, J. I. 1981. *Edgar J. Goodspeed, Articulate Scholar*. Biblical Scholarship in North America 4. Chico: Scholars Press.
Cooper, K., and J. Hersey. 1997. *The Complete Book of Floorcloths: Designs & Techniques for Painting Great-Looking Canvas Rugs*. New York: Lark Books.
Cromwell, J. 2014. "Walter Ewing Crum (1865–1944): A Coptic Scholar 'sui generis.'" In *Christlicher Orient im Porträt: Wissenschaftsgeschichte des christlichen Orients*, edited by P. Bukovec, 2:407–422. Hamburg: Dr. Kovač.
Cronon, W. 1991. *Nature's Metropolis: Chicago and the Great West*. New York: W. W. Norton.
Danker, F. W. 1988. *A Century of Greco-Roman Philology*. Atlanta: Scholars Press.
Davis, S. J. 2001. *The Cult of St Thecla: A Tradition of Women's Piety in Late Antiquity*. Oxford: Oxford University Press.
Davis, T., et al. 1907. *The Tomb of Iouiya and Touiyou*. London: Archibald Constable.
Deuel, L. 1965. *Testaments of Time: The Search for Lost Manuscripts and Records*. New York: Knopf.
Dillmann, A. 1899. *Grammatik der äthiopischen Sprache*, 2nd ed. by C. Bezold. Leipzig: C. H. Tauchnitz.
Dindorf, G., and F. Blass, eds. 1885. *Demosthenis orationes*. Vol. 1. 4th ed. Leipzig: B. G. Teubner.
Dixon, H. L. 1903. *"Saying Grace" Historically Considered, and Numerous Forms of Grace Taken from Ancient and Modern Sources*. Oxford and London: James Parker.
Dora, C. 2005. "Adolf Fäh." *Historisches Lexikon der Schweiz*. https://hls-dhs-dss.ch/de/articles/042372/2005-10-24/
Drower, M. 1995. *Flinders Petrie: A Life in Archaeology*. 2nd ed. Madison: University of Wisconsin Press.
———, ed. 2004. *Letters from the Desert: The Correspondence of Flinders and Hilda Petrie*. Oxford: Aris and Phillips.
Echenberg, M. J. 2007. *Plague Ports: The Global Urban Impact of Bubonic Plague, 1894–1901*. New York: New York University Press.
Edgar, C. C. 1905. *Graeco-Egyptian Coffins, Masks, and Portraits: Catalogue général des antiquités égyptiennes du Musée du Caire, nos. 33101–33285*. Cairo: Institut français d'archéologie orientale.
Egypt and How to See It. 1907. New York: Doubleday, Page.
Egyptian Ministry of Finance. 1914. *Atlas of Egypt Compiled at the Offices of the Survey*. 2 vols. Cairo: Government Press.

Falcetta, A. 2018. *The Daily Discoveries of a Bible Scholar and Manuscript Hunter: A Biography of James Rendel Harris (1852–1941)*. London: T&T Clark.
Farrar, F. W. 1889. *Lives of the Fathers: Sketches of Church History in Biography*. 2 vols. Edinburgh: Adam and Charles Black.
Gallazzi, C., and G. Hadji-Minaglou. 2000. *Tebtynis I: La reprise des fouilles et le quartier de la chapelle d'Isis-Thermouthis*. Cairo: Institut français d'archéologie orientale.
Galsworthy, J. 1995 [1922]. *The Forsyte Saga*. Oxford: Oxford University Press.
Garstin, W. E. 1900. *Report upon the Administration of the Public Works Department for 1899*. Cairo: National Printing Department.
Gertzen, T. L. 2012. "Giant of Egyptology, 28th of a Series: Friedrich Wilhelm von Bissing (1873–1956)." *KMT: A Modern Journal of Ancient Egypt* 23.2:76–82.
Gill, D. W. J. 2011. *Sifting the Soil of Greece: The Early Years of the British School at Athens (1886–1919)*. Bulletin of the Institute of Classical Studies Supplement 111. London: Institute of Classical Studies.
Gilman, A. G., and M. G. Gilman. 1927. *Who's Who in Illinois: Women-Makers of History*. Chicago: The Eclectic Publishers.
Goldschmidt, A. 2000. *Biographical Dictionary of Modern Egypt*. Boulder: Lynne Rienner.
Goodspeed, C. T. B. 1932. *Thomas Wakefield Goodspeed*. Chicago: University of Chicago Press.
Goodspeed, E. J. 1897. "Description of an Unedited Syriac Manuscript of the New Testament." B. D. thesis, University of Chicago.
———. 1898a. "The Ayer Papyrus: A Mathematical Fragment." *American Journal of Philology* 19:25–39.
———. 1898b. "The Washîm Papyrus of *Iliad* Θ 1–68." *American Journal of Archaeology* 2:347–356.
———. 1899a. "The Newberry Gospels." *American Journal of Theology* 3:116–137.
———. 1899b. "Work and Workers." *Biblical World* 14:446–449.
———. 1900a. "From Haifa to Nazareth." *Biblical World* 16:407–413.
———. 1900b. "A Papyrus Fragment of *Iliad* E." *American Journal of Philology* 21:310–314.
———. 1901a. "The Book of Thekla." *American Journal of Semitic Languages and Literatures* 17:65–95.
———. 1901b. *The Book of Thekla*. Chicago: University of Chicago Press.
———. 1902a. "How Ancient Records Are Dug Out of the Sands of Egypt." *Chicago Tribune*, Sunday, 16 November 1902:41.
———. 1902b. "Karanis Papyri." *Studies in Classical Philology* 3:1–66.
———. 1902c. *The Newberry Gospels*. Chicago: University of Chicago Press.
———. 1903a. "Alexandrian Hexameter Fragments." *Journal of Hellenic Studies* 23:237–247.
———. 1903b. "The Ayer Papyrus." *American Mathematical Monthly* 10:133–135.
———. 1903c. "A Fourth-Century Deed from Egypt." *Biblia* 15:333–337.
———. 1904a. "Greek Ostraca in America." *American Journal of Philology* 25:45–58.
———. 1904b. "Papyrus Digging with Grenfell and Hunt." *The Independent* 57:1066–1070.
———. 1905. "Greek Documents in the Museum of the New York Historical Society." In *Mélanges Nicole*, edited by P. Moriaud et al., 177–191. Geneva: W. Kündig.
———. 1908. "Karanis Accounts." *Classical Philology* 3:428–434.
———. 1910. "The Harrison Papyri." *Classical Philology* 5:320–322.

———. 1923. *The New Testament: An American Translation*. Chicago: University of Chicago Press.
———. 1935. *The Curse in the Colophon*. Chicago and New York: Willett, Clark.
———. 1953. *As I Remember*. New York: Harper.
———. n.d. "Abroad in the Nineties." Unpublished typescript with handwritten emendations, SCRC, University of Chicago.
———, and E. C. Colwell. 1935. *A Greek Papyrus Reader with Vocabulary*. Chicago: University of Chicago Press.
Goodspeed, T. W. 1916. *A History of the University of Chicago Founded by John D. Rockefeller: The First Quarter-Century*. Chicago: University of Chicago Press.
———. 1926. *Ernest De Witt Burton: A Biographical Sketch*. Chicago: University of Chicago Press.
———. 1928. *William Rainey Harper: First President of the University of Chicago*. Chicago: University of Chicago Press.
Gosse, E. 1984 [1907]. *Father and Son: A Study of Two Temperaments*. Harmondsworth: Penguin Books.
Grant, F. C. 2004. "Lake, Kirsopp (1872–1946)." *Oxford Dictionary of National Biography*, 23 September 2004. https://doi.org/10.1093/ref:odnb/34375
Graves, F. P. 1904. "The Recent Commemoration at Oxford." *The School Review: A Journal of Secondary Education* 119:673–685.
Grene, D. 2007. *Of Farming & Classics: A Memoir*. Chicago: University of Chicago Press.
Grenfell, B. P. 1896–1897. "Oxyrhynchus and Its Papyri." *Archaeological Report (Egypt Exploration Fund)*:1–12.
———, and A. S. Hunt. 1897. ΛΟΓΙΑ ΙΗΣΟΥ: *Sayings of Our Lord from an Early Greek Papyrus*. London: Henry Frowde.
———. 1898. *Menander's ΓΕΩΡΓΟC: A Revised Text of the Geneva Fragment with Translation and Notes*. Oxford: Clarendon Press.
———. 1900. "A Large Find of Papyri." *Athenæum*, 12 May 1900, 3785:600–601.
———. 1900–1901. "Graeco-Roman Branch: Excavations in the Fayûm." *Archaeological Report (Egypt Exploration Fund)*:4–7.
———. 1901. "A Large Find of Ptolemaic Papyri." *Archiv für Papyrusforschung* 1:376–378.
———. 1901–1902. "Graeco-Roman Branch: Excavations in the Fayûm and at El Hîbeh." *Archaeological Report (Egypt Exploration Fund)*:2–5.
———. 1902–1903. "Graeco-Roman Branch: Excavations at Hîbeh, Cynopolis and Oxyrhynchus." *Archaeological Report (Egypt Exploration Fund)*:1–9.
Griffith, P. 2009. "Oman, Sir Charles William Chadwick (1860–1946)." *Oxford Dictionary of National Biography*, 8 October 2009. https://doi.org/10.1093/ref:odnb/35312
Grossman, R. 2016. "Chicago Flashback: The Wheel Deal." *Chicago Tribune*, Section 1, 15 May 2016:23.
———. 2018. "Chicago Flashback: Disneyland's 1890s Forebear." *Chicago Tribune*, Section 1, 14 January 2018:23.
Haeberlin, C. 1897. "Griechische Papyri." *Zentralblatt für Bibliothekswesen* 14:1–13.
Hagen, F., and K. Ryholt. 2016. *The Antiquities Trade in Egypt, 1880–1930: The H. O. Lange Papers*. Scientia Danica, Series H, Humanistica 4, vol. 8. Copenhagen: Det Kongelige Danske Videnskabernes Selskab.

Hallwas, J. 2011. "The Remarkable Tunnicliff Sisters." *McDonough County Voice*. 1 ("Lawyer and Scholar Helen Tunnicliff"): 13 August 2011; 2 ("Sarah and Ruth"): 20 August 2011.
Hanson, A. E. 2001. "Text & Context for the Illustrated Herbal from Tebtunis." In *Atti del XXII Congresso Internazionale di Papirologia*, edited by I. Andorlini et al., 1:585–604. Florence: Istituto papirologico "G. Vitelli."
Harnack, A. von. 1900. *Das Wesen des Christentums: Sechzehn Vorlesungen vor Studierenden aller Facultäten im Wintersemester 1899/1900 an der Universität Berlin gehalten*. Leipzig: Hinrichs.
Harrauer, H. 2007. "Carl Wessely (1860–1931)." In *Hermae: Scholars and Scholarship in Papyrology*, edited by M. Capasso, 1:71–75. Pisa: Giardini.
Hart, G. E., and D. A. Pacyga. 1979. *Chicago: A Historical Guide to the Neighborhoods: The Loop and South Side*. Chicago: Chicago Historical Society.
Hearst, K. 2005. "Phoebe Apperson Hearst: The Making of an Upper-Class Woman, 1842–1919." Ph.D. dissertation, Columbia University.
Heinze, H., et al. 1892. *Souvenir Map of the World's Columbian Exposition at Jackson Park and Midway Plaisance*. Scale not stated. Chicago: A. Zeese.
Hickey, T. M. 2014. "A Misclassified Sherd from the Archive of Theopemptos and Zacharias (Ashm. D. O. 810)." *Tyche* 29:45–49.
———. 2017. "Grenfell and Hunt in the Fayyūm: Two Letters to J. Gilbart Smyly." *Bulletin of the American Society of Papyrologists* 54:219–235.
———, and J. G. Keenan. 2016. "At the Creation: Seven Letters from Grenfell, 1897." *Analecta Papyrologica* 28:351–382.
Hickey, T. M., and K. A. Worp. 1997. "The Dossier of Patermouthios *sidêrourgos*: New Texts from Chicago." *Bulletin of the American Society of Papyrologists* 34:79–109.
Hoffman, A., and P. Cole. 2011. *Sacred Trash: The Lost and Found World of the Cairo Genizah*. New York: Nextbook and Schocken.
Holmes, R. 1985. *Footsteps: Adventures of a Romantic Biographer*. New York: Viking.
Hombert, M. 1933. "Le commerce des papyrus en Égypte." *Chronique d'Égypte* 8:148–154.
Howat, G. M. D. 2011. "Grace, William Gilbert [W. G.] (1848–1915)." *Oxford Dictionary of National Biography*, 6 January 2011. https://doi.org/10.1093/ref:odnb/33500
Humphreys, A. 2011. *Grand Hotels of Egypt in the Golden Age of Travel*. Cairo: American University in Cairo Press.
———. 2015. *On the Nile in the Golden Age of Travel*. Cairo: American University in Cairo Press.
Hunt, A. S. 1920. "J. P. Mahaffy." *Aegyptus* 1:217–221.
Hyde Park Union Church [1989]. Pamphlet describing the Church's stained-glass windows.
Imaging Papyri Project. 1998. "Grenfell's Cigarettes Invoice." *Oxyrhynchus: A City and Its Texts*. Online exhibition. http://www.papyrology.ox.ac.uk/POxy/VExhibition/introduction/cigarettes.html
Irwin, R. 2008. *Dangerous Knowledge: Orientalism and Its Discontents*. New York: Overlook Press.
Jacoby, A. 1900. *Ein neues Evangelienfragment*. Strassburg: Karl J. Trübner.
James, L. R. 1963. "In the Country: Controlling the Rook." *Punch*, 8 May 1963, 244:676.
Johnson, A. H., and P. R. H. Slee. 2004. "Burrows, Montagu (1819–1905)." *Oxford Dictionary of National Biography*, 23 September 2004. https://doi.org/10.1093/ref:odnb/32199

Johnson, W. A. 2004. *Bookrolls and Scribes in Oxyrhynchus.* Toronto: University of Toronto Press.

Karabacek, J., et al. 1894. *Papyrus Erzherzog Rainer: Führer durch die Ausstellung.* 2nd ed. Vienna: Sammlung der Papyrus Erzherzog Rainer.

Kaser, M. 1964. "Gradenwitz, Otto." *Neue Deutsche Biographie,* 6:702–703. Berlin: Duncker & Humblot.

Keenan, J. G. 1971. "Two Papyrus Fragments of the *Odyssey.*" *California Studies in Classical Antiquity* 4:199–202.

———. 2003. "Deserted Villages: From the Ancient to the Medieval Fayyūm." *Bulletin of the American Society of Papyrologists* 40:119–139.

———. 2009. "The History of the Discipline." In *The Oxford Handbook of Papyrology,* edited by R. S. Bagnall, 59–78. Oxford: Oxford University Press.

Kendrick, T. D., et al. 1952. "Sir Frederic Kenyon, G.B.E., K.C.B." *British Museum Quarterly,* December 1952, 17.4:63–70.

Kenyon, F. G., ed. 1891a. ΑΘΗΝΑΙΩΝ ΠΟΛΙΤΕΙΑ: *Aristotle on the Constitution of Athens.* London: British Museum and Longmans.

———, ed. 1891b. *Classical Texts from Papyri in the British Museum, Including the Newly Discovered Poems of Herodas.* London: British Museum and Longmans.

———, ed. 1897a. *The Letters of Elizabeth Barrett Browning.* London: Smith, Elder.

———, ed. 1897b. *The Poems of Bacchylides, from a Papyrus in the British Museum.* London: British Museum and Longmans.

———, ed. 1897c. *The Poetical Works of Elizabeth Barrett Browning.* London: Smith, Elder.

———. 1899. *The Palaeography of Greek Papyri.* Oxford: Clarendon Press.

Kersel, M. M. 2010. "The Changing Legal Landscape for Middle Eastern Archaeology during the Colonial Era, 1800–1930." In *Pioneers to the Past: American Archaeologists in the Middle East, 1919–1920,* edited by G. Emberling, 85–90. Oriental Institute Museum Publications 30. Chicago: Oriental Institute of the University of Chicago.

Kimber, G. 2021. "Nastiness and Joy: A Virtuosic Biography of D. H. Lawrence." *Times Literary Supplement,* 28 May 2021, 6165:3, 5.

Kludas, A. 1986. *Die Geschichte der deutschen Passagierschiffahrt.* Vol. 1. Schriften des deutschen Schiffahrtsmuseums 18. Hamburg: E. Kabel.

———. 1991. *Die Seeschiffe des Norddeutschen Lloyd.* Vol. 1. Herford: Koehler.

Larson, E. 2003. *The Devil in the White City: Murder, Magic, and Madness at the Fair That Changed America.* New York: Crown Publishers.

Law, G. 2004. "Charles, Robert Henry (1855–1931)." *Oxford Dictionary of National Biography,* 23 September 2004. https://doi.org/10.1093/ref:odnb/32370

Lawrence, T. E. 1935. *Seven Pillars of Wisdom: A Triumph.* Garden City, NY: Doubleday, Doran.

Lehnus, L. 2007. "Bernard Pyne Grenfell (1869–1926) e Arthur Surridge Hunt (1871–1934)." In *Hermae: Scholars and Scholarship in Papyrology,* edited by M. Capasso, 1:115–141. Pisa: Giardini.

Lightfoot, J. B. 1889–1890. *The Apostolic Fathers,* 2nd ed. Part I (1890) in 2 vols. Part II (1889) in 3 vols. London and New York: Macmillan. Reprint Hildesheim: Georg Olms Verlag, 1973.

Lockwood, F. C. 1929. *The Life of Edward E. Ayer.* Chicago: A. C. McClurg.

Ludwich, A., ed. 1902. *Homeri Ilias*. Vol. 1. Leipzig: B. G. Teubner.
Lutz, H. F. 1930. *Egyptian Statues and Statuettes in the Museum of Anthropology of the University of California*. University of California Publications: Egyptian Archaeology 5. Leipzig: J. C. Hinrich.
Lyon, D. J., comp. 1976. *The Denny List*. Vol. 2. London: National Maritime Museum.
Macintosh, F., and C. Kenward. 2020. *Agamemnon: A Performance History*. Oxford: Archive of Performances of Greek and Roman Drama. Downloadable through Apple Books.
Macmillan & Co. 1905. *Guide to Egypt and the Sûdân*. 3rd ed. London: Macmillan.
Maddison, I., comp. 1917. *Bryn Mawr College Calendar: Register of Alumnae and Former Students*. January 1917, vol. 10.1. Bryn Mawr: Bryn Mawr College.
Manning, F. 1990 [1929]. *The Middle Parts of Fortune: Somme and Ancre, 1916*. New York: Viking Penguin.
Marden, P. S. 1912. *Egyptian Days*. Boston and New York: Houghton Mifflin.
Margoliouth, D. S. 1912. *Cairo, Jerusalem, and Damascus: Three Chief Cities of the Egyptian Sultans*. New York: Dodd, Mead.
———, and R. T. Stearn. 2015. "Conybeare, Frederick Cornwallis (1856–1924)." *Oxford Dictionary of National Biography*, 28 May 2015. https://doi.org/10.1093/ref:odnb/32537
Mark Twain Project. 2007. "Guide to Editorial Practice (MTDP 00005)." *Mark Twain Project Online*. August 2007. http://www.marktwainproject.org:8080/xtf/view?docId=letters/MTDP00005.xml
Martin, V. 1940. *La collection de papyrus grecs de la Bibliothèque publique et universitaire et ses fondateurs Jules Nicole – Edouard Naville*. Geneva: Imprimerie Privat.
Maspero, G. 1892. "The Dog in Ancient Egypt." *Biblia* 4:333–335.
———. 1902. *Guide du visiteur au Musée du Caire*. Cairo: Institut français d'archéologie orientale.
McAdam, Jr., E. L., and G. Milne. 1963. *Johnson's Dictionary: A Modern Selection*. New York: Pantheon Books.
Meliadò, C. 2008. «*E cantando danzerò*»: PLitGoodspeed 2. Orione 1. Messina: Dipartimento di scienze dell'antichità.
Mencken, H. L. 1977. *The American Language: An Inquiry into the Development of English in the United States*. Abr. ed. New York: Alfred A. Knopf.
Metzger, B. M. 1997. *Reminiscences of an Octogenarian*. Peabody, MA: Hendrickson Publishers.
Michell, R. L. N. 1877. *Egyptian Calendar for the Year 1295 A. H. (1878 A. D.)*. Alexandria: Imprimerie française.
Milne, J. G. 1935. "Report on Coins Found at Tebtunis in 1900." *Journal of Egyptian Archaeology* 21:210–216.
Ministère des finances: Direction de la statistique. 1910. *Annuaire statistique de l'Égypte*. Cairo: Imprimerie nationale.
Montserrat, D. 2007. "News Reports: The Excavations and Their Journalistic Coverage." In *Oxyrhynchus: A City and Its Texts*, edited by A.K. Bowman et al., 28–39. Graeco-Roman Memoirs 93. London: Egypt Exploration Society.
Morris, J. 1979. *Pax Britannica: The Climax of an Empire*. London: Penguin Books.

Murray, K. E. M. 1979. *Caught in the Web of Words: James Murray and the Oxford English Dictionary*. Reprint Oxford: Oxford University Press.

Mutzafi, H. 2014. *Comparative Lexical Studies in Neo-Mandaic*. Leiden: Brill.

Neilson, K. 2011. "Kitchener, Horatio Herbert, Earl Kitchener of Khartoum (1850–1916)." *Oxford Dictionary of National Biography*, 6 January 2011. https://doi.org/10.1093/ref:odnb/34341

Nickliss, A. M. 2018. *Phoebe Apperson Hearst: A Life of Power and Politics*. Lincoln and London: University of Nebraska Press.

Nicole, J. 1897. "Le Laboureur (Γεωργός)" de Ménandre: Fragments inédits sur papyrus d'Égypte. Basel and Geneva: Georg & Co. [1898 erroneously appears on the title page.]

Nöldeke, T. 1879. *Geschichte der Perser und Araber zur Zeit der Sasaniden*. Leiden: E. J. Brill.

Nongbri, B. 2018. *God's Library: The Archaeology of the Earliest Christian Manuscripts*. New Haven: Yale University Press.

Oates, J. F., et al., eds. 2021. *Checklist of Editions of Greek, Latin, Demotic, and Coptic Papyri, Ostraca, and Tablets*. http://papyri.info/docs/checklist

O'Connell, E. R. 2007. "Recontextualizing Berkeley's Tebtunis Papyri." In *Proceedings of the XXIVth International Congress of Papyrology*, edited by J. Frösén et al., 2:807–826. Commentationes Humanarum Litterarum 122. Helsinki: Societas Scientiarum Fennica.

Office of Geography [U. S.] 1959. *Egypt and the Gaza Strip: Official Standard Names Approved by the United States Board on Geographic Names*. Gazetteer no. 45. Washington, DC: U. S. Government Printing Office.

Officer, L. H. 2018. "Dollar-Pound Exchange Rate from 1791." *MeasuringWorth*. http://www.measuringworth.com/exchangepound/

Oliphant, L. 1882. *The Land of Khemi: Up and Down the Middle Nile*. 2nd ed. Edinburgh: W. Blackwood and Sons.

Olson, L. 2017. *Chicago Renaissance: Literature and Art in the Midwest Metropolis*. New Haven: Yale University Press.

Orsenigo, C. 2010. "Turning Points in Egyptian Archaeology, 1850–1950." In *Egypt and the Pharaohs: From the Sand to the Library: Pharaonic Egypt in the Archives and Libraries of the Università degli Studi di Milano*, edited by P. Piacentini, 115–172. Milan: Skira.

Ottman, F. C. 1920. *J. Wilbur Chapman: A Biography*. New York: Doubleday, Page.

Packman, Z. M. 1992. "The Westminster College Papyri." *Bulletin of the American Society of Papyrologists* 29:41–56.

Parsons, T. 1961. "Alfred L. Kroeber, 1876–1960." *American Journal of Sociology* 66.6: 616–617.

Pedley, J. G. 2012. *The Life and Work of Francis Willey Kelsey*. Ann Arbor: University of Michigan Press.

Pellé, N. 2007. "Frederic George Kenyon (1863–1952)." In *Hermae: Scholars and Scholarship in Papyrology*, edited by M. Capasso, 1:97–105. Pisa: Giardini.

Perale, M. 2020. *Adespota papyracea hexametra Graeca*. Vol. 1. Sozomena 18. Berlin: De Gruyter.

Petrie, W. M. F. 1899. *Catalogue of Antiquities from the Excavations of the Egypt Exploration Fund at Diospolis, and a Loan Collection of Prehistoric Vases, Exhibited by Permission of the Council at University College, Gower Street, London, July 10th to July 19th, 1899*. London: Egypt Exploration Fund.

———. 1900. *Catalogue of Antiquities from Excavations at Abydos, Found by the Egypt Exploration Fund and the Egyptian Research Account, Exhibited by Permission of the Council at University College, Gower St., London, W.C. (Close to Gower Street Station), July 2nd to July 28th, 1900*. London: Egypt Exploration Fund.

Pintaudi, R. 2016. "Schêch Farag el-Badawi." *Analecta Papyrologica* 28:383–390.

Pirozzi, M. E. A. 2003. *Herculaneum: The Excavations, Local History, and Surroundings*. Translated by M. Weir. Naples: Electa Napoli.

Poethke, G. 2007a. "Ulrich Wilcken (1862–1944)." In *Hermae: Scholars and Scholarship in Papyrology*, edited by M. Capasso, 1:81–96. Pisa: Giardini.

———. 2007b. "Wilhelm Schubart (1873–1960)." In *Hermae: Scholars and Scholarship in Papyrology*, edited by M. Capasso, 1:193–205. Pisa: Giardini.

Powell, W. R. 1978. "Romford." In *A History of the County of Essex*, edited by W. R. Powell, 7:56–98. Oxford: Oxford University Press.

Praetorius, F. 1886. *Äthiopische Grammatik mit Paradigmen, Litteratur [sic], Chrestomathie und Glossar*. Karlsruhe and Leipzig: H. Reuther. Simultaneously published in Latin.

Pridmore, J. 2013. *Building Ideas: An Architectural Guide to the University of Chicago*. Chicago: University of Chicago Press.

Quirke, S. 2010. *Hidden Hands: Egyptian Workforces in Petrie Excavation Archives, 1880–1924*. London: Duckworth.

Ragan, J. S. 1922. "Report of an Epidemic of Gastro-Enteritis at Indiana Boys' School." *Indianapolis Medical Journal* 25:9–12.

Rand, McNally and Co. 1893. *Rand, McNally & Co.'s New Indexed Standard Guide Map of the World's Columbian Exposition at Chicago (Ill.), 1893*. 1:7,320, 1″=610′. Chicago: Rand, McNally.

Rathbone, D. 2007. "Grenfell and Hunt at Oxyrhynchus and in the Fayum." In *The Egypt Exploration Society – The Early Years*, edited by P. Spencer, 199–229. Occasional Publications 16. London: Egypt Exploration Society.

Raven, M. J. 2018. *The Most Prominent Dutchman in Egypt: Jan Herman Insinger and the Egyptian Collection in Leiden*. Papers on Archaeology of the Leiden Museum of Antiquities 19. Leiden: Sidestone Press.

Regional Cultural History Project. 1959. *Frank C. Stevens: Forty Years in the Office of the President, University of California, 1905–1945*. Berkeley: General Library, University of California. https://bancroft.berkeley.edu/ROHO///collections/subjectarea/univ_hist/fac_adm_reg.html

Regional Oral History Office. 1986. *Robert Gordon Sproul Oral History Project*. 2 vols. Berkeley: Regional Oral History Office, The Bancroft Library, University of California. https://bancroft.berkeley.edu/ROHO///collections/subjectarea/univ_hist/fac_adm_reg.html

Reid, B. L. 1990. *Necessary Lives: Biographical Reflections*. Columbia: University of Missouri Press.

Reid, D. M. 2002. *Whose Pharaohs? Archaeology, Museums, and Egyptian National Identity from Napoleon to World War I*. Berkeley and Los Angeles: University of California Press.

———. 2015. *Contesting Antiquity in Egypt: Archaeologies, Museums & the Struggle for Identities from World War I to Nasser*. Cairo: American University in Cairo Press.

Renberg, G., and F. Naether. 2010. "'I Celebrated a Fine Day': An Overlooked Egyptian Phrase in a Bilingual Letter Preserving a Dream Narrative." *Zeitschrift für Papyrologie und Epigraphik* 175:49–71.

Rotberg, R. I., and M. F. Shore. 1988. *The Founder: Cecil Rhodes and the Pursuit of Power.* New York and Oxford: Oxford University Press.

Ryholt, K. 2013. "The Illustrated Herbal from Tebtunis: New Fragments and Archaeological Context." *Zeitschrift für Papyrologie und Epigraphik* 187:233–238.

Sattin, A. 1988. *Lifting the Veil: British Society in Egypt, 1768–1956.* London: J. M. Dent & Sons.

Schröder, W.-A. 2012. "Schöne, Hermann Immanuel," 26 October 2012. http://www.teuchos.uni-hamburg.de/interim/prosop/Schoene.Hermann.html

Schubart, W. 1901. "Fritz Krebs." *Biographisches Jahrbuch für Altertumskunde* 24:28–35.

Schubert, P. 2000. "La collection papyrologique de Genève." In *Papyrus Collections World Wide [sic]*, edited by W. Clarysse and H. Verreth, 43–46. Brussels: Koninklijke Vlaamse Academie van België voor Wetenschappen en Kunsten.

———. 2003. "Les papyrus de la Bibliothèque publique et universitaire de Genève." In *Voyages en Égypte de l'Antiquité au début du XXe siècle*, edited by J.-L. Chappaz and C. Ritschard, 241–258. Geneva: La Baconnière/Arts and Musée d'art et d'histoire de Genève.

Sharkey, H. J. 2008. *American Evangelicals in Egypt: Missionary Encounters in an Age of Empire.* Princeton: Princeton University Press.

Skerrett, E. 2008. "Morgan Park." In *Chicago Neighborhoods and Suburbs: A Historical Guide*, edited by A. Durkin Keating, 216–217. Chicago: University of Chicago Press.

Society for the Promotion of Hellenic Studies. 1900. "Session 1899–1900." *Journal of Hellenic Studies* 20:xiii–xliii.

Stanford, W. B., and R. B. McDowell. 1971. *Mahaffy: A Biography of an Anglo-Irishman.* London: Routledge & Kegan Paul.

Steevens, G. W. 1899. *Egypt in 1898.* New York: Dodd, Mead.

Storr, R. J. 1966. *Harper's University: The Beginnings.* Chicago: University of Chicago Press.

Teeter, E. 2010. "Egypt in Chicago: A Story of Three Collections." In *Millions of Jubilees: Studies in Honor of David P. Silverman*, edited by Z. Hawass and J. H. Wegner, 303–314. Supplément aux *Annales du Service des antiquités de l'Égypte*, cahier 39. Cairo: Conseil Suprême des Antiquités de l'Égypte.

Tomlinson, R. 2015. *Amazing Grace: The Man Who Was W. G.* London: Little, Brown UK.

Toynbee, J. M. C. et al. 2004. "Gardner, Percy (1846–1937)." *Oxford Dictionary of National Biography*, 23 September 2004. https://doi.org/10.1093/ref:odnb/33328

Trevor-Roper, H. 1973. *Christ Church Oxford.* 2nd ed. Oxford: Governing Body of Christ Church.

Turner, E. G. 2007. "The Graeco-Roman Branch." In *Oxyrhynchus: A City and Its Texts*, edited by A. K. Bowman et al., 13–26. Graeco-Roman Memoirs 93. London: Egypt Exploration Society.

Turner, F. J. 1986 [1893]. *The Frontier in American History.* Tucson: The University of Arizona Press.

Turner, J. 2014. *Philology: The Forgotten Origins of the Modern Humanities.* Princeton: Princeton University Press.

University of Chicago. 1897–1898. *Annual Register*. Chicago: University of Chicago Press.

———. 1898. *University Record*, 5 December 1898, vol. 3, no. 36. Chicago: University of Chicago Press.

———. 1899. *University Record*, 8 December 1899, vol. 4, no. 36. Chicago: University of Chicago Press.

———. 1899–1900. *Annual Register*. Chicago: University of Chicago Press.

———. 1900a. *University Record*, 29 June 1900, vol. 5, no. 13. Chicago: University of Chicago Press.

———. 1900b. *University Record*, 6 July 1900, vol. 5, no. 14. Chicago: University of Chicago Press.

———. 1904–1905. *Annual Register*. Chicago: University of Chicago Press.

———. 1920. *Circular of Information: The Divinity School*. Vol. 20. Chicago: Illinois Divinity School of the University of Chicago.

———. 1930. *Announcements: The Divinity School*. Vol. 31. Chicago: University of Chicago Press.

Urquhart, J. 1901. "The Earliest Date." *The Sunday School Journal and Bible Student's Magazine* 33:19.

Verhoogt, A. M. F. W. 1998a. "Family Papers from Tebtunis: Unfolding a Bundle of Papyri." In *The Two Faces of Graeco-Roman Egypt: Greek and Demotic and Greek-Demotic Texts and Studies Presented to P.W. Pestman by Alumni of the Papyrological Institute*, edited by A. M. F. W. Verhoogt and S. P. Vleeming, 141–154. Papyrologica Lugduno-Batava 30. Leiden: Brill.

———. 1998b. *Menches, komogrammateus of Kerkeosiris: The Doings and Dealings of a Village Scribe in the Late Ptolemaic Period (120–110 B.C.)*. Papyrologica Lugduno-Batava 29. Leiden: Brill.

———. 2017. *Discarded, Discovered, Collected: The University of Michigan Papyrus Collection*. Ann Arbor: University of Michigan Press.

Walters, C. C. 1989. "Christian Paintings from Tebtunis." *Journal of Egyptian Archaeology* 75:191–208.

Whitaker, J. 1899. *An Almanack for the Year of Our Lord 1899*. London: J. Whitaker.

Wilamowitz-Moellendorff, U. von. 1900. "Neue Bruchstücke der hesiodischen Kataloge." *Sitzungsberichte der Königlich preußischen Akademie der Wissenschaften zu Berlin*, 839–851.

Williamson, S. H. 2021. "Seven Ways to Compute the Relative Value of a U.S. Dollar Amount, 1790 to Present," April 2021. www.measuringworth.com/uscompare/

Wilcken, U. 1901. "Fritz Krebs." *Archiv für Papyrusforschung* 1:375.

Wilson, J. A. 1964. *Signs & Wonders upon Pharaoh: A History of American Egyptology*. Chicago: University of Chicago Press.

"World's Currencies, The." 1899. *Sound Currency* 7, no. 8:122–152.

INDEX

(initial compilation by Michael Hendry, revised by the authors)

Notes for the user:
- An "f" in a reference, e.g., "23f," does not mean "23 and following" but refers to a figure (map or photograph) on page 23.
- A **bold** page reference or footnote number indicates the most important reference, usually one in which a person's full name, dates, and references to further reading are given.
- References like "54n140" mean that the person, place, or thing indexed is mentioned only in the note (thus n. 140 on p. 54), while "54+n140" (sometimes "54+nn140–142") indicates that the indexed entity is mentioned in the text, with additional important information in the note (or notes) specified.
- The names of the three most important people in the book are frequently abbreviated: Edgar J. Goodspeed as "EJG," Bernard P. Grenfell as "BPG," and Arthur S. Hunt as "ASH." Grenfell and Hunt working together, as they typically did, are indexed as "Grenfell and Hunt'" and abbreviated as "G&H."
- In short lists, some items appear in logical rather than alphabetical order. For example, the subentry "EJG's visit to his [Petrie's] camp (Abydos)" has "planned" before "accomplished."
- Some of the largest entries (e.g., EJG's) have **bold** subentries, again in logical (or temporal) order.
- Some topics are grouped together for easier searching: "hotels and other lodging," "papyrus dealers," "transportation (selected)," etc.

ʿAbbās Ḥilmī, khedive, 3+n9
Abū Jirāb (Abu Gurob), 43n43, 45n57
Abydos, Petrie's excavations at, 26+n83, 36+n7
   EJG spends time "in the trenches" there, 41+n35
Acts of Thekla. See Thekla, Acts of
Adams, Henry
   low opinion of Berlin, 20n62
   regarding the World Columbian Exposition, 8
Alexander, Rev. J. R., 16+n41, 17+n48
   Alexander papyri, 18n49, 19n61
Alexander, William Hardy, 150–152
Alexandria, EJG arrives at, 36
ʿAli Muhammad es Suefi, 131+n48
American Mission, Cairo, 44+n51, 69n4
"Americanisms," EJG to avoid in translations for *P.Tebt.* II, 143
Andrews, Emma, 14n35, 42n39, 43n43, 56n114
Andromeda papyrus ("Andromeda"), 44n51, 85–91, **87n76**, 96+n118, 100, 103–105, 111–113, 115
   EJG judges neither Homeric nor Hesiodic, 84+n62

EJG proposes to name for Joseph Bond, 84+n61
   contrasted with Berlin Hesiodic papyrus, 87+n75, 91
   Friedrich Blass supports Hellenistic date, 112
antiquities (other than "mummies" and "papyri," both indexed separately)
   alabaster vessels, 137, 139, 147+n6
   beads, 137, 147+n6
   bronze objects, 63+n128, 129, 136, 147
   coffins, 137, 147–148
   coins, 51, 135–136
   glass, 136, 147
   jewelry, 76n30
   ostraka, 13n31, 40
   portraits, 76+nn30–31, 139+n46
      with a sketch or description on back, 139+n47
   rings, 136
   scarabs, 137, 147
   statuettes, 51, 135+n20
Antiquities Service, Egyptian, 3–4, 38+nn15&19, 39n22, 53n99

Archiv für Papyrusforschung, 89+n83
Arnold, Matthew, quoted, 69+n1
Arsinoe, ruins of, Madīnet, 56, 60f, 126–127
Ashmunên (ancient Hermopolis Magna), 53+n100
Aswan (Assouan), 32, 35, 39–40, 41n32
Asyūṭ (Assiut), 16, 17n48
Athenæum, 77–78, 133–140nn *passim*, 147
Athens, EJG visits, 74
Ayer, Edward E., 13+nn30–33, 14n36. *See also* Ayer papyrus
   co-founder, first president of Field Columbian Museum, 13
   grateful for having the Ayer papyrus named after him, 13n33
   letter to EJG about Ayer papyrus, 121
   spending on antiquities, 121–122
Ayer, Emma (wife of previous), 120–121
Ayer papyrus, 13+n33, 123f
   acquisition, 46
   chronology, 120–124
   contents and difficulties of, 13
   EJG's 1898 edition, 22n68, 86n67
   EJG's first sight of, 12–13
      beginning of papyrology in America, 120
      date uncertain, 120, 122, 124
   EJG's introduction to papyrology, 18, 118–119
   inspires EJG to collect papyri himself, 14–15, 122

Baden-Powell, Colonel Robert Stephenson Smyth (founder of the Scouting Association) and his half-brother Baden Henry B.-P., 83+n51
badingan (eggplant, aubergine), 54+n103, 55n107
Ballerini, Francesco, 46n60
Baring, Sir Evelyn, Lord Cromer, 3+n9
Baring-Gould, Sabine, *Mehalah*, 114n36
Behnesa (ancient Oxyrhynchus), 133. *See also* Oxyrhynchus, G&H's excavations (1896/1897)
Beman, Wooster Woodruff, 122
Berlin, "almost intolerably drab and dull" (EJG), 20+n62
Berlin, University of, pinnacle of the German system, 10n14
"Berlin disaster" (Berlin's acquisition of Hesiodic papyrus, "Gizeh tragedy"), 52–53, 72+n10, 85
   EJG blames Ludwig Borchardt, 52
   EJG still bitter half a century later, 53n96
   EJG tries to compensate for by buying more papyri, 72–73
Betteridge, Mary Caroline Allen, 102+n141
Bible
   EJG's allusions to, 14n35, 25, 107nn166–167, 114n38, 115n44
   influence of King James Version on EJG's writing, 27n8
   noncanonical Ascension of Isaiah, 104
Big Tom (bell of Christ Church), Oxford, 87+n74
biographer, first duty of, 1+n1
Birmingham, EJG visits, 31
Bissing, Friedrich Wilhelm Freiherr von ("the Baron"), 43–50, **43n43**, 45nn54&57, 53, 73
   other possible references to, 38n16, 44n50
   joined Nazi party, later expelled, 43n43
   "the most amiable youth in the world," 73
   transcribes Hesiodic fragment for Wilamowitz, 53n94
   unclear whether EJG identified him as villain of "Berlin disaster," 53n96
Blass, Friedrich, **34n119**, 77n34, 85, 104, 112+n26, 143
Bodleian Library (Bodley's), 25, 86, 90, 92+n97, 97, 100, 109+n11
Boer War, 81, 88
Bond, Elfleda. *See* Goodspeed, Elfleda Bond
Bond, Joseph (EJG's benefactor and soon-to-be father-in-law), **21+n66**
   pays $500 for EJG's travels in Egypt and Holy Land, 21–22+n67, 32n112, 49, 52
Bond papyri (later Bond Homer, Bond *Iliad*), 84+n61, 88, 92–94
   plan to name them, 86+n67
Borchardt, Ludwig, 43n43, 45+n57, **45n59**, 53nn94&98
   outbids Quibell for "Epic" fragment ("Berlin disaster"), 52
Boxer Rebellion, 100+n131
Brandenburg Gate, Berlin, 20
Breasted, James Henry, 9n11, **13n29**
   Ayer gives him permission to publish Ayer papyrus, 13n32
   "Breasted-Crandall bungle" (Clarke Crandall writes letter to Petrie at Breasted's "hasty and ill considered suggestion"), 39, 41
   calls Egyptian Museum "old tinder-box," 3n10
   EJG first sees Ayer papyrus in his office, 12–13
   facilitates purchase of papyri for EJG, 16–18
   "finds" Ayer papyrus in Field Museum, 122, 124

friend of EJG, 13n29
helps EJG unroll his papyri, 18
studies in Germany, 10n14
writes a "stupid" letter to EJG, 75+n22
British Museum, 4–5, 16n41, 21–22, 74, 77, 109, 115
EJG delighted with Oriental room, 24
Browning, Elizabeth Barrett and Robert, Kenyon's editions of, 22, 24n69
Brugsch Bey, Emil Charles Adalbert, 38–39, 43–44, 46, 49–50, 53–54, 121+n4
keeper of the Egyptian Museum, 38n15
"the old boy" (EJG), 53
Budge, E. A. Wallis, 4–5, 16n41, 32, 94
By Nile and Tigris, 4+n16
EJG meets him, 25
his guidebook, 38+n18
his smuggling methods, 4n16
Burton, Ernest De Witt, 9+**n9**, 122
correspondence with EJG, 10n17, 30–32
pressures EJG to change doctoral concentration, 9
visits BPG in Oxford, 143
By Nile and Tigris (Budge), 4+n16

Cairo, map of, in EJG's time, 37f
Cairo Museum. *See* Gizeh Museum
California, University of (Berkeley)
possible opposition "from California" (Mrs. Hearst and U.C.) to EJG editing the Tebtunis papyri, 29+n96, 69+n2, 73, 129
Tebtunis papyri shared between U.C. and Gizeh Museum, 140
Cambridge (United Kingdom), EJG visits, 108, 110–111+n20
Camp, Walter, 25+n78
Carter, Howard, 36n8
Casa di Aristides, Herculaneum, 35n2
Caton-Thompson, Gertrude, letters from ASH, 137n32
transcribed in full, 146–148
Catterall, Ralph Charles Henry (married to Helen Tunnicliff), 74n20
EJG helps him get permission to use the Bodleian, 109+n11
EJG meets him and family in London and then Oxford, 100n130, 108+n4
his son Ralph, 74n20, 108+n4, 113, 114n37
Chapter Library, Toledo (Spain), 10n18
Charles, R. H., and his wife Mary (née Lilias), 86–87, **86n69**, 94, 116n45
R.H. helps EJG with Thekla. *See Thekla, Acts of* (EJG's edition), advice and assistance from other scholars, Charles (R. H.)
their household, 104
Cheyne, Thomas Kelly, 84
Chicago
Goodspeed family moves to, 7
Great Fire, 7
Chicago, University of, *passim*
newly resurrected (1892), 7
cigarette boxes, tin, used to pack papyri, 17, 63n127
Coffin, Fulton, 26+**n82**, 27+n86, 30, 101
Colwell, E. C., 118n56
Congress of Orientalists, XII International (Rome, 1899), 32–33, 35–36, 45n59
Conybeare, Frederick, 28+n93
Cook's travel agency ("Cook's," Thomas Cook & Son), 41+n33, 43, 49, 52, 72
Coptos (Keft, Qift), 76n30, 134n12
Coptos tariff, 141+n3
Corfu, EJG visits, 74
Corinth, EJG visits, 74
Crandall, Clarke Eugene, 36+n7, 38–39, 41+n35, 50
meddles in EJG's plans, 38–39+n21, 41
Crawford, Earl of, his manuscripts, 97n127, 100, 105n160
crocodile god, Sebek, 135
crocodile mummies. *See under* mummies
Crocodilopolis (*see also* Medinet [modern name]), 126+n9
Cromer, Lord (Sir Evelyn Baring), 3+n9
Crum, Walter Ewing, 101+n133

Damascus, EJG visits, 50
Damian (Damyān, Dānyāl), train stop, 54, 62, 65n132, 127
David, Rev. Albert Augustus, 106+n163
De Angelis, Sabatino, 121n8
Delegacy for the Extension of University Teaching, 27+n84, 31
Dendera, 36
Denison University, EJG's alma mater, 8+n6
EJG bequeaths books to its library, 116n48, 118n56
Diamond Jubilee, Queen Victoria's, 3+n7
disciplinary boundaries, more rigid in EJG's time, 2
Douglass, Frederick, 8n5
Dragulin, Wilhelm Eduard, 96n121, 114

Edinburgh, 109+n7
Egypt Exploration Fund (Society), 4nn12–13, 13n34, 34n119, 48n66, 51+n87, 76+n30, 119n60
Egyptian Museum, 3–4. *See also* Gizeh Museum
Egyptology, distinguished from papyrology and classical philology, 2
Egyptomania, 121n4
Elephantine, EJG visits, 40
Erman, Jean Pierre Adolphe (Adolf), 45n54, 75+**n23**
Euhemereia, 62n121

Fäh, Adolf, 75
Farrar, Frederic William, 115+n44
Fayoum (Fayyūm), map of, in EJG's time, 57f
Ferris Wheel (first), 7, 8n4
Field Columbian Museum, 120–121
  Ayer papyrus, 123f
    acquired for its collection, 120–122
    change of name from Field Columbian Museum to Field Museum of Natural History, 13n30
    some of Ayer's ostraka now there, 13n31
First Oasis, probably EJG's alternative name for Fayyūm, 126+n10
Flaubert, Gustave, 36n11
Florence, EJG visits, 75
food
  EJG's basket of vegetables for G&H, 125+n4
  meals at G&H's excavation, 128, 130
Friends' Summer School (Birmingham), 31
Froude, J. A., *The Two Chiefs of Dunboy*, 89+n85

Galilee, EJG visits, 132n54
Galilee, Sea of, EJG visits, 50
Gardner, Percy, 28+n93
Geneva, EJG visits, 33
Germany, EJG visits its universities, 20+n62
Gharak (Gherac), Fayyūm, 7, 42, 48
  as a provenience in Hearst Museum records, 76n32
Gibson, Margaret Dunlop, 103+n146
Gifford, Edward Winslow, 152+n8
Gildersleeve, Basil Lanneau (editor of *American Journal of Philology*), 10n17, 86+n67, 89, 92, 95–96, 105, 124n13
Gizeh Museum (Cairo Museum, Egyptian Museum), 18n56, 52, 121, 139–140
  EJG socializes there, 39
  EJG transcribes papyri there, 43, 46–47+n62, 49, 53–54

ideal conditions for reading papyri, 47
library collection inadequate for research, 45, 47
recipient of *partage*, **4+n13**, 140+n51, 147+n6
Goodspeed, Charles Ten Broeke (brother of EJG), 8n6, 10
  buys camera for EJG, 18
  letters to and from EJG, 10+n17, 11+n22, and *passim*
Goodspeed, Edgar Johnson (EJG)
  portraits of, young and old, 6f, 153f
  camera the constant companion of his travels, 18
  first meeting with G&H, 27–28
  visit to Petrie's camp at Abydos, 35, 41+n35
  Education
    A.B. in Classics (Dennison, 1890), 8+n6
    graduate study at Yale (1890-1891), 8
    Bachelor of Divinity (Chicago, 1897), 9
    PhD, New Testament Studies (Chicago, 1898), 9
      March or April conferral, 9n11, 122
  Foreign Languages
    Arabic, 8, 26
    Ethiopic, 21, 24+n72, 49, 94+n109, 100–101, 116n45
      needs "to verify every letter" of manuscript, 94
      brother sends him a grammar, 43+n47
    French, inadequate for conversation, 33
    German, 18+n56, 39
    Greek (ancient), 8 and *passim*
    Hebrew, 8
    Latin, 8
    Semitics, 9
    Syriac, 9
  Other Study and Expertise
    cursive writing (Greek papyri of Roman period), 43 ("former facility"), 84, 90
    dogma, history of, 10
    early Christian literature, 10
    legal literature of the Old Testament, 8
    meter, only dactylic hexameter, 44
    New Testament, 9 and *passim*
    "only American" qualified to work on papyri, 7, 55
  Teaching
    Owen Academy (1891), 8
    University of Chicago (1898-1937)
      joins faculty as Assistant in Biblical and Patristic Greek, 9
      desire for paid leave from, 30+n98

170 INDEX

promotion to Associate in Biblical and Patristic Greek, 9n13
G&H identify him as "Assistant Professor of New Testament and Patristic Greek," 116
University of California at Los Angeles (1940-1942), 149+n1
Collecting
personal collection, 4, 22n67
Ayer papyrus as inspiration for, 14, 16
purchases papyri through Breasted and Alexander, 16-18, 30n100
   story in *Chicago Daily Tribune*, 17n48
visits papyrus dealers in Egypt, 40, 46, 69, 72-73, 126
blue glaze lion from Tebtunis, 79
Editing (Papyri)
abandons, 118+n56
at the Gizeh Museum, 43-73 *passim*
at Oxford, 81-114 *passim*
BPG advises not to worry about "cruxes," 143
BPG's proposal for EJG to edit Tebtunis papyri. *See* **Grenfell, Bernard Pyne (BPG)**, proposes EJG's work on Hearst papyri.
G&H tell him to work on easier pieces, 107, 117
leaves England craving a respite from papyri, 114-115+n44
not invited to edit more papyri after *P.Tebt.* II, 118
not listed as editor in *P.Tebt.* II, 116-117+n48
wants BPG's approval of work on Hesiodic papyrus, 45
Writing
"Abroad in the Nineties" (unpublished memoir), 12+n24
   revisions and their possible dates, 12n25
   differs from *As I Remember*, 12, 20n62, 30n97, 62n120, 73, 116n45
As I Remember (1953 memoir), 2, 11, 116, 118, 120, 149
   as a mature reflection, 116
   two typescripts preserved among his papers, 11n22
      discrepancies, 20n62, 120
   differs from correspondence and other evidence, 2, 73, 149n1. *See also* "Abroad in the Nineties" (unpublished memoir), differs from *As I Remember*

EJG wonders about accomplishments in years abroad (rhetorical question), 108, 118
omits mention of his Oxford summer (1900), 73
The Curse in the Colophon, 18n56
Greek papyrus reader, 118+n56
"Karanis Accounts," 118+n54
planned publication venues
   American Journal of Archaeology (for the "Gizeh study"), 91
   American Journal of Archaeology (for the *Odyssey* fragment), 54
   American Journal of Philology (publishes Bond *Iliad*), 86+n67
   American Journal of Semitic Languages and Literatures (publishes "Thekla"), 104n153
   Journal of Hellenic Studies (for the "Epic" fragment), 49-50, 52
   Journal of Hellenic Studies (publishes "Andromeda"), 86n67, 89, 91
   Journal of Philology (for the "Epic" fragment), 49
popular accounts of G&H's excavations at Tebtunis, 55-56
sonnet mentioning Andromeda and Thekla, 96+n120, 103
"Student Travel Letters"
   vol. 1 (lost), 2, 9n10, 10, 116n45
   vol. 2, 2, 10-12, 20n62, 25n78, 27n84, 73, 87n76, 93n101
   diary-like, 81+n49
   discovery by authors, 2
   general description, 10-11+nn19-21
   less informative at end of Oxford summer (1900), 108
   preserved by brother Charles, 11
   supplements memoirs, 73
   use for memoirs, 11-12+n22
worries about joint vs. single authorship, 30+n101
worries over adequacy of papyrological abilities, 79, 106-107, 117
Health
cold, "beastly bad back" from too much canoeing, 111-112
eyesight problems, lifelong, 24n73, 117+n50
moth flies in ear, 39
sore throat and cold, blamed on trip to London, 101-102
toothache, 39

Athletic Interests
in general, 84n60
boating in Oxford and Cambridge, 108, 111, 113
cycling tour in England, 25
disappointed by Chicago athletes' lack of success at Paris Olympiad, 105+n158
enjoys Oxford boat races, 85
football, American, 84n60
goes to London for English track and field championships, 100+n129
    meets Amos Alonso Stagg and Chicago athletes, 101+n136
walks in Oxford, 17, 88, 91, 113
watches "swimming demonstration" on the Isis, 102+n142
would have abandoned papyri to watch W. G. Grace play cricket, 84+n60

Attitudes, Character Traits, Judgments: Select Examples
ambition
    getting into print, 74 and *passim*. *See also* **Writing**, planned publication venues
    networking ("lion hunting"), 26, 36, 38
ambivalent attitude to smoking/tobacco, 29n95, 101, 109+n13
Anglophilia (celebrates British relief of Mafeking [Boer War]), 81, 83. *See also* Oxford
antipathy toward W. L. Phelps, 112n25
aversion to alcohol, 29n95, 79
enjoys food, talk at Queen's College, 85, 106
ethnic remarks
    Egyptians, 36, 45
    Germans and German-Americans, 87+n75, 115
    Poles, 115+n43
extroversion, 26n79
feelings of inadequacy, 32, 52, 106–107, and *passim*
quick to identify friends, 13n29, 19n58, 22, 47, and *passim*
patriotism 86, 100 (celebrates the Fourth of July)

Goodspeed, Elfleda Bond (wife of EJG), 10, 22n67, 144+n21, 149
Goodspeed, George S. (cousin of EJG), 41n36, 89+n83, 128+n25
Goodspeed, Henry S., Captain (EJG's uncle), 44+n52
Goodspeed, Mary Ellen, née Ten Broeke (mother of EJG), 7

EJG and Breasted unroll papyri in her kitchen, 18
Goodspeed, Thomas Harper (son of EJG's cousin George), 41n36
Goodspeed, Thomas Wakefield (father of EJG), 7+**n1**, 109n13
Gradenwitz, Otto, 112+n28
Granger, Edna ("stunning Buffalonian"?), 26+n79
Greek authors
    Aeschylus, *Agamemnon* performed at Bradfield College, 92–93+n101
    Bacchylides, 4n16
    Demosthenes, 95+n113 (EJG: "some Greek historian"), 110+n17, 143
    Herodotus, on size and depth of Lake Moeris, 137, 146n1
    Homer, 18, 69, 72+n6
    Iliad, 16, 27+n88, 33+n18, 74, 83–86, 84nn59&61, 85n65, 86n67, 88–89, 92, 94–97, 102–103+n147, 105, 110n18, 143
    Odyssey, 49+n78, 53–54+n101, 97+n123
    Menander, *Georgos*, 33–34+nn118–119
    Pseudo-Aristotle, *Constitution of Athens*, 3, 22n68
    Strabo, 126n10
Gregory, Caspar René, 9+**n10**, 75, 90+n89, 96n118, 101n139, 105+n160
    asks EJG to examine New Testament manuscripts, 92+n95, 97+n127, 100, 103
Grenfell, Alice Pyne (mother of BPG), 28–29+n94, 104
    EJG escorts to see *Agamemnon* at Bradfield College, 93
Grenfell, Bernard Pyne (BPG). *See also* Grenfell and Hunt *for the two working together*
pictures
    formal portrait, 15f
    in the field with workmen, 64f
EJG consults on Ayer papyrus, 13–14
EJG's description of, 14, 129
    fast walker, 65+n132, 129
    height, 63+n126
honorary degrees, 94+n106
ill health postpones publication of *P. Tebt.* III, 146–147
proposes EJG work on Hearst papyri, 28–30+nn96–98, 43, 51 52, 54–55, 63, 129
wit, 33–34, 117+n53
Correspondence to EJG, 7, 14, 41–43, 48, 50–51, 54–55+nn107–108, 117n50, 141–144

appends Greek subscription to letter, 51+n88
consoles EJG on loss of "Epic," 54–55
Publications, 13–14+n34. *See also* papyri, published volumes (selected), G&H (and collaborators)
Grenfell, John Granville (father of BPG), 29n94
Grenfell and Hunt (G&H)
 division of labor in the field, 65+n129
 EJG's final dinner with them, 114+n36
 Grenfell confident, Hunt cautious, 29+n96
 Hunt as designated conservator of duo, 112n31
 "incomparable decipherers" (E. G. Turner), 89+n81
 instructors of EJG in "papyrus palaeography," 90+n89
 introduce translations to papyrus editions, 48n66
 rooms at Queen's College as "the book factory," 89, 91
Excavations, Tebtunis. *See* Tebtunis
 conditions at camp, 62, 128
Publications. *See* papyri, published volumes (selected), G&H (and collaborators)
 popular, 13n34 (*Logia*), 133–140 (*New York Journal*)

Haifa, EJG visits, 50
Hamilton, David Gilbert
 funds purchase of Ayer papyrus, 122
 position in life, 122n10
Harnack, (Carl Gustaf) Adolf von, 19+**n57**
 "Essence of Christianity" (*Das Wesen des Christentums*), 105
Harper, Robert Francis (brother of next), 104+n153, 115
Harper, William Rainey
 approves of EJG's ventures (according to J. R. Harris), 111
 EJG's letters to, 20n64, 26n82, 36n7
 EJG's teacher at Yale, 8, 13n29
 influenced by German university model, 10n14
 president of University of Chicago, 8+n7
 sends EJG abroad, 9
Harris, James Rendel, 24n71, 31+nn104–106, 32, 110+n15, 111+n23, 116n45
Hawara, 14n36, 139
 pyramid of, 14n36, 127 (EJG sees)
Hearst, Phoebe Apperson (Mrs. Hearst)
 benefactress of University of California, 28+n90

 correspondence with George Reisner, 42n41, 55n106, 69n2, 76n30
 funds G&H's expedition to Fayyūm, 28, 134, 151 ("financing of Reisner Egyptian Expedition")
 G&H as "Directors of the Phoebe A. Hearst Exploring Expedition," 133
 list of objects sent to her by Reisner, 135n20
Hearst, William Randolph (son of previous), editor of *New York Journal*, 78n38
Hearst Museum, Berkeley, 76n32
Henley Regatta, 25+n77
Herakleopolis, 45n57, 119n59
Herculaneum, EJG visits, 35
Hermopolis Magna (Ashmunên), 53n100
Hermopolite nome, 106n165
Hesiodic *Catalogus mulierum* (EJG's "Epic"), 44–50, **53n94**
 associated with Keneh, 47 (its dealer there), 75
 BPG encourages EJG to publish it, 52
 edited by Wilamowitz. *See under* Wilamowitz-Moellendorf, Ulrich von
 EJG learns it is Hesiodic, 77+n34
 fine uncial hand, 44, 49
 lost to Germans, 52–53. *See also* "Berlin disaster"
Hibeh, G&H's excavations at, 144
Holy Land. *See* Palestine
hotels and other lodging
 Angleterre (Cairo), 132+n53
 10 Bedford Place (London), 22, 23f, 75, 100, 114
 Hotel Bristol (Cairo), 36+n10, 38, 41, 48, 131, 132n53
 "Cook and Son" hotels, 41n33
 Eden Palace Hotel (Cairo), 66+n133, 132+n53
 "Isis" Boarding Establishment (Oxford), 79, 81–82ff, 87n84, 88, 90n87, 91, 93, 100, 101n139, 112–113, 118
 Hotel Karoon (Karoun), Madīnet al-Fayyūm, 42+n39, 56, 58f, 126
 Luxor Hotel, 41+n33
 Hôtel du Nil, 36+n11
 Shepheard's Hotel (Cairo), 4+n15, 41, 69n4, 120+n3
 Pension Sima (Cairo), 125+n4, 131
 Villa Victoria (Cairo), 36, 131, 132n53
Hu, 36
Hunt, Arthur Surridge (ASH). *See also* Grenfell and Hunt *for the two working together*
 advises EJG on excursion to Toledo (Spain), 10n18

INDEX 173

descriptions of, 14n35
family in Romford, 78–79+n41
letters to Gertrude Caton-Thompson, transcribed in full, 146–148
  his map of Tebtunis, 147
nickname "Huggins," 127n15
picture of, in the camp at Tebtunis, 68f
processing papyri in camp, 50+**n82**, 129–130
shoots rooks, 79+n43
sick with influenza, 76, 79
Hunt, Francis John (brother of ASH), 77+n36
Hyde Park (Chicago neighborhood), 7
Hyde Park Baptist Church (succeeded by Hyde Park Union Church), 10+n16

Independent, The, 55–56
Ismāʿīl, khedive (1863–1879), 3
Italy, EJG's tour of, 75

Jackson Park, Chicago, 7
Jerusalem, EJG's visit to, 21n66, 50, 52
Jouguet, Pierre, 117n53

Karabacek, J., 20n64
Karanis (modern Kawm Aushīm, Washim), 17n47, 22n68, 47n62, 55n108
Kase, Edmund H., Jr., 151
Kawm Aushīm. *See* Karanis *and* Washim
Kawm al-Khamsīnī (Khamsin, ancient Kerkethoeris), 76n32, 139n48
Kelsey, Francis Willey, 63n126, 91n91, 119n61, 126n14
Keneh (Qena, Qinā), 47+n65, 49
Kenyon, Frederic G., **22+n68**, 24–27+n69, 50, 52, 55+n107, 77, 79, 89, 91, 96, 100
  his *Palaeography*, 47
khedive, 3+n9
Kitchener, Lord (Horatio Herbert, Earl Kitchener of Khartoum), 25+n76
Krebs, Friedrich ("Fritz") Maximilian, 19–20, 27, 75n22, 117, 119n59
  EJG learns of his death from ASH, 79+n44
  EJG writes because his papyri related to some in Berlin, 19n61
  EJG's papyrological mentor, 19+**n58**, 90n89
  includes EJG's editions in *BGU*, 19+n60
Kroeber, Alfred L., 150–152+n5
Krüger, (Hermann) Gustav, 116n45
Krueger, Stephanus Johannes Paulus ("Oom Paul"), 81, 83n51

Lake, Isabel Monica Strong (sister of following), 83+n58, 100

Lake, Kirsopp, 29n95, 83n58, 100
Lange, Hans Ostenfeldt, 42n39, 46n60, 49, 126n14
Lange, Jonna (wife of preceding), 46n60, 72n11
Lewis, Agnes Smith, 103+n146, 110
Lightfoot, Joseph Barber, 115+n44
Los Angeles, University of California at (UCLA)
  EJG teaches there, 149
  EJG's proposal to transfer some Tebtunis papyri there, 149–152

Mace, Arthur Cruttenden, **36+n8**, 38, 101, 130, 131n46
MacIver, David Randall, 131+n46
Mafeking, siege of, 81, 83n51
  Galsworthy's description of celebration, 83n53
Magrath, John Richard, 114+n36
Mahaffy, John Pentland, 27+n89, 117, 133, 134n3
Mainz (EJG: "horrible town"), 21+n66, 52
Manning, Frederick, *The Middle Parts of Fortune*, 54n104
Mansour (Mansoor), Mohammed (Mahmoud), 62, 65+n130, 127, 130
  possible confusion about name, 65n130
  possible picture of, with train, 61f
manuscripts. *See also* papyri
  Arabic, 111
  Codex Alexandrinus, 111
  Codex Bezae, 111+n22
  Codex Vaticanus, 111
  Cairo Genizah, 103n146, 110–111
  Coptic, 46, 111
  Ethiopic. *See Thekla, Acts of*
  Hebrew, 46, 111
  Newberry Gospels, 9
  Syriac, 9+n8, 25, 31n105, 111+n23
Mariette Pasha, François Auguste Ferdinand, 38+n19
Maspero, Gaston, 38–39, 44, 46–49
  director, Antiquities Service, 3, 38n15
  EJG meets for the first time, 38
  gives EJG permission to work on papyri at Egyptian Museum, 38
  "the great man" (EJG), 53
  keeps papyri locked up on boat, 53+n99
Mathews, Shailer, 21, **22n67**, 86+n67, 95–96
McKinley, President William, 3
McMahan, Una, 93–94+**n103**, 100, 110n16, 111–115
  despite knowing Greek and architecture, "a very jolly girl," 96

Medinet (Madīnet, Madīnet al-Fayyūm, Medina)
  its mud-brick bridge, "veritable rialto," 59f, 126
  pictures, 70–71ff
  picturesqueness, 126
  waterwheels, 56, 126
Merneptah, opening of the mummy case of, 53
Michigan, University of, 122
  center of renaissance of papyrology in America, 119n61
Midway Plaisance, Chicago, 8
Mills, Florence (wife of George S. Goodspeed), 18n56, 41+n36
Mills, Sarah Ellen (EJG's maternal cousin, daughter of next), 11+n23
  EJG's correspondence with, 14, 19+n58, 20n64, 33–34, 41, 48
Mills, Sarah née Ten Broeke (EJG's maternal aunt), 11n23
missionaries involved in papyrus trade, 16+n41
Moeris, Lake
  modern Birket el Kurun, 137
  debate about historical water levels, 137, 146–148+n1
Moore, Eliakim Hastings, helps decipher the Ayer papyrus, 124n13
Morgan Park (Chicago neighborhood), 7–8, 11n23, 27n89, 109n6
Mouski (street in Cairo), 36+n11, 38
mummies
  crocodile, 63, 116n48, 128–130+n39
  sham, 138+n41
  size range, 138
  story of discovery, 62n120, 138n45
  human, 63, 76n30, 137–139
  papyrus cartonnage used for, 133–134, 137
Munro, J. A. R., 51n88
Murch, Rev. Chauncey, 16n41
Murray, James, and his scriptorium, 97+n126

Naples, EJG's visit to, 35, 41, 43n47
Naplia (Nafplio), EJG visits, 74
Narmouthis, 42n41
Naville, Edouard, 33+n113
Nazareth, EJG visits, 50
"Nefertiti affair," 45n59
New Testament Club (University of Chicago), 12n28
  EJG first hears of Ayer papyrus there, 12, 122, 124
Newberry Library (Chicago), 9n12, 120n2

newspapers (selected)
  Chicago Chronicle, 124n13
  Chicago Tribune, 17n48, 121
    Sunday, 24n72
  coverage of Tebtunis excavation, 56+n110, 78n38
  Inter Ocean, 120n3, 121n5
Nicole, Jules, 27n89, **33+n113**, 34, 83, 117
  G&H reedit his Menander, 34
  their dedication to him, 34f+n120
  wife and niece, 33
Nile cruise, EJG's, 32+n112, 40–41
Nöldeke, Theodor, 10n17, 21+**n65**, 24nn71–72, 32, 75, 88, 90

Old Colony Building, Chicago, 121+n6
Olympia, EJG visits, 74
Oom Paul ("Uncle Paul"). *See* Krueger, Stephanus Johannes Paulus
Ottoman Empire
  quarantine problems in ports, 50
  sultan, 3
Oxford
  agrees with EJG "beautifully," 84
  EJG's "Oxford bondage," 73
  EJG's treatment of summer 1900 in later works, 73
  lovelier than Venice according to EJG, 83
  map of, in EJG's time, 80f
Oxford University Gazette, used by ASH when flattening papyri, 91+n91, 96n122
Oxyrhynchus, G&H's excavations in 1896/1897, 4+nn12–13, 128, 133–134
  unrivaled for Roman and Byzantine papyri, 133

Palestine (Holy Land), EJG's tour of, 2, 9, 35–36+n7, 43, 47, 49–50
  partly on horseback, 50
  prospect has "abysmal effect," 21n66, 52
  prospect is very pleasant, 35
  turns out "more important for me than any other land," 52
papyri
  "paps," a Grenfellism EJG adopts, 94
  "papyruses," another Grenfellism, 83
  market for, 4
  collections
    Alexander's (Westminster College), 18n49
    Amherst (= Lord Amherst's), 51+n87, 81, 143
    Archduke Rainer (Vienna), 20

INDEX 175

Berkeley (Tebtunis/Hearst), 134–140, 142–143, 145, 149–152, and *passim*
Berlin, 19+n61
Cairo, 4 and *passim*
Geneva and Jules Nicole's, 33+n113
Goodspeed's, 16–18+nn and *passim*
individual (select examples)
    Andromeda papyrus. *See above*
    Bacchylides, 4n16
    Cairo *Odyssey* fragment, 49, 53–54+n101
    Christian prayer, 47+**n62**, 49
    Gordian, "letter" of Emperor, 97+n125, 99f
    Hesiodic *Catalogus mulierum*. *See above*
    "immense Tebtunis Iliad," 85+n65, 103+n150, 110+n18
    "letter to a potter's wife," 114+n35
    magical papyrus, "extraordinary," 96–97+n122, 98f
    "nice horoscope," 108+n3
    papyrus with "stunning" legal language, 47–48+n66
languages/scripts of
    Arabic, 46, 54n100
    Coptic, 39, 44, 46, 54n100
    Demotic, 45–46, 50, 133, 135+n18, 137–139+n43, 140n51
    Greek, *passim*
    hieroglyphic, 135
    Latin, 75
prices of, 13n31, 16–17+n46, 40, 41n32, 46+n60, 48–49, 52, 69, 72, 121
published volumes (selected)
    EJG
        P.Cair.Goodsp., 4n11, 18n49, 43n45, 49n76, 54n101, 74n18, 86n67, 113n33, 141+nn1–2
        P.Chic., 4n11, 84n62, 86n67, 116nn46–47
        P.Kar.Goodsp., 4n11, 17n48, 18n49, **19**+n61
    G&H (and collaborators)
        P.Amh. I, 81n50, 87n72
        P.Amh. II, 51n87, 116n48
        P.Cair.Cat., 43n45, 143+n19
        P.Oxy. II, 39, 42–43+n42, 143n17
        P.Oxy. III, 51n87, 142
        P.Tebt. I, 51n87, 62n120, 116n48, 143n17
        complimentary copy sent to EJG, 141
        P.Tebt. II, 50n82, 116+n48, 145
        BPG writes to EJG about his contributions, 142–143
        P.Tebt. III, publication delayed, 118n56, 146–147
    other
        BGU (series), 19+nn60–61, 27, 101
        P.Lond. II, 22n68
papyrifer, a likely Grenfellism, 129+n38
papyrographer, papyrography, 20
    earliest reference, 20n63
papyrology
    early practitioners essentially self-taught, 90n89
    EJG's "Greek Papyri" course, 118n55
    EJG's withdrawal from the field, 116+nn47–48, 117–118+n56, 119+n60
    Hilfsmittel for Religious Studies, 118
    this book's relation to history of, 2
papyrus dealers
    Ali el-Arabi (Ali Abd el-Haj el-Gabri, "Ali in Giza"), 69+n3, 72n10
    Farag Ali, 46n60, 72n11
    Farag Ismaïn ("Old Sheikh Farag"), 46+n60, 72+nn7&11
    discounts prices, 46+n60
    Kasira (Casira), Michel, 44n51, 69+nn4–5, 72+n10, 84nn61–62
    Mohasseb, Mohammed (Luxor), 40+n31
    Refsbai (Rafaa, Rafar, Rifaa, Rifai, Riffai), Mahmoud (Mahommed, Mohammad, Mohammed), 126+n14, 127n15
    most likely Refā'ī, 126n14
    unnamed (Cairo), 38–39
    unnamed "old Arab Sheik," 17n48
    unnamed "old codger" (Luxor), 40, 41n32
papyrus mounting, 19n61, 75+n27, 151
papyrus smuggling, Budge's methods, 4n16
papyrus storage
    EJG's
        papyri from Alexander arrive in cigarette tins, 17
        tin box made in Cairo, 72
    G&H's, 27, 63n127, 79
Paris, EJG visits, 75
Paris Olympiad, 100n129, 105
partage, 4, 139–140+n51
Paul, St., 24
Petrie, William Matthew Flinders, 4, 17n48, 26+**n81**, 36, 62n117, 101, 134n12
    BPG's workers pleased that EJG knows him, 130
    Crandall writes at Breasted's suggestion, 39+n21
    EJG's visit to his camp (Abydos)
        planned, 35, 36n7
        accomplished, 41+n35
    excavations at Gurob, 133+n2

his methods
  "bakshish" for workers' finds, 134
  local market day his day of rest, 128
  spartan life in camp, 128+n23
Petrie, Hilda (wife of previous), 41n35
Pettitt, George Albert, 150–152
Phelps, William Lyon and Annabel Hubbard Phelps (wife), 100n130, 108–109+n4, 112–113+n25
Philae, 40n29
philology, classical, historically separate from Egyptology, 2
Platz, Harold H., 12n28
plum cake, 54+n104, 55n107
Plum Lake, Goodspeed family summer home, 30+n99
Port Said, 50
Pretoria, capture of (Boer War), 88
Prince of Wales (future Edward VII), 25+n78
Pyrgos, EJG visits, 74

Qasr es-Sagha, 147
Quakers, 31
Quibell, James Edward, 39+**n22**, 43–46, 48–49, 52–53, 130
Quincy, Illinois, 7, 11n23, 96
quotidian, biographers' fascination with, 1+1n

Reid, B. L., *Necessary Lives*, quoted, 1
Reisner, George A., 29n96, 55+n106, 131n46
  BPG's negotiations with, 76+n30
  consents to EJG's work on Tebtunis papyri, 76
  correspondence with Mrs. Hearst, 42n41, 69n2, 76n30, 135n20
  "Reisner Egyptian Expedition" financed by Mrs. Hearst, 151
Revillout, (Charles) Eugène, 27+n89, 117
Rhodes, Cecil, 25+n76
Roman authors (writing in Latin or during the imperial period)
  Dictys Cretensis, 136n22
  Eusebius Gallicanus, 75n27
  Isidore of Seville, 75+n27
  Petronius, quoted, 35
  Terence (Publius Terentius Afer), EJG quotes, 52
"Roman cursive," 90
  "worst Greek to read," 84
Roman emperors
  Antonines, 94
  Augustus, 129+n32, 136
  Domitian, 141

Gordian III, 97+n125
Tacitus, 44, 47
Vespasian, 16
Rome, EJG visits, 74–75
Romford (ASH's birthplace; family home), 77–79+n35, 101 (Romford Hall)
Rubayyat (site in Egypt), 139
Rubensohn, Otto, 126n14

Sayce, A. H., 16+n44, 114+n36
  advises Alexander on papyrus purchase, 16
  ancestor claims descent from Julius Caesar, 114n36
  Ishtar, his *dhahabīyah*, 16n44
Schäfer, (Johann) Heinrich, 44n50, 45–46+n59, **45n57**, 49, 53n98
Schechter, Solomon, 102, **103n146**, 110–111+n21
Schöne, Hermann Immanuel, 90n89
Schubart, Wilhelm, 19+n58
Sebek, 135
Seknebtunis, 135
Shakespeare, EJG's allusions to, 33+n115, 44+n49, 96+n17
Sheldonian Theatre, 25
Sidon, EJG visits, 50
Smyly, J. Gilbart, 29n96, 51n88, 63n123, 140n50
  coedits *P.Petr.* III, 134n3
  considered better papyrologist than Mahaffy, 27n89
  letters from BPG, 29n96, 76nn30&32, 94n106, 116n48, 117n53
Society for the Promotion of Hellenic Studies (Hellenic Society), 77+n34
Sproul, Robert Gordon, 150–152+n4
St. Gallen convent library, 75
Stagg, Amos Alonso, 84n60, 105, 109n6
  EJG meets, 101
Stevens, Frank Clifford, 152+n7
Strassburg (Straßburg), 21 (EJG visits), 75
"Street in Cairo," exhibit at World Columbian Exposition, 7, 8n4
Sue, "cousin Sue" (probable maternal cousin of EJG), 11+n23, 29, 35, 50
Swiss Institute in Cairo, 45n59
Switzerland, EJG's visits to, 33, 75

Talthybius, 93
Tebtunis, 42 and *passim*
  less commonly "Teptunis," 42, 51n89
  modern name Umm el-Baragât, 42, 137
  BPG's descriptions, 41–42, 134

cemeteries, 147
  ASH's sketch map, 147f
  Middle Empire, 147
  New Empire (two), 147
  Ptolemaic, 137–138, 147
  Roman, 139, 147
Coptic churches, ruins of, 51+n86, 128, 136+n27
  EJG's visit, 55–66, 125–132
  BPG on what to bring, 42, 51
  BPG's travel instructions, 42–43, 54
  EJG's washstand there,130+f
  G&H's finds divided between Cairo and Berkeley, 139–140+n51, 147
  G&H's finds double the number of Ptolemaic papyri, 138
  G&H's newspaper account of excavation, 78+n38, 133–140
  pharaonic remains, 136–137
    ASH's letters to Caton-Thompson concerning, 146–148+n1
  photos of G&H's camp, 67–68ff
  staffing of G&H's excavation, 129, 131, 134–135
    Bedouin vs. *fellāḥīn*, 135+n14
  temple, ruins of, 135
Thayer, Joseph Henry, 90n87
Thayer, Miss ("the adorable Miss Thayer," daughter of preceding), 90+n87
Theadelpheia, 62n121, 134n4
Thekla, Acts of (EJG's edition), **24+n71**
  advice and assistance from other scholars, 79n45 (necessity for)
  Budge, 25+n75, 32
  Charles (R. H.), 24nn71–72, 86, 88, 90, 92, 94, 104, 115
  Harris, 32
  Nöldeke, 24nn71–72, 32, 88, 90, 94
  Charles (brother) sends Ethiopic grammar to help, 43+n47
  competes with "palaeography" for EJG's attention, 30, 32
  "different from any known version," 78
  EJG restores corrupt passage "better than Charles," 97
  EJG tempted to finish under Nöldeke, 75
  EJG writes to R. F. Harper about, 104+n153
  "no ordinary martyrological piece," 83
  plates, 88–89
  proofs, 114–115
  publication of and publicity for, 24n72
  sidelined while EJG in Egypt, 49
  text posted to printer, 102

translation, 79, 115
  work on it in Oxford, 81, 83, 86, 88, 90, 95–97, 102, 106n164
"thick description," 2
Thomas, Ralph, 102+n142
Thomas Cook & Son, Ltd. *See* Cook's travel agency
Thompson, E. M., 4n12
Tiergarten ("Thiergarten"), Berlin, 20
Tims, Thomas, 108n2
Tom Brown at Oxford (Thomas Hughes), 30+n100
transportation (selected)
  cab (two-horse carriage, Cairo), 45, 47
  camel, mentioned, 62, 127
  donkeys, mentioned, 42
    local donkeys inferior (BPG), 54
  ships and boats
    Bohemia (S.S.), 75
      renamed *Pompei*, 75n29
    Cleopatra (Nile steamer), 39+n24
    Fürst Bismarck (S.S.), 120
      ports called at, 121n5
    Grosser Kurfürst (S.S.), 115
    Ishtar (Sayce's *dhahabīyah*), 16n44
    Khedivial Mail Steamship Line, 50+n80
    Queen Olga, 74+n19
    Umberto Primo, 35+n3
  trains
    Cairo to al-Wāsṭah, sights, 125–126
    Egyptian train in station, 61f
    Erie Railroad from Chicago to New York, 18+n53
    narrow-gauge from Madīnet, 42, 56, 127–128
    train from al-Wāsṭah to Madīnet, 56
  tram, 38+n14 (Cairo), 111 (Cambridge)
  underground (London), 101
  walking
    as a good way to study "Arab life," 45
    dangers of dogs in Egyptian hamlets, 62, 127
    to and from G&H's camp, 62, 65+nn131–132, 127, 130
Tunnicliff, Damon George, and family, 74n20
Tunnicliff, Sarah Bacon (Damon's middle daughter), 74+nn20–21, 92–94, 105, 108–111, 114–115+n39
Turner, E. G., 89n81
Turner, Frederick Jackson, 8n5
Tutankhamun, 36n8
Tyre, EJG visits, 50

Umm el-Baragât, 42+n41, 48, 134, 137. *See also* Tebtunis
Unter den Linden, Berlin, 20
Urkunden. *See* papyri, published volumes (selected), other, *BGU* (series)

Victoria, Queen, 3+n7
Vienna, EJG visits, 20
Villa dei Papiri, Herculaneum, 35n2
Vinylite, used to mount papyri, 151
Votaw, Clyde W., 12+n28

Wadham College, EJG's dinner there, 92
Washim (Kawm Aushīm, ancient Karanis), 17+n47
Wasta (Wastah, al-Wastah, al-Wāsṭah, el-Wastah), 56, 65, 125, 129–130
Wessely, Carl Franz Joseph, **20+n64**, 27, 117
Westermann, William Linn, 119n61
"Westminster sisters," 103+n146. *See also* Lewis, Agnes Smith
Wilamowitz-Moellendorf, Ulrich von
  announces Hesiodic papyrus at Hellenic Society meeting, 77
  edits Hesiodic papyrus, 53n94, 77n34
Wilcken, Ulrich, 27+n89, 45n57, 79n44, 89+n83, 117
  only rival of G&H as documentarian, 119+n59
Wollaeger, Dr., 132+n54
World Columbian Exposition (Chicago), 7–8+n4, 121n4
Wright, John Henry (editor of *American Journal of Archaeology*), 86+n67, 88–89, 91, 95–96, 100
Wyant, Andrew ("Polyphemus"), 109–110+n6